Neighborhood Conservation

Neighborhood Conservation

A handbook
of methods
and techniques

Editors: Robert H. McNulty and Stephen A. Kliment AIA
Design: Ivan Chermayeff and Stephan Geissbuhler

The Whitney Library of Design
An imprint of Watson-Guptill Publications, New York

First published 1976 in New York by The Whitney Library of Design,
an imprint of Watson-Guptill Publications,
division of Billboard Publications, Inc.
1515 Broadway, New York, N.Y. 10036

Manufactured in U.S.A.

Library of Congress Cataloging Publication Data
Main entry under title:
Neighborhood conservation.
    Includes bibliographical references and index.
    1. Urban renewal—United States. 2. Architecture,
Domestic—United States—Conservation and restoration.
3. Neighborhood. 4. Cities and towns—Planning—
 United States. I. McNulty, Robert H. II. Kliment, Stephen A.
HT175.N396 1976   309.2'62'0973   76-7607
ISBN 0-8320-7380-7

First Printing, 1976

Preface

The publication

This book is designed as a guide to the key administrative, legal, financial, social, and physical design issues governing the present and future of neighborhood conservation. The narrative is complemented by case studies of 45 American cities with a record of activity in neighborhood conservation, along with a detailed compendium of printed resources arranged by issue and subject matter. The case studies of Chapter V are in a notebook form of shorthand to save the reader time.

The issues and options chapter (III) has numerous entries in the margins; these refer to the city case studies of Chapters V and VI. Key governmental programs are defined briefly in the Index.

Publication credits

The research and detailed city data on which much of this work rests was a team effort. Originally, some 109 cities were reviewed by the firm of Abeles, Schwartz and Associates of New York City. Following a winnowing process, Harry Schwartz and Judy Scherer conducted site visits and extensive telephone interviews. These efforts were supplemented by research conducted and chronicled by Gordon Binder, Clark Kellogg, Clint Page, and Robert Coombs. Richard Morris undertook the complex problem of research and writing on the problems and promise of neighborhood conservation in New York City, and Roberta Gratz augmented the New York City case study for this edition. Phyllis Myers researched and wrote the case studies for Cincinnati and Seattle.

Merrill Ware prepared the chapter describing the states' role in neighborhood conservation, with general help from Robert Stipe and Robert Rettig, and Roy Berkeley contributed the essay "The City in Folksong." Robert McNulty wrote Chapter I and Stephen Kliment Chapters II and III.

Ivan Chermayeff and Stephan Geissbuhler of Chermayeff & Geismar Associates, New York, designed this book as well as all materials for the 1975 New York Neighborhood Conservation Conference, which is referred to below and throughout the book. Their suggestions have been key in every aspect of this work.

Danae Voltos researched the photographs for this book and helped in their selection. Editorial and research support was provided by Suzanne Fogelson, Cleo Mastacouris, and Luella Boddewyn.

On the staff of Whitney Library of Design, Frank DeLuca's special efforts made possible the timely publication of a preconference working edition of this book, and Susan Braybrooke and Susan Davis cooperated freely in the planning that produced this definitive edition.

Coordination credits

Singular credit should be given to Jane Clark, who as overall project coordinator for the cosponsors of the New York Conference developed the ideas and questions into working tasks that led to the research, the conference, and this edition.

Eugenie Cowan served not only as the coordinator for the Conference but, with great skill and efficiency, kept the work on schedule over the 18-month planning period. She was assisted by Kathryn Higgins, Margaret Hobler, and Constance Sheppard, and worked directly with the Cultural Council Foundation of New York City in the fiscal management of this program.

The sponsors

Many people and organizations supported the work of the Neighborhood Conservation Conference from which this book was in part prepared.

The project was a cosponsored interest of the National Endowment for the Arts, the New York City Landmarks Preservation Commission, the state of New York, and The Conservation Foundation. Nancy Hanks, Chairman of the Arts Endowment, has been extremely supportive of this program, and came to address the conference in New York. Bill Lacy, Director of the Endowment's Architecture and Environmental Arts Program, provided invaluable advice throughout the course of research, conference, and publication. Thanks should also be extended to Robert Wade, General Counsel for the Endowment, Bill Potter, Grants Project Officer, and Chris Chamberlain, Betty Principe, and JoAnn Taylor of the Architecture Program. Special credit goes to Merrill Ware of the Endowment; she was associated with editor Robert McNulty in his role as Conference Director and also worked extensively on this publication.

The city of New York, through its Landmarks Preservation Commission, chaired by Beverly Moss Spatt, was Conference host and a cosponsor of the research leading to this publication. Beverly Spatt showed a strong personal commitment to neighborhood conservation and to this book. Adele Chatfield-Taylor, Special Assistant to Beverly Spatt, was among the first to begin to lay the groundwork for the book; she also served creatively as Assistant Director for the Conference. Commission member Stephen Lash, and Patricia Rich and Marion Ryan of the Commission staff also contributed time and effort.

The state of New York was represented by three groups. The first of these was the New York State Council on the Arts, chaired by Joan Davidson. Constance Eiseman, Director of the Council's Architecture and Environmental Arts Program, was particularly helpful in the work of the conference and on this book. The Office of Parks and Recreation's Division for Historic Preservation, directed by Frederick L. Rath, Jr., played an active role. And Mario Cuomo, Secretary of State for New York State, became the leader in the state's sponsorship. Gary Levi of Mr. Cuomo's staff and Edwin Friedman of the former State Office of Planning Services gave useful help as well.

The Conservation Foundation, through its president, William K. Reilly, played an extremely important role in the research and publication. Through a grant from the Rockefeller Family Fund, Foundation staff prepared extensive case studies in three cities. We have used their work on Seattle and Cincinnati, researched and written by Phyllis Myers of the Foundation staff and found in this book. Gordon Binder, Assistant to the President, was critical to the preparation of this publication and thoroughly researched the Annapolis case study. Additional administrative support was provided by Janet Fesler.

Besides the sponsors, several Federal agencies took an active part in shaping the book and in supporting the 45 city case study research effort.

Other participating agencies

The President's Council on Environmental Quality, chaired by Russell Peterson, was the first federal agency to respond to the request for assistance. William Matuszeski, Assistant Staff Director, and Marilyn Klein, Senior Staff Member, arranged CEQ's financial support for the research and writing of the conference publication and commented helpfully on form and substance.

The Department of Housing and Urban Development, through the Assistant Secretary for Research and Policy Development (formerly Michael Moskow and now Charles Orlebeke) provided generous financial support and advice for the research, conference, and conference publication. Particular credit goes to Edwin Stromberg, and Charles Gueli and Pamela Hussey for their close support and sustained assistance. Lawrence O. Houstoun, Jr., Acting Director, Office of Planning and Management Assistance, has long been a close associate in this area and has provided valuable guidance and leadership in our efforts.

The President's Advisory Council for Historic Preservation served early as the coordinator of research on all federal programs influencing the conservation of older neighborhoods. Ann Webster Smith, former Director of the Office of Intergovernmental Programs and Planning, was a strong supporter. Harvey Blumenthal of the Council staff produced a separate 89-page publication entitled *Federal Programs for Neighborhood Conservation*, which contributed substantially to the present edition.

Colleagues at The National Trust for Historic Preservation, notably James Biddle and Russell Keune, were helpful allies at the research stages.

The Urban Reinvestment Task Force, a joint project of the Department of Housing and Urban Development and the Federal Home Loan Bank Board, through its Neighborhood Preservation Project, directed by Harry Brunett, helped us by recommending communities where across-the-board neighborhood programs were taking place.

Plus

Comments made by several individuals during the conference helped the editors rethink certain issues. These individuals included Rep. Henry S. Reuss (D., Wis.), Richard Babcock (Chicago), Ronald Lee Fleming (Cambridge, Mass.), Marjorie McCann (Philadelphia), Richard A. Miller (Chicago), Arthur J. Naparstek (Washington, D.C.), Charles A. Noon (Baltimore), Carolyn J. Odell (New York City), and Peter Williams (Washington, D.C.).

Last, thanks are due to all those who contributed their advice and criticism to the development of this book. Since this means well over 200 people, we can only acknowledge their help collectively. To them, we extend our sincere thanks and appreciation.

The Whitney Library of Design nobly assisted the cosponsors of the conference by assuring the on-time publication of the paperback pre-conference working publication, *Neighborhood Conservation—A Source Book*.

Soon thereafter, talks began with Whitney about the publication of a hardcover, rewritten and reedited edition of that preliminary book, which had been designed chiefly for use by conference participants. This book is the result.

The editors hope that these tools and tactics for neighborhood conservation will benefit city agencies and private groups across the country. Many ideas exist and have been tried with varying degrees of success. But only you, in your own community, know which ones—and in which combinations—can apply to your problems.

The Editors
March 17, 1976

Table of Contents

Statement
Nancy Hanks

In one sense, the Endowment's commitment to neighborhood conservation may be seen simply as a response to a rapidly growing demand by the American people for advice and support in their attempts to deal with an ever-changing environment—by preserving what is worthwhile from the past, and by creating communities that are livable and lively.

Our interest springs as well from our conviction that the arts, defined broadly, possess enormous potential for stimulating humaneness, economic health, and new life in our communities. Recognizing that cities are going to be with us for many years to come, the Endowment has adopted as one of its primary goals the reinforcement of those positive attributes in our cities which set them apart and which make them appealing places for residents and visitors alike. We see the arts as a vital tool in recapturing the qualities that have always drawn people to the city. And we feel that the neighborhood level is a manageable and hopeful setting for the process to take place.

It is within this context, then, that the Endowment's Architecture and Environmental Arts program has undertaken a many-faceted initiative to encourage the enhancement of older urban neighborhoods. In keeping with the program's broad objective of improving the visible characteristics of the built environment, the emphasis of its neighborhood conservation efforts is not merely on preserving the past, but, more important, on the sympathetic adaptation of older structures to generate new vitality.

There are other programs in the Endowment whose concern for the neighborhood environment goes beyond its physical features. To name just a few, we have supported neighborhood and community based arts programs in which citizens find opportunities for cultural expression through participatory exhibits, performance, and training programs. In an attempt to broaden distribution of arts resources, the Endowment has also sponsored residencies in neighborhoods by poets, painters, and performing artists.

Cities are extremely complex organisms, and we recognize that the arts alone can never provide the whole answer. Cooperative efforts are required from all spheres of society. The September 1975 New York Conference on Neighborhood Conservation demonstrated such cooperation, and I am pleased that the Endowment could work together with our three cosponsors in making it happen. I am confident, too, that the same cooperation will continue as we seek to realize our hopes for neighborhoods throughout the country.

Nancy Hanks
Chairman
National Endowment for the Arts

Statement

Russell W. Peterson

Nearly all of us live in a neighborhood. It could be a few square blocks of a large city that have resisted the hustle of urban life and remained a residential enclave. Or it could be an old residential area of a smaller city where the trees have survived the traffic engineers and the houses have aged with dignity. It could be a piece of the suburbs that has somehow established an identity that separates it from surrounding subdivisions. Or it could be the west end of a small town on the prairies. There are almost as many categories of neighborhoods as there are neighborhoods; each seems to be at least a little different from any other. And that is one of the most important reasons for preserving them.

The focus in this document is on the preservation of urban neighborhoods in cities and towns of all sizes. Our attention is drawn not only to those neighborhoods with a unique history or architecture that have received considerable attention in the past, but to the full range of places—old and new, rich and poor, distinctive and nondescript—which try to serve the traditional purposes of a neighborhood.

What are those traditional purposes? They relate to giving the residents a sense of community, identity, security, and diversity in their surroundings. A neighborhood is first of all a community on a human scale—a place where residents have the chance to get to know others who live there and run the shops and services. A neighborhood also gives identity to residents, so that as they go about the city and region they can refer and relate to the place where they live in a way that adds some background to who they are. "I'm from Greenwich Village" means something in New York, as does "I'm from Browntown" in Wilmington. Too often in recent years our society's entirely appropriate rejection of stereotypes has been carried too far and has made us almost embarrassed to ask someone what neighborhood he lives in. Instead, in a society as richly diverse as ours, one's neighborhood should be a matter of pride and general interest.

A good neighborhood is one that has a special character. It can derive from the buildings, the street life, the commerce, parks or natural features, or the people who live there. Whatever the source of this character, it is something the residents feel and have an almost instinctive desire to preserve. It is the essence of what makes a neighborhood unusual to all and at the same time familiar and comfortable for those who live there.

If we have learned anything about neighborhoods of all types in recent years, it is their essential fragility. Urban freeways and renewal projects, unless planned and executed with excruciating care and sensitivity, can destroy the vitality of a neighborhood virtually overnight. It is tragic that government—and especially the federal government with its billions for public works projects—has so often been unaware of how the economic, social and environmental elements of a neighborhood can be irreparably thrown out of equilibrium by one out-of-scale or poorly designed project. New federal programs for community development and a more flexible approach to transportation—which emphasize local participation and an understanding of how one action relates to others—are expected to offer the opportunity for bgtter choices by those at the local level.

Much like a natural ecosystem, the challenge of a neighborhood is to adapt to changes over time. No neighborhood is or should be stagnant and unchanging; at any given time parts of it are deteriorating and, one hopes, parts are being fixed up. Changes within and changes at the edges affect all of them. The real effort to preserve neighborhoods is not to freeze them in time or even in style or demographic composition. Rather, it is to assure that our neighborhoods are capable of maintaining a necessary degree of stability while at the same time acting as viable and dynamic parts of the cities and towns which they occupy. This may mean some outright preservation in each neighborhood—of structures, of land uses, or of traditions. But it also means assuring adequate, safe, and comfortable housing and services for the residents. And it means making sure that new public works projects and other pressures for change are kept on a scale which the neighborhood can accommodate.

What this publication is all about is how to make neighborhoods work as attractive places to live. Not everyone wants to live in the elegant French Quarter in New Orleans, or in Little Italy in Cleveland, or on a quiet, shady street in a midwestern town, or in a subdivision along the Santa Monica Freeway in Los Angeles. But for at least some of us each represents a choice of neighborhood. The important thing is for government and citizens to work together to develop and bring to bear the resources to keep our neighborhoods viable.

Russell W. Peterson
Chairman
The President's Council on
Environmental Quality

Statement
Beverly Moss Spatt

To understand how the New York City Landmarks Preservation Commission came to be concerned with neighborhood conservation, it is necessary to know how the Commission defines the word *landmark*.

According to New York City Local Law 46, a landmark is "... any improvement, any part of which is thirty years old or older, which has a special character or special historical or aesthetic interest or value as part of the development, heritage or cultural characteristics of the city, state, or nation. . . ."

According to *Webster's*, a landmark is "(1) a mark designating a boundary; (2) a conspicuous object on land that marks a locality, . . . a structure used as a point of orientation in locating other structures; (3) an event which marks a turning point. . . ."

Up to now, the Commission has been occupied with the specific business of identifying and saving landmarks—landmarks threatened by a whole range of urban dangers. By 1975, more than 11,000 properties in both public and private ownership had been designated landmarks, including 27 historic districts.

In the ten years of its existence, the Commission discovered that the process of designation and preservation achieved what some planners have been unable to accomplish, namely, the preservation of neighborhoods. This factor makes the business of landmarks preservation one of the most important tools in government planning today.

The first clue to this far-reaching effect came from the communities themselves which began petitioning for designation in large numbers from all over the city. They included communities in transition, in danger of being altered by outside forces such as clearance and renewal projects; prosperous neighborhoods that were in danger of being disrupted by development; neighborhoods conscious of an identity they merely wished to have certified.

The reason is obvious.

Landmarks provide ballast in a neighborhood. They steady it and bring out its character. A designation alone is sometimes enough to check a certain kind of deterioration in the quality of life. If you know a building, a street, a neighborhood will stay, *you* are more likely to stay. The result has been psychological, social, physical, and fiscal reinvestment.

The change that this discovery has brought about is a change in city consciousness. Community continuity must color all the Commission's programs in the future, and the multiplier effect will go a long way toward preserving not only landmarks but the character and stability of the communities that contain them. For it is neighborhoods that give a city life, and it is life that is the only guarantee of permanence.

This book is a shorthand study of a number of neighborhood conservation techniques employed across the United States, only one of which is the technique of historic preservation. The urgent need for these efforts is one major finding of this work; the limited funding, and the technical and administrative tools available, are also revealed; but the most compelling discovery is how people involved in a life-or-death struggle for their neighborhoods have been able to improvise and achieve remarkable results with very little outside help.

The book is, therefore, a notebook—and, I hope, an inspiration as well as a reminder of the great human resources that are saving American neighborhoods, and the appropriateness of that investment.

Beverly Moss Spatt
Chairman
New York City Landmarks Preservation
Commission

Statement
William K. Reilly

The 1975 New York Neighborhood Conservation Conference and this publication reveal a range of positive contemporary models of urban life whose basis seems to be a deeper understanding of the life and death of communities.

Some skeptics have suggested that these models are temporary and that business as usual—neglect and decay of the old and familiar, new development thrusts into the cornfields at the urban periphery—will resume when recession, high mortgage rates and suburban no-growth policies ease. But I believe the strong forces underlying this vitality—the new demographic realities (particularly the increase in single-person households and childless couples), the revival of interest in the old, the greater regard for history and existing physical assets, the growing sense of how to use these assets as focal points for neighborhood pride and community regeneration—will not decline.

While the unusual commitment to urban conservation we are seeing today is largely a middle-class phenomenon, in-depth research sponsored by The Conservation Foundation in Seattle, Cincinnati, Boston, and Annapolis reveals that this movement can widen its embrace to include diverse activities and people as well as physical structures. The relevance of neighborhood conservation as a broad urban strategy depends on this integrated approach.

Further evidence of the seriousness and strength of the conservation movement comes from its worldwide character. For the past two years, The Conservation Foundation has been engaged in a major international comparative land use research program. One of our findings, not quite expected, is that urban residents around the world are coping with problems similar to those we face in the United States. Often viewing themselves as victims of intrusive change that disrupts and uproots, citizens are demanding policies that respect the old, the untidy, and the small, and are succeeding in getting a larger voice in what happens in their neighborhoods. Planning controversies in the Rocks neighborhood in Sydney, the Covent Garden Market in London, the Marais in Paris, and in Amsterdam, Munich, even in Warsaw, are forcing modification or shelving of large-scale, "bash-and-build" projects and emphasizing instead renewal and recycling of the familiar.

In this country, as in others, there is new emphasis on *local* efforts and on the validity of *local* aspirations and ideas about community conservation. This raises practical problems of allocating limited resources (in one neighborhood the choice was between improving a public housing project or paving and lighting a "gray" area), of ensuring that efforts to produce locally defined quality are not racially exclusionary, of sorting out appropriate governmental responsibilities.

One feature of neighborhood conservation efforts throughout the democracies is a tendency to distrust government, to be skeptical about professionals, and to place more faith in popular initiatives. Some find this trend disturbing, and it surely can impair needed change. But to some extent, it stems from reduced expectations and greater self-reliance, both worthy of encouragement. If harmonizing demands within a system consists of lowering expectations, or redirecting them so they don't tax the system's resources as much, then decentralized coping is likely to be a fair and practical way of allocating scarce resources. Citizens must do something about the problems that too-high and even contradictory expectations impose on their societies, especially in a new era of scarcity.

In self-renewing urban communities, we may find some help in forging new values that place greater emphasis on cooperation, community self-government, citizen participation, and personal involvement. This is the challenge confronting cities in 1976: to nurture the sense of involvement and participation in urban life on the part of people who decry big government, big business, and remote institutions of all sorts.

This is a time of trial-and-error, experimentation—and also failure. Conservation activities, while widespread, are admittedly limited in their impact. What is most exciting is that many neighborhoods in many cities, despite all the constraints, feel they are on the way to better answers than they have had before. Governments on all levels, and private investors—both individual and corporate—are beginning to think differently, too. The result could just be stronger, more lively communities.

William K. Reilly
President
The Conservation Foundation

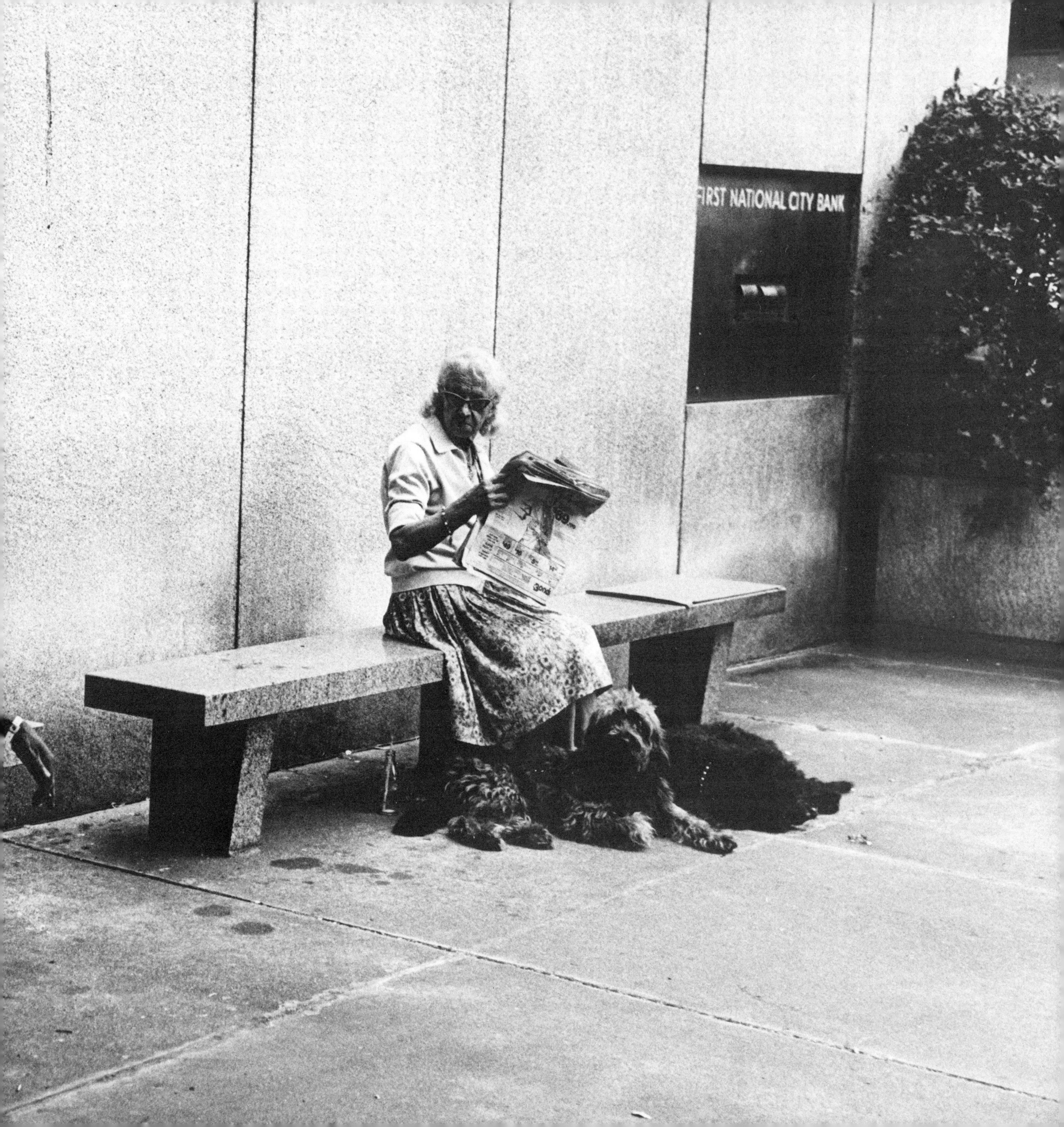
FIRST NATIONAL CITY BANK

Chapter I

The
Making
of a
Constituency

The Making of a Constituency

Preservation of the built environment has been a subject of concern in America, first to private and later to public groups, for the last one hundred and twenty years. It began in 1853 with the Mount Vernon Ladies Association, which mounted a national fund-raising campaign to save Mount Vernon when both federal and state governments declined to provide any assistance for its preservation.

The federal government takes a hand

Since then the federal government has evolved its own approach to historic preservation. The 1906 Antiquities Act, the 1916 Park Service Act, and the 1935 Historic Sites Act represent preservation by federal ownership. The National Register (established under the 1935 Historic Sites Act), the Surplus Property Act amendment in 1948, and the creation of the National Trust for Historic Preservation in 1949 were aimed at stimulating greater state, local, and private involvement in historic preservation—through education, recognition, and gifts of museum quality property.

The era of self-regulation began with the passage of the 1960 Reservoir Salvage Act, and broadened with the Historic Preservation Act of 1966 and its Advisory Council on Historic Preservation. It continued with the Transportation Act of 1966, the Demonstration Cities and Metropolitan Development Act of 1966, and culminated in the National Environmental Policy Act of 1969.

Through these laws the government has tried to avoid, or at any rate limit, the adverse impact of its activities upon historic properties and areas. Some have been purely remedial. Others have required a sizeable amount of preplanning by the federal government.

At the same time it tried to curb its own actions to forestall harm to historic sites, the federal government began slowly to develop programs to promote active preservation programs at the state and local levels. The opening up of the National Register to properties of local, state, and regional significance—coupled with grant programs to fund state surveys, preservation plans, and actual preservation projects—has had the effect of stimulating and coordinating the states' preservation efforts. The Department of Housing and Urban Developement's former preservation grant and open space programs, and its funding of historic surveys by regions and communities, had a correspondingly good influence at the local level. Funding programs by the National Endowment for the Arts and the National Endowment for the Humanities have proved of value. The 1972 amendment to the 1944 Surplus Property Act has opened a new door to federal assistance to communities by allowing economic and preservation goals to comingle and reinforce one another.

Direct and positive action by the federal government itself to conserve and promote the vitality of entire historic sites and areas had, except for the Old Georgetown Act of 1950, been meager. However, in 1971, the president started a trend with his executive order on "Protection and Enhancement of the Cultural Environment." Henceforth the federal government was to provide the lead in preserving, restoring, and maintaining the historic and cultural environment of the nation. All federal agencies were directed to set up procedures which would make sure that federal plans and programs helped preserve and enhance nonfederally owned sites, structures, and objects with historical and architectural meaning. This policy statement is important in terms of setting a fresh federal tone for conserving our historic resources. All too often, federal initiatives, in the form of building or highway alignments, have displayed, on the contrary, an insensitive attitude to vital neighborhoods and districts of historic or cultural worth.

The motives, purposes, and tools for preserving the past have also undergone great changes in the last few years, broadening the constituency of those concerned and, significantly, shifting the leadership to the cities.

The decade of the 1970s brought about a

broader, more inclusive approach to environmental quality. Going beyond the problems of air, water, noise, and solid waste pollution, the American public has shown its concern for the more aesthetic, intangible elements of daily life. The arts and leisure-time pursuits have become necessary ingredients in the daily mix that makes up the quality of life. The environment in which we live and work—the built environment—has been rediscovered. The sterile, look-alike nature of new development and growing suburban sprawl has at last produced a voice for quality design in sympathy with human scale. This recognition has dramatically enlarged a constituency hitherto concerned largely with *historic* preservation.

The Housing and Community Development Act of 1974
On August 22, 1974, the president signed into law the Housing and Community Development Act of 1974. This replaced the Department of Housing and Urban Development's categorical grants programs (which up to that date had funded urban renewal, planning, historic preservation, open space, and other federally assisted community development [CD] activities) with a comprehensive block grant program. The primary objective of this new program is the development of viable urban communities by providing decent housing, a suitable living environment, and expanded economic opportunities, particularly for persons of low and moderate income. Seven specific objectives include conservation and expansion of the nation's housing stock, and historic preservation.

Every city that wants CD funds must prepare a program which outlines proposed activities and costs. Each program must include a housing assistance plan for the community. In selecting locations for assisted housing, the act requires "furthering the revitalization of the community, including the restoration and rehabilitation of stable neighborhoods to the maximum extent possible." What is more, citizens must participate in deciding program priorities. Thus the cities and their citizens have a flexible resource

which can be tailored to meet neighborhood conservation objectives.

Of course, the prospects for large-scale success of purely physical alterations in older cities are bleak unless the element of economic dependency of many of the people who live there is improved. The redevelopment of cities will lag unless something is done to improve the quality of life on urban streets, in the schools, and in the parks—both for those who live there now and for those the cities hope to attract.

The Housing and Community Development Act will not solve these problems. The accumulation of social, economic, and physical decay that now burdens central cities cannot be remedied by any one piece of legislation or funding program. And yet this act, with its focus upon rehabilitation and conservation, and its requirement for public participation, comes at an opportune time in terms of forcing a rethinking of how to improve our cities and in the value of small-scale planning.

The city as nerve center
Twentieth-century technology, by permitting a daily breakout in all directions where land could be built on or the automobile could reach, introduced a new factor into urban decision-making. The access requirements of the truck, and the efficiency of single-floor, continuous-flow manufacturing processes requiring great amounts of horizontal space, diminished the appeal of the cities for much of industry. Instead of fixed environments, cities became nerve centers, elements in a communications and transportation network whose principal purpose was to transmit creative human energy and to exchange information. Physical monuments to fixity, massive sunk investments in steel and concrete, the cities' functions changed faster than their various plants and services could.

At the historical moment when cities should have begun to modernize their physical plants— their parks, streets, and public transportation fa-

Urban renewal and the reaction

cilities—they were obliged to direct their budgetary priorities to the needs and problems of large numbers of newcomers. Unfortunately there was a tendency to confuse the problems of people and the problems of places. Thus the earliest response of those cities to heavy immigration by the rural poor was directed at upgrading *property*, not helping *people*. Buildings were seen to be falling into disrepair. The people in them were overlooked. Clearance of slum housing became the project, with little or no attention paid to employment or supporting services. Some cities bulldozed block after block of human-scale row housing for new buildings that typically were larger and more imposing, but out of reach to the poor, as well as far less interesting and less accessible than those they replaced.

During the 1960s a reaction among urban planners set in against these redevelopment priorities. According to its critics urban renewal was a costly subsidy to downtown businessmen, while the forced relocation of the poor to make room for new stores, parking garages, and luxury housing resulted in disrupting low-income families and neighborhoods and increasing the price the poor had to pay for a reduced supply of slum-type housing. The highway program caused even greater disruption in the poorer neighborhoods, whose docility too often won for them the lottery of highway corridor location. Yet the very places in cities that were once seen as obsolescent—older row houses, waterfronts, decaying factory buildings—have the potential for the things cities alone can offer—a residential, neighborhood environment, characterized by relatively high density, and adapted to the pedestrian.

Commercial redevelopment

There are also new attitudes on commercial redevelopment in cities. These stress the need to adapt built-up areas to pedestrian uses, subdue and segregate the automobile, and reduce the scale of buildings to more human dimensions. Few downtown districts today offer accessible outdoor places for pause or retreat. Surfaces are hard and unfeeling. Trees are typically scarce or stunted, and relief from the summer sun is most likely to come from the impersonal shadow cast by a building several hundred feet away. Streets are noisy and congested and polluted by automobiles, trucks, and buses. Downtown areas contain blocks of uninterrupted office buildings whose street floors too are largely confined to nine-to-five uses.

But times are changing. The residential neighborhood and the old low-rise commercial district set in its midst have been, in a sense, reaccredited for contemporary use. The American Institute of Architects, through its National Policy Task Force led by Archibald C. Rogers, proclaimed in 1972 that the appropriate "growth unit" was the *neighborhood,* that "America's growth and renewal should be designed and executed not as individual buildings and projects, but as human communities with the full range of physical facilities and human services that ensure an urban life of growth."

In its 1973 report "The Use of Land," the Rockefeller Task Force on Land Use and Urban Growth went even further. It proposed an English planning technique that empowers local authorities to designate parts of the community as "conservation areas," insuring close public scrutiny of development and redevelopment proposals which affect these special precincts. The President's Council on Environmental Quality, as evidence of its concern for the built environment in cities, gave over the lead chapter in its 1973 annual report to "Urban Environment—Towards Livable Cities," focusing upon the role of older neighborhoods.

Return to center city

A new immigration is occuring in many cities. In part due to the physical blandness and lack of diversity of most suburban settings, people are returning to the center city and seeking out as residences and work spaces these older, "more interesting" buildings and neighborhoods. Frequently there is nothing historic or architecturally significant about these areas—except that the old buildings provide nonstandard space, and a grouping of such buildings into a neighborhood provides identity and continuity. Redevelopment and demolition of such buildings runs counter to the very reason these newcomers returned to the city. Thus historic district designation, a hybrid of general municipal zoning authority, is now increasingly sought to provide greater public control over development proposals that could cause collective harm to the inhabitants of such areas.

But what about the people who were living and working in these neighborhoods before in-migration of more affluent and more influential residents? What about the people who never left the city and whose ethnic neighborhood or community is suddenly "rediscovered"? Rediscovery brings higher property values and a greater tax burden. Displacement, without real choice, may occur to the very people whose lives in a neighborhood made it a vital, stable community. Here too is an important arm of the new conservation constituency.

Neighborhood conservation: a milestone conference

A notable milestone in the development of such a constituency was the occasion of the National Conference on Neighborhood Conservation held from September 23 to 26, 1975 in New York City. Initiated by the National Endowment for the Arts and cosponsored by the Conservation Foundation of Washington, D.C., the State of New York, and the New York City Landmarks Preservation Commission, the conference gathered together a cross section of political, economic, design, and social action representatives from across the nation. Included were public officials concerned with urban planning, preservation, and economic development, as well as architects and planners, economists and sociologists, lawyers, developers, and bankers. There were leaders of public interest, community, and environmental organizations.

The three-day agenda of workshops and panel discussions covered the uses and potential of zoning power and tax policy; the problems of financing, commercial district revitalization, and delivery of city services; the pros and cons of such tools as the transfer of development rights; urban homesteading; imaginative uses of community development block grants; the challenges of organizing government for neighborhood conservation; and the means to greater cooperation among levels of government.

The slots of time left between and after the sessions brought strangers in this growing neighborhood conservation constituency together for the first time, in informal exchanges that laid the groundwork for future cooperation.

Speakers
Speakers included Nancy Hanks, chairman of the National Endowment for the Arts, Rep. Henry S. Reuss (D.-Wis.), chairman of the House Committee on Banking, Currency and Housing, and Charles Orlebeke, HUD assistant secretary for development and research. David Crombie, mayor of Toronto, spoke of his city's successful neighborhood conservation program. Richard Babcock, a Chicago attorney, stressed the key role of the corporate partner in conserving neighborhoods. The mayors of Dallas, Louisville, and Lewiston, Maine, were the chairmen of sessions on municipal leadership. Donald D. Burns, secretary of the Business and Transportation Agency of the State of California, described state regulations that would help prevent state-chartered savings and loan associations from rejecting home loan applications in declining neighborhoods. New York City Mayor Abraham D. Beame was conference host.

The story of New York City neighborhood conservation was presented by a panel moderated by Beverly Moss Spatt, chairman of the city's Landmarks Preservation Commission. The Cincinnati story was related by four Cincinnatians, with William K. Reilly, president of the Conservation Foundation, as moderator. Leading special issue symposiums were: John E. Zuccotti, then chairman of the New York City Planning Commission and later first deputy mayor of the city, on the topic "Special Zoning for Special Neighborhoods"; John R. Price, Jr., vice-president, Manufacturers Hanover Trust Corporation, on "Inner City Financing and the Lending Institutions"; and Mario Cuomo, secretary of state of New York State, on "State Actions to Support Neighborhood Conservation."

Why multiple sponsorship?
What were the intent and meaning of this conference? Through multiple sponsorship representing the diverse interests of a private environmental foundation and of municipal, state, and federal governments, the different sectors involved in neighborhood conservation had the opportunity to report back to their large and many-sided constituencies and memberships.

For example, the Conservation Foundation is an organization in the environmental area whose own interest in the last few years has focused sharply on land use, growth issues, and energy conservation. And this has led it towards a more rational approach to *urban* form and growth.

New York City was represented through its Landmarks Preservation Commission. This was important since this Commission has been a pioneer of neighborhood conservation, and its chairman, a planner rather than a preservationist, is a vocal spokesman for people-oriented urban conservation policies.

The state of New York was represented both by the Office of the Secretary of State and by the State Council on the Arts. Increasingly, with the shift from preservation to conservation, the legislative and fiscal powers of states have become keys to resources that local communities can use. Land-use planning authority, enabling acts for special districts or historic district zoning, housing finance agencies, tax abatement programs—all are part of the state's role (the state's role is discussed in Chapter IV).

In forming the conference the sponsors assumed as a base point that certain neighborhoods have special values. They may be significant from a historic or cultural point of view, or from a de-

sign perspective. Or they may be merely frameworks for a tightly knit social structure of a group or segment of the community. They may house a traditional activity or pattern of life associated with their city. They may be representative of a character or a style of building and material use peculiar to that city or region. Or they may house a community trying hard to insure a continuing residency in their city.

These diverse features have usually involved different constituencies, and these frequently do not see eye to eye. Their interests are seen as competing against one another for municipal support. Each interest group has developed its own special tools and talents for securing its ends. Each has its own representation at city hall.

But these groups have much more in common than they realize. Each is tied to a physical backdrop—its neighborhood. Each is forced to seek a broad range of political, financial, and social tools to accomplish its objectives. The conference sought to define this common cause of shared strategies and shared goals. Moreover, it sought an increased role for the municipality in using its powers to advance efforts in these neighborhoods.

The conference was a participatory event—as many as 150 of the 350 invited persons played a formal part in the program. The many-faceted range of this program and the subject precluded answers to many specific problems. But the conference served as a symbolic event in certifying the goal of neighborhood conservation and in highlighting, through its participants, the wide range of people needed to make neighborhood conservation a reality.

As seen by the press
Writing in *The New York Times* of September 27, 1975, reporter and urban affairs critic Paul Goldberger saw some danger signals as well as opportunities in the Conference which:

". . . pointed up the crucial problem facing all

urban programs right now—there is no money. Our problem is not what to do, and it is not how to do it. It is that whatever we decide to do we will probably not be able to afford.

"Dr. George Sternlieb, director of the Rutgers University Center for Urban Policy Research, was one of few participants willing to acknowledge this. 'We are at the end of 35 years of housing subsidies,' he said. 'Society is just not interested any more—there is no political clout to the cities and the best we can do is optimize a wasting asset.'

"Dr. Sternlieb at one point suggested that the conference would have been perfect in 1953 and his remark has a certain validity, since the long night of urban crisis was merely beginning then, and we might have benefited more then from some of the policy discussions going on today.

"Right now there is general agreement about the direction that urban renewal should take—it is toward gradual, incremental renewal, with a strong emphasis on conservation of existing resources and the independent identity of neighborhoods.

"But of course this new conventional wisdom could never have existed in 1953. It came about slowly, in part because of planners' reluctant recognition that traditional and more sweeping approaches to urban renewal failed, in part because of the growing social consciousness that affected many areas of society in the nineteen-sixties. And this was spurred by the decline of the economy in the late sixties, when it was realized that it cost at least a little less to restore than to rebuild.

"But now that there is so little money around even for restoration, and that the battle to change the direction of American planning is largely won, what is the point of such conferences as last week? There are two main reasons why the session was a good idea.

"First, assuming that something eventually will happen to improve both the overall economy and the political clout of cities, now is the ideal time to lay groundwork for a rational planning philosophy.

"Second, and perhaps more important, planners must constantly be on guard to prevent the development of a new orthodoxy, which the present approach to neighborhood-oriented planning often threatens to become.

"Small scale, preservation-focused planning on a neighborhood level is indeed more humane than, and generally preferable to, the cataclysmic urban renewal of a decade ago, but it is not always right. There are often citywide factors against which a neighborhood's desires must be balanced, and a too-simple formula directed only toward neighborhood preservation ignores this.

"Moreover, each neighborhood is different; the problem in some is physical preservation of quality architecture, in others it is jobs, in others it is social stabilization.

"It is vital that planners keep this in mind and never fall prey to the belief that, as one speaker at the conference said, 'all old neighborhoods are to be treated like Georgetown.' "

The certifying event has come and gone. There is now a growing acceptance of the value of conserving neighborhoods. The real work is now up to the newly conscious constituency, which must use limited funds along with complicated legal, financial, administrative, social, and physical design tools, to push back the stubborn frontier of physical, financial, and visionary decline in our cities and neighborhoods.

Chapter II

An Introduction to Neighborhood Conservation

An Introduction to Neighborhood Conservation

Background

Buried in the haystack of urban statistics there lies one very sharp needle. It comes from the U.S. Census Bureau and points out that since 1970, for the first time, more people have moved out of our metropolitan areas than have moved in. This simple fact has major implications because it shows that the long-time net outflow from our central cities is now occurring on a metropolitan-wide scale. How will this affect the central city's long-term ability to provide services in line with revenues from the property tax and from other sources tied to the income and purchasing power of those who live and work there? How has it shifted the political balance of cities and their influence on the state and national scene? What will the exodus of industry do to jobs and morale among low-income groups and minorities left behind by the exodus?

The trend is expected to continue and even accelerate in the decades ahead. Practical responses to these questions, therefore, can spell the difference between a lively, thriving city, and a city marked by an ever-widening gap between a shrinking enclave of high-income residents and the underemployed poor; by a rising ratio of deteriorating, underused urban housing; and an ever-dwindling tax base that more and more curtails the city's ability to come to the rescue.

Two kinds of resources lost
The fact is that most central cities (and by that we mean that nuclear part of a metropolitan area administered by a single government) are fighting an increasingly costly battle with consistently waning resources. This depletion of resources is not solely financial. True, business and industry have been moving out, along with their taxes and their sources of jobs; middle-class families (mostly white but including minorities) have left for the suburbs (though still often using the city as a source of income), taking with them another substantial slice of municipal taxes paid via excise levies on purchases, taxes on income (in some cities), and the benefits of multiple turnover of their spending dollars. Moreover, as school enrollments stabilize and decline, state and federal support geared to enrollments drop

also, exerting a further squeeze on scarce resources.

(A measure of this is reflected in Census Bureau figures which show that for the six largest Standard Metropolitan Statistical Areas—SMSAs—in the north and east of the nation, the ratio of central city median family income to total SMSA median family income declined sharply by 13%—from a mean of 0.95 in 1949 to 0.83 in 1969.)

But this depletion of resources goes beyond the strictly financial. There has been also a depletion of skills, stamina, and initiative. Many of the residents who remain in the neighborhoods are elderly. Yet even more serious is the rising ratio of unskilled labor that remains in central city neighborhoods or has moved in from outside the city. As manufacturing left taking many unskilled jobs with it, demand in central cities has come to be more and more for white-collar jobs or jobs in the skilled service fields (such as computer, auto, and appliance servicing)—skills short among most low-income and minority groups. This emphasis has limited sources of work to largely sporadic, very low-paying jobs with little future, raised unemployment to extraordinary levels, and, aside from burdening the city's welfare budget (a Rand Corporation study of June 1974 showed that 38% of New York City's population fell below the "low-income threshold"), has also had a far more insidious effect: it has distorted the attitudes of many residents towards their neighborhoods, leading to increased vandalism, street crime, drug use, littered streets, and abused buildings.

The high cost of housing
As the population of many central city neighborhoods declined, the problem of housing began to shift from one of *scarcity* to one of *cost*. It was not that low- and moderate-income families couldn't find decent housing—they merely couldn't afford it. The high cost of new construction made it difficult even with the aid of various federal, state, and local subsidy programs to bring rental costs down to within the budgets of

even many middle-income families, let alone the poor. Concurrently, the costs of renovating the existing housing stock had risen also, placing upon many landlords the dilemma of whether to renovate, raise rents and lose tenants, or to cut maintenance to the bone, "milk" the property, and eventually abandon it, driving the tenants out to find costlier or seamier quarters elsewhere.

The reluctance of lending institutions to make purchase and renovation loans in many high-risk areas has tended to discourage owners who might otherwise have been inclined to upgrade properties in the hope of later refinancing or selling at a profit. The toll of abandoned properties has been very high, leaving a residue of housing that is increasingly either high-cost or uninhabitable. One of the major breakthroughs in what is left of this decade would be a full-scale effort to rehabilitate the huge supply of still rescuable housing and cast it, at far less cost than by building afresh, back on the market at a price modest-income families can afford.

A waste of energy
The energy impact of the movement to the suburbs (and beyond) is one of considerable waste. A well-established urban neighborhood infrastructure of utilities, roads, parks, schools, and public transportation is underused due to the exodus and in many cases abandoned, while whole new systems must be built (or enlarged) in the suburbs to accommodate out-migrating families as they increase the density patterns of existing suburbs or move on into once open country.

Policy of government
Another background factor of some import is the changing nature of government policy, especially in such areas as the decision to delegate the discretion on spending federal urban aid funds, increasingly, to state and local government. The federal community development (CD) block grant program is still too recent to assess, but it is quite clear that those citizens and groups concerned with conserving neighborhoods are having to compete fiercely with other municipal interests for a piece of their city's slice of the CD block grant pie.

Still, if intent becomes reality and broad-stroke priorities are translated into specific action, the CD block grants may well pave the way for a more intensive conservation of residential neighborhoods. A report issued by HUD Secretary Carla A. Hills in January 1976 indicated that $2.5 billion had been allocated to communities as block grants in 1975. A HUD survey of 880 entitlement recipients showed that 67% of the total funding for the category of metropolitan cities would go—according to priorities indicated by recipients—for "prevention of blight" and "the conservation and expansion of the housing stock." On the other hand, urban counties—another category of recipients—stated as their top priority "construction and improvement of sewer and other public facilities."

The Secretary's report also pointed out that local governments would direct 57% of CD block grant funds to minority neighborhoods, and 71% to low- or moderate-income areas.

Environmental laws
At the same time, as mounting concern for the environment has in the past few years finally been incorporated into statutes, there is promise now of a strong urban impact of these laws; but due to fewer economic and administrative obstacles, they at first tended to make more headway in low-density and rural settings. However, the president's Council on Environmental Quality has become more and more conscious of the fragility of urban neighborhoods. Using the power given it under the 1969 National Environmental Policy Act to review environmental impact statements by federal agencies, the council is stepping up its focus on urban neighborhood conservation.

From preservation to conservation
Not least among the various background factors

is the gradual shift in attitude that began to emerge in the early 1970s. Until that time a wide gulf tended to separate the preservation of historical, cultural, and architectural landmarks in certain of our more distinctive urban neighborhoods, from the concept of saving not only these but also the many less distinguished neighborhoods for the benefit of their own residents. The latter concept, as expressed in the public policy of the 1960s, saw the solution largely in terms of new construction of housing and office buildings on land made available through wholesale demolition and clearance.

Of course, building code enforcement and rehabilitation were always alternatives in redevelopment thinking in the post-World War II era, even while the 1949 Housing Act was planned and passed (inspiring the reckless renewal projects associated with redevelopment policies). These alternatives became legislation in the 1954 Housing Act and later came to dominate much redevelopment planning. But the net outcome of the 1960s, as most of us are now painfully aware, was quite the opposite: few neighborhoods managed to retain their character by the time the dust settled, and low-income families, displaced on a large scale, overloaded the facilities of poorer neighborhoods with their presence and their needs.

The gulf between the preservationist and the people-oriented neighborhood conservationist began to narrow with the growing seriousness of the urban problems. There were the rising outflow of many middle-class families from the central cities; the huge cost inflation (reaching 12% in some years) in the building industry; the economic problems of preserving landmarks. But there were also signs that a nucleus of professional upper-middle-income families liked city living and was returning. Meanwhile, a growing nostalgia for the nation's past made itself felt—a sentiment measurable in the sales of certain books and records, attendance at films and plays on historic themes, and the prodigious membership growth of such groups as the National Trust for Historic Preservation.

What happened, in short, was that by the early 1970s there had emerged a new constituency for conservation, setting the stage for formal expression through public policy at federal, city, and, to some extent, state levels of government. The shaping of this constituency, its legislative and private-sector antecedents, and its first major manifestation at the 1975 Neighborhood Conservation Conference in New York are the subject of the preceding chapter.

The platoons that march today under the banner of neighborhood conservation are in surprising agreement as to what they mean by *neighborhood* and what it means to conserve it. Some feel the term *neighborhood* is too limiting, that *conservation area* is better in that it expands the strict residential meaning many attribute to *neighborhood*, so that it encompasses commercial and industrial districts too.

In seeking to define neighborhood conservation, Michael Middleton of Britain's Civic Trust told the National Trust for Historic Preservation, meeting in Cleveland in 1973:

"A town is more than a collection of important buildings. To seek to preserve a limited number of outstanding buildings, while failing to retain and enhance the more modest streets and spaces which form their proper setting, has been likened to keeping the cherries out of the cake and throwing the cake away. The quality and character of a town reside in the sum of its multiple and often fragmented inter-relationships—in the spaces between buildings no less than in the buildings themselves; in its uses of land and juxtaposition of functions; the social mix of its communities; in the workaday objects and structures with which we furnish it; with the wider landscape setting in which it finds itself—the views into, and out of, the town. These inter-relationships are not to be placed in a glass case, isolated in a place of safety. . . .

"What is essential is that, somehow, we achieve much more purposeful control over the proc-

What is neighborhood conservation?

esses of change, so that what is best from the past is retained, and what is less than good is replaced by something better—thus constantly enriching the environment rather than eroding and diminishing it.

"This is why *I* prefer the term 'conservation' to 'preservation'—after all, in the kitchen, to 'preserve' is merely to keep from decomposition. Conservation can be seen as a total, purposeful creative philosophy, embracing, of course, the evidence of time past and luxury objects of beauty, but also the whole environmental problem with all its social, demographic, economic, political, and administrative connotations. . . ."

How do you identify such a conservation area? One of the best sets of criteria was offered in 1973 in a speech at the University of California at Berkeley by Lawrence O. Houstoun, Jr., acting director of the Office of Planning and Management Assistance of the U.S. Department of Housing and Urban Development. His 8-point checklist asks:

• Does the area have a variety of facilities and opportunities for residence, employment, shopping, recreation, and education?

• Is the area associated with groups of existing or former residents who because of their common employment or heritage have contributed significantly to the city's development?

• Is there a special activity associated with the area—a central market, an educational or transportation facility, wharves, warehousing?

• What is the overall effect of structures and spaces in the area on its utility as well as its attractiveness?

• Is the sense of place enhanced significantly by some important natural or man-made feature such as a canal or river, a hillside, vistas, a park, or public square?

• Do the people who live, work, and shop there have a clear and consistent sense of the area as an identifiable urban place with definable boundaries?

• Can it house people of various incomes? Will restoration permit those who have made it a home to stay there if they wish? Are there distinctive social as well as economical characteristics?

• Are residents attached enough to the area to support one or more active organizations that want to enhance the neighborhood and/or do something for the well-being of the residents?

In 1973, the President's Council on Environmental Quality, in proposing a new classification for the National Register of Historic Places, introduced the term "neighborhoods with special charm." "Sometimes," CEQ said, "these neighborhoods attract in part because of the historic role they have played in the life of the city, but usually the houses are more comfortable than elegant, the neighborhood more put together than restored."

This trio of definitions makes an attempt to capture the essence of neighborhood conservation. But it still remains a rather elusive concept when compared to the relative exactness of historic preservation. This looseness admits of a huge range of manifestations, from Chicago's tightly cohesive Pullman neighborhood, New York's large and more diversified Clinton, and the physical contour-oriented districts of Cincinnati and San Francisco, all the way to an area of a half-dozen commercial blocks in downtown Austin and the citywide, people (rather than locale) oriented approach of cities such as Boston, Peekskill, New York, or Hoboken, New Jersey.

This broad range poses certain difficulties for policymakers, planners, and economic interests. Thence, despite a general consensus on what neighborhood conservation is, there has yet to emerge a comprehensive set of viable statutes to translate this consensus into action.

However, there is, no question about the nature and severity of the problems still to be over-

A look at the obstacles

come. The following summary identifies these and breaks them down into manageable categories. (Chapter III explores them in detail.) These categories are: political/administrative, legal, business/financial, social, and physical design.

a. Political/administrative

On the administrative side, the decisions facing local government would tax the wisdom of a Solomon. Torn between the claims of its citizens for improved services, a dwindling property tax base, a rising clamor for increased neighborhood representation in decision-making, a steadily aging housing stock, and, in many cases, a reservoir of underemployed that usually doesn't fit the job demands, city fathers must resolve a great many issues when they decide to embark on a program of neighborhood conservation.

Singling out particular neighborhoods for a concentration of conservation tools and tactics—from designation to special zoning to special subsidy programs—risks alienating other city voters not benefiting from this emphasis.

After coming to grips with this issue, the city must then choose between the politically equally hazardous alternatives of focusing its efforts on a neighborhood well down the road to decay, or on one whose fate lies in the balance, where judicious use of tools could swing it back to health. Should the city devote its conservation resources, on economic grounds, to reversing the flight of white middle-class families to the suburbs; or should it seek through training programs to make poor or minority families a stronger, better-skilled factor in the local job market; or should the effort go into improving the quality of its housing stock by means of code enforcement, tax, and other incentives? The answers are elusive and costly.

What degrees of real autonomy should a city grant its neighborhoods? Where tried, decentralization schemes have run into snags from overlapping jurisdiction of city services, super-participation by some groups and disinterest by others; and many realized that a major overhaul of a city's charter would be needed before such decentralization was ever to be more than a benevolent gesture.

One of the main administrative challenges facing local government is how to meld federal funds and programs into local circumstances, which vary widely as to construction costs, income levels, vacancy rates, and the extent of state-delegated authority. As one instance: housing cash subsidies, pilot-tested in several communities, are said to have worked well in Kansas City where the housing vacancy rate was quite high; where the rate is low, such subsidies merely serve to inflate rents.

Similarly, HUD Section 8 subsidies (which allow builders to reduce rents to families that meet prescribed income requirements) work better in areas where costs are not so high that the bulk of available funds is used up on a few projects.

And bureaucratic procedures, defended by some as ensuring fairness and productive use of the taxpayer's dollar, tend on the other hand to cause delay, raise the costs of rehabilitation and administration, accelerate the abandonment of properties, destroy a project's momentum through inertia, and damage the faith of neighborhoods in government.

b. Legal

On the legal side, local government risks court challenges on constitutional grounds as it seeks to expand pioneering approaches in the use of its delegated police power along untested channels. *Overlay zoning* (which allows greater planning freedom on a given site); *special district zoning* (which singles out city areas to promote or retain something of value, such as retail businesses or a long-term resident population); *incentive zoning* (which offers a developer a density bonus in exchange for amenities such as open space, planting, etc.); and *transfer of development rights* (under which a landmark owner can sell unused air rights for development on another site, using the proceeds to make up for lost development revenues)—all these legal tools have been tried on a relatively limited scale. All face possible challenges in the years ahead on grounds such as taking without due process.

Indeed, the very issue of *designation* which singles out a limited area or building for protection (as set against the citywide scope of traditional zoning) is an explosive legal issue. So is a property owner's right to a fair return on investment if impaired by the act of designation. Several cases now in the courts are expected to clarify a still hazy picture.

c. Business/financial

The key business and financial issues in neighborhood conservation are "redlining" and business disinvestment; the need for a just response to development pressures; the mixed impact of local property taxes; the underused potential of federal real estate tax depreciation allowances; and, in some cities, the controversial impact of rent control on landlords and tenants.

Redlining (the withholding of bank loans from high-risk areas) is an especially vital issue, for it defies what we should call the First Law of Neighborhood Conservation, namely, that a program will fail in the long term unless methodically backed by the private sector. Hence one of the main policy tasks facing government is to develop incentives, large enough and flexible enough, to cause lending institutions and businesses to put their money into marginal areas. Zoning changes, local and federal tax concessions, an improved infrastructure, sensitive code enforcement, incentives to hold property for gain, and clearly manifest signs of commitment on the part of the neighborhood itself (this last perhaps most of all) must be explored if neighborhood conservation is to stand a chance in any but the most historic or most prosperous of neighborhoods.

d. Social

The ultimate benefits of neighborhood conservation are social, resulting in people with a sense of community, living in decent surroundings, at a cost they can afford.

We are a long way from this ideal because the still imperfect tools in current usage often breed all kinds of negative social consequences. The displacement of existing residents is one such problem—one hard to resolve because it so often is the by-product of success. Successful upgrading of an area usually raises assessed valuations, property taxes, and, in due course, rents, either causing tenants to pay more for rent than they can afford or forcing a move to a cheaper neighborhood. People will be displaced when large old mansions are reconverted from multiunit to single-family use, and when private developers (as well as many historic landmark foundations) buy houses and may legally evict tenants at the end of their leases. City housing rehabilitation programs also often lead to dislocation if repairs are extensive, and displacement can happen because the structure is no longer fit to live in.

The basic issue of displacement must be attacked on a number of fronts. One is to take a fresh look at the legal rights of tenants, which are minimal and still largely derived from the medieval doctrine of "caveat lessee." (It wasn't until August 1975 that a bill requiring a landlord to keep leased premises in proper repair became law in the state of New York.) The issue, explored in detail in another chapter, could lead to a tenant receiving a "guarantee of habitability" and automatic recourse to the courts.

Another social concern is the need to place far greater public and private resources into providing adequate non-housing services to urban neighborhoods—crime and fire protection, sanitation, schools, public libraries, day-care facilities, parks, recreation, and health-care centers for low-income households. Because housing is such an easily visible target, an unduly large ratio of resources has gone into upgrading it; yet a HUD-sponsored survey found that schools, crime, and clean streets often outranked housing as an incentive to households to move into or to leave a neighborhood.

Concurrently, channels for civic participation that are more than cosmetic must be evolved and tested.

Finally, more must be done to build up experience and ability of neighborhood property owners to maintain and, in case of rental property, manage their properties. Much social (as well as financial) hardship has stemmed from incompetent management, and the remedies, discussed in another chapter, need urgently to be tried and tested.

e. Physical design

The physical or design problems facing neighborhood *conservation* vary from place to place and, unlike historic *preservation,* are difficult to group in any coherent way. Among the most consistent tasks is the regulation of the urban design aspects of a neighborhood so as to preserve its vistas, enhance its open spaces, and protect strategic buildings such as a church or community hall. Special district zoning and other new tools are being used to make sure this happens, but the process is still imprecise, and much depends on the quality and clout of city planning staffs and the caliber of the professional consultants.

Another issue involves the protection of the buildings themselves and the wide variety of tools—from facade easements to design guidelines—available to help protect landmark-quality structures. One hazard arises when the enabling ordinance contains language that reflects a bias against a particular style, such as Victorian additions to colonial structures. This kind of sanction may swiftly decimate the character of a district if callously enforced. Complicating the matter of architectural conformance is the monetary issue of compensation, in the form of loans, grants, or tax credits to the owner for the cost of altering property to conform to guidelines. Lack of such mechanisms in many cities has imperiled the physical upgrading of properties in designated districts.

Several other physical problems remain. They include the matter of proper design controls over fringe areas of designated districts. There is also a very high toll that design controls exact when they are so strict in their demands for historic authenticity (especially in commercial districts) that architectural creativity is stifled, and business decides that the benefits of conforming rarely catch up with the costs.

Finally, it is easy to forget that as neighborhood conservation picks up converts, these newly identified neighborhoods will not possess the kinds of easily identifiable "protectible" features that has simplified, to some degree, the work of landmarks preservation commissions to date. One approach is to continue to apply the same kinds of guidelines used for historic preservation (height, bulk, materials, openings, color, texture) to the often nondescript, even poor quality (visually and physically) of houses found in many nonhistorical neighborhoods.

Another way, more geared to this phenomenon, is to develop detailed, block-by-block criteria to be applied in cases of (a) cosmetic alterations, (b) gut renovation, and (c) replacement, so as to cover structural and safety standards (by references to the building and housing codes); a cost range (to insure quality but preclude "luxury" upgrading that could trigger displacement); and architectural guidelines that allow for a greater range of solutions than possible under most historic district guidelines.

Conclusions

As the movement to conserve urban neighborhoods takes shape, certain general conclusions and caveats begin to stand out. They must be attended to if the promise is not to be thwarted by a mass of unrealistic measures. We must recognize:

That any viable policy has to pass three tests: *economic*, political, and *judicial.* Failure in any one of these is enough to cast serious doubt on the the long-term prospects of any policy.

That despite general agreement on many of the definitions and concepts of neighborhood conservation, there is still a virtual absence of any comprehensive, realistic, forceful statutes to translate this concern into action.

That any new federal neighborhood development programs which ignore the widely varying nature and problems of neighborhoods (because of differences in geography, demography, price levels, income, and politics) will lead to an extravagant misdirection of funds and to meager results.

That it is shortsighted to view neighborhood conservation as a discrete problem that can be approached in a large measure of isolation from what is going on in other sections of the nation. For the fact remains that industry and vital middleclass families are leaving our older cities in growing numbers, and even whole metropolitan areas for the first time are losing more people than they are gaining. This basic fact of life must be a constant reminder to public officials, planners, and businessmen as they seek to forge the right measure of land-use controls, investment, and tax climate that will conserve the nation's urban neighborhoods for their citizens.

Chapter III

Neighborhood Conservation: Issues and Options

Political / Administrative

Legal

Business / Financial

Social

Physical Design

Neighborhood Conservation: Issues and Options

This chapter identifies and reviews the principal issues that confront decision-makers—municipal, state, and federal officials, bankers and businessmen, neighborhood people, planners, legal experts, architects—as they seek to guide the still irresolute youth of neighborhood conservation into maturity.

The issues are divided for convenience according to five key groups of factors and activities that shape neighborhoods. These are:

1. Political/administrative issues;

2. Legal and constitutional issues;

3. Business, financial, and other economic factors;

4. Social issues—participation, housing and non-housing-oriented factors, and the consequences of conservation;

5. Physical design and related factors.

It is logical to link these five categories to the interest groups whom they most concern. Such an approach has been followed in this chapter. The political/administrative and legal issues are seen in terms of the concerns of the public officials charged with promulgating and carrying out conservation programs. The economic issues are studied from the viewpoint of the businessman (a category that can range from landlord to lender to developer). The social issues are discussed in the light of their impact on the actual residents of the neighborhood. The design issues are seen from the standpoint of planners, designers, and preservationists whose concern is the physical fabric.

Each issue contains a brief discussion, and policy options are indicated where appropriate. The names of cities often appear in the margins next to a particular issue. Refer to the city case studies (chapters V and VI) for details on how that city dealt with the issue.

Political / Administrative

The political climate and administrative practices are essential elements in setting the stage for a conservation program. The extent to which local elected and key appointed officials (and agency staff who administer programs) are sympathetic to the conservation concept is crucial.

The preservation focus of the 1960s usually found its initiative in the private sector. As the focus begins to shift to conservation, it is clear that the complex economic, legal, social, and administrative policies and mechanisms needed to make conservation work, and the growing role of neighborhood groups of all backgrounds applying pressure through their elected representatives, will inevitably move the major responsibility to local government.

The actual and potential impact of local government on conservation is very large. It resides chiefly in its application of land-use controls, its discretion as to choice of districts for attention, its direct financial support through use of tax revenues and as a conduit for state and federal funds, its powers of code enforcement and use of the property tax, its ability to expand or reduce the power of local subdepartments such as community boards, and its power to shape the quality of program planning and execution via its staff appointments.

The use of local public powers in the name of conservation can range from designation, which involves the use of police powers under a justification of general welfare (similar to zoning), to the direct acquisition of buildings or facade easements, which involves the expenditure of tax funds to preserve buildings deemed to be of value to the public. Within this range, but mainly at the police power end of the scale, certain issues arise. These include such questions as the extent to which public powers (in the form of designation, usually) should be used to protect an area from development and change, when such protection may lead to lower tax revenues to the municipality; the manner in which use of these powers to benefit residents of one neighborhood is seen by the larger community; and the equity in placing the burden for preserving a building upon an owner without offering some form of compensation.

However local government is structured, it is important that it tie in with state and federal government programs, reach out to the private sector, and keep in touch with constituents through skillful communication.

In recent years, several new mechanisms have been developed. They permit local government to tailor its general welfare powers more closely to the special requirements of different types of neighborhoods, than can be done through conventional land use controls. It is true that zoning remains the basic regulatory tool over the use of land. In its favor are the facts that it is widely accepted politically and, from the standpoint of city government, it's free. Against it is the fact that in its traditional form it is not geared, except through an often complicated appeals procedure, to dealing with specific alleged inequities.

The new tools give government the initiative to promote special neighborhood goals, such as necessary but uneconomic uses (e.g., theaters); to protect an existing public investment (parks, a cultural center); to preserve public amenities in an area ready for future development; to preserve retail stores; to avoid major changes in the socio-economic composition of a stable neighborhood; or to protect landmarks against development pressures.

Incentive zoning (a developer is given a density bonus in exchange for providing specified amenities) and transfer of development rights (air rights over a landmark are sold for use on another site and the proceeds used to maintain the landmark) are not the only pioneering tools government can use to direct public development, even though they are the best known. Other tools include these:

1. Privately reimbursed exercise of eminent domain (the city condemns a property holdout on a site assembled for development, and is reimbursed by the developer in exchange for certain public amenities);

2. Restrictions running with the land or "conditional zoning" (the city reclassifies an owner's property for a new use on the condition that the owner improves, in perpetuity, the impact of new development on neighboring properties);[1]

3. Development easements geared to smaller, growing communities. Property owners are temporarily restricted from building, pending development of a proper infrastructure (schools; sewers; roads. In return they receive a tax abatement and the prospects of a major rise in future valuation).[1]

As these activities of local government break new ground, they are subject to legal challenge on constitutional grounds. Some of the key issues, such as taking, zoning vs. designation, and use of eminent domain, are taken up later in the legal section of this chapter.

Not all these powers of the municipality have such direct legal implications, however. They also include administrative options such as choice of tactics for initiating conservation projects, the pros and cons of a clustered vs. scattered approach in the use of the city's resources, the political implications of focusing programs on marginal rather than highly deteriorated areas, problems of citizen participation, and of allocation of federal subsidy moneys.

These issues are taken up below.

An important initial decision faced by many municipalities is whether to focus preservation and conservation efforts on one or two key neighborhoods, or to spread limited resources over the municipality as a whole.

To cluster or scatter conservation efforts

Discussion
In recent years it has become clear that the problems both of landmarks preservation and of rehabilitating declining neighborhoods are, in most cases, best handled on a neighborhood-wide basis, as opposed to a site-by-site approach.

The concept of focusing scarce municipal resources on certain neighborhoods and ignoring other areas is, however, a politically difficult one for officials whose constituency is the entire city, or whose districts do not embrace the impacted area. Even though most municipalities are more conscious than before that marginal but still good areas must be saved if the housing stock of a city is to withstand erosion, in many communities political pressures from designated districts and the scarcity of resources threaten to dilute the concentration most observers feel is needed to conserve key areas.

In any case, prospective conservation neighborhoods must be integrated into an overall city planning process, including traffic planning, zoning policy, and official attitudes in general. Conservation areas cannot stand alone, grafted onto a general planning process as an extra.

Focus on deteriorated vs. marginal neighborhoods

Many groups in severely deteriorated neighborhoods are uneasy over conservation efforts that are aimed at reasonably sound areas and neighborhoods on the fringes of the deteriorated area rather than at the area itself. They feel their problems are being ignored and in some cases suspect a policy of deliberate containment.

Discussion
In some cities neighborhood conservation was seen as the middle- and white working-class equivalent of the model cities program. Whereas model cities was a mechanism aimed largely at the more deteriorated areas in cities, neighborhood conservation has sought to focus resources on those areas not yet in serious trouble.

As funding for model cities and anti-poverty efforts has dwindled, concern has grown among minority groups that local governments are channelling resources into borderline areas that should go, instead, to hard-core areas where social and housing problems are deepest. Others feel that neighborhood conservation is often an effort to preserve a white demography in areas that might otherwise experience ethnic change.

Anacostia
Boston
Dallas
Hoboken
Pittsburgh
Troy

These perceptions should recognize that neighborhood conservation areas, at least in the largest cities, are for the most part populated by minority groups.

This concern poses constraints on policymakers who often find it necessary to balance neighborhood conservation programs with model cities and other antipoverty efforts. As competition for community development block-grant dollars sharpens, this push-pull is likely to become more fierce.

Option
One city (Philadelphia) selects conservation areas according to detailed neighborhood profiles arrived at by measuring three informational elements: (a) vacancy rate; (b) economic disinvestment; and (c) inspection and violation reports. Using census and municipal data, these profiles serve as a basis for pinpointing neighborhood problems and for evolving solutions.

The political and administrative question of how much planning responsibility and how much operating power should be assigned to neighborhood units faces many local governments in a period of rising demand for participating government.

Discussion
The question as to what degree of decentralization works best in stabilizing neighborhoods is still largely unresolved. By and large, municipal decentralization is intended to improve city services or to provide recipients with greater control over services delivery. It can lead to greater grass-roots involvement in planning. A study by Robert Yin and Douglas Yates[2] found that of over 200 cases studied, two-thirds showed some link between decentralization and better services; some 60% showed an increased flow of information between city hall and neighborhoods concerning services needed and services offered. But only 25% of cases admitted to "greater satisfaction," while a sizable minority felt services had worsened. Just under 25% felt localized control over services had improved.

Berkeley
New York
Richmond
St. Paul

Decentralization— how much is best?

The issue of decentralization is sometimes complicated in large cities such as New York by the concurrent operation of two forms of neighborhood government—an elected community board charged largely with making planning recommendations; and local "cabinets" or mini-city halls made up of the local heads of citywide departments (such as police, sanitation, and health services). The problem has been one of liaison between the two kinds of groups, perhaps largely because the perceived role of the boards is planning and policy recommendations, whereas that of the mini-city halls is performance and delivery of services.

Cincinnati
Dallas
Detroit
Minneapolis
New York
Pittsburgh
Seattle

Also, the boundaries of service districts do not always coincide (e.g., between the school district, police precinct, and health services district). A New York City charter review commission has proposed coterminous service districts and the election of community councils with wide powers.

Options
Establish by local ordinance a municipal department of neighborhood conservation to coordinate stabilization, preservation, and development activities in neighborhoods and to coordinate resource programs offered by state and federal agencies.

Explore creation, by federal or state legislation, of neighborhood government corporations as legal entities whose responsibilities would include conservation.

The tactics of project initiation

The timing, setting of geographical limits, and choice of initial projects for a neighborhood conservation program have a big bearing on its short- and long-term accomplishments.

Discussion
Conservation action is frequently a response to one or more of the following: (1) the threatened or actual loss of an important building which people have organized to rescue; (2) proposed new development, such as a highway, shopping center, high-rise building, drastic urban renewal, or structures with discordant uses and styles that are considered disruptive to the existing community; (3) social and economic changes perceived as adverse—such as conversion of houses to multifamily and rooming house residences, abandonment, crime, development pressures.

Seattle

A city agency or private preservation group will tend to select projects or tactics with great prudence, avoiding the risk of controversy, and advancing only those projects that will help build public and private confidence. For example, a *scattered* rehabilitation approach with its "seeding" benefits may be foregone in favor of a more viable, *concentrated* plan. Especially in the case of historic preservation, winning early public acceptance and reducing the threat of court challenge would dictate a cautious approach. In other words, a low-profile tactic, with time to build up a constituency, and early recourse to legal counsel are important.

Timing, too, is a factor. Sometimes there are advantages in delay. Since local historic designation is often accompanied by the imposing of strict time limits on owners to restore properties (it can also lead to rapid escalation of property values and hence increased front end costs) premature designation may become a hindrance in carrying out a total plan. Savannah's experience shows that local historic designation is *not* essential to preservation. Instead Savannah relied on the clear, natural boundaries of its historic district and the influence of a very active private group, the Savannah Foundation. The Foundation made the first investment, through its revolving fund, in historic preservation and protected both its goals and its efforts with restrictive covenants. Only after its initial efforts succeeded did private owners and the city, through urban renewal, follow the lead and undertake large-scale restoration and conservation activities in the old city. The city did not enact a historic ordinance until restoration was already established, socially, economically, and politically.

Detroit
Troy
Savannah

New York

In New York City it was a broad groundswell of concern for architecturally and historically important buildings in the early 1960s that spurred creation of a Landmarks Preservation Commission in 1965, with power over both buildings and districts and, eight years later, over publicly used interiors as well.

Boundary designation itself can be an issue, with widespread due-process and physical impact connotations. Even though a majority of residents in a district may seek designation, a minority may object on the grounds that designation is an undesirable limitation on their ability to use their property. Such a minority, if geographically concentrated and politically strong, can either defeat designation or insist on having its portion excluded from the proposed district.

Oklahoma City

It is important for private groups never to lose sight of the political implications of any conservation activity, and to seek support from their representatives as soon as broad local support has been assembled.

Should most Section 8 funds be allocated to new or old buildings?

How to apportion rent subsidy dollars allocated to local governments under the 1974 Housing and Community Development (HCD) Act poses a key question to local officials. The choice between subsidizing rents largely in newly constructed buildings or in renovated existing buildings can have long-term implications for neighborhood stability.

Discussion
The allocation of HUD Section 8 subsidy dollars is a key question not only for local government but also for local owners and business interests. Unfortunately renovation, beyond the most superficial, tends to drive up rents in many conservation areas above levels tolerable by current tenants, leading to a choice between an inadequate physical plant or an unmarketable one.

Section 8 rent subsidy dollars offer an important alternative in that they permit renovation to the degree required without a major rent rise.

The discretion granted under Section 8 of the HCD Act is unusually broad, permitting these resources to be used for rent subsidy of newly built as well as substantially renovated housing units.

Neighborhood conservation advocates have strongly urged use of such funds for renovation in selected target neighborhoods. They note that lower costs of renovation when compared to the cost of new construction make it possible to subsidize the rents of as many as five renovated units for each subsidized newly constructed unit. They argue further that the leverage inherent in preserving a building in a neighborhood that is on the verge of decline may far outweigh an isolated subsidy of an independent newly built housing project.

On the other hand, pressures from developers of housing, the building industry, and labor unions (all of whom are traditionally geared up to new construction) are strongly in favor of allocating large sums of Section 8 money to new buildings. Yet very steep subsidies are required in many high-cost cities to bring newly built housing within the rental range of families with incomes below the prescribed ceilings. This limits the quantity of units that can be helped.

These pressures are particularly strong when government funds have been used for mortgage financing of the construction projects. Thus government on occasion finds itself with the choice of according the developer the subsidy he needs to help him market his apartments, or defaulting on its own mortgage.

New York

If local administrators consistently allocate such aid to newly built units rather than to renovations in conservation areas, existing neighborhoods will suffer. To landlords the prospects of any real renovation will diminish, further reducing their willingness to treat ownership as anything other than a short-range, cash-flow-oriented proposition.

Competition for CD block grant monies

Preservation and stabilization programs hitherto funded under the old system of categorical programs now must compete with other, citywide programs for their share of support.

Discussion
Applying the conservation uses permitted under CD block grant regulations raises hard questions for city government. The rescinding of categorical programs puts the burden of resolving priorities upon the mayors and city councils. Requests for support of historic preservation, rehabilitation, concentrated code enforcement, and similar neighborhood stabilizing purposes compete in the local political arena for CD block grant funds with such uses as the construction of utilities and other public works, real estate acquisition, administration, etc.

Again, local government leaves itself open to criticism on constitutional grounds if it singles out particular neighborhoods for a disproportionate share of CD block grants, with inherent political risk to those officials elected citywide.

How to compel renovation of deteriorated buildings

Many municipalities face the problem of coping with badly deteriorated properties in the midst of neighborhoods selected for conservation. How to compel the owners of such properties to maintain or renovate them is a key political and administrative issue.

Discussion
In any neighborhood-based conservation program, the administration dilemma posed by the deteriorating structure situated in a target district needs careful handling. Yet, beyond the relatively limited weapon of code enforcement (discussed below), many localities find themselves ill-equipped to cope with this issue.

Several means exist to take the property from a negligent landlord. Some cities have receivership laws, and many can use condemnation in designated districts.

Yet the key problem remains a dearth of new

potential owners. Many localities find few alternatives to the proverbial "slumlord." Homesteading, co-oping, and community ownership are frequently explored alternatives, but most experience to date indicates that these work best only when property has not substantially deteriorated prior to conversion.

Some states are exploring the possibility of state-sponsored ownership cooperatives tied to management corporations. Failing such tools, however, local government often finds itself with no option but to refrain from using its legal power to take property, and to deal, instead, with an owner in whom it has little confidence. The further question then arises of lending such an owner additional funds for renovation: Should local officials allow a building to deteriorate and risk jeopardizing a program, or bet on the chance that in enough cases such a financial gamble will succeed?

New York

Option
One approach is use of an anti-neglect ordinance. The city assumes the right to enter and fix up a delinquent property, attach the bill as a lien on the building, and take over the property if the lien is not satisfied.

Seattle

A double-edged weapon, code enforcement can either improve housing quality or expedite displacement (and ultimately, abandonment) as landlords pass the costs of compliance on to tenants in the form of higher rents.

Code enforcement

Discussion
The catch phrase "sensitive code enforcement" does little to resolve the dilemma over the real impact of active code enforcement. Given a climate of readily available improvement loan money, good long-term prospects for refinancing or selling the property, and the presence of rent-subsidy funds, code enforcement is a stabilizing influence on neighborhoods.

Atlanta
Dallas
San Francisco
Seattle

On the other hand, in declining neighborhoods, where code infractions are the most common, enforcement is a hardship both on landlords and the low-income tenants. But is there a price for "lax" enforcement? According to the authors of a 1974 article in the *AIP Journal:*[3]

"Code enforcement may in some instances lead to abandonment, but abandonment will often occur on a large scale without code enforcement. The costs of not enforcing codes and of the abandonment process are part of the same problem— the deteriorating quality of inner city housing, and the conflict between landlords' profit motives and the housing needs of low-income people.

"To deal with this situation by not enforcing codes for fear of causing abandonment is passively to accept the status quo and inflict high costs on low-income tenants. More aggressive measures that attack the problems of abandonment as well as code enforcement, such as transfer of ownership, are the only means to begin resolving the problem."

One must ask, therefore:

1. Are standard incentives such as low-cost loans and tax forgiveness enough to trigger code-generated improvements, if the penalties for noncompliance in many cities are no more painful than a parking ticket?

2. Could an intermediary, such as a Special District Board, serve to adapt compliance orders issued by the Building Department to individual circumstances? Or should such flexibility of attitude be a part of all inspection training programs? Some cities (Baltimore, for example) are given discretionary authority under their Housing Code to grant certain waivers in cases that involve preservation of a historic structure. The waiver is usually for a particular occupancy, and the city reserves the right to change it if the occupancy changes. Any broad-scale use of this authority in a district of architecturally undistinguished, highly deteriorated structures is open to question, and in many cases the legal matter of inspector liability, should casualties or damage occur as the result of a waiver, must be taken into account.

In two other developments, the State of California now has a State Historical Building Code which controls the fate of historic structures, with special concern for cost-effective approaches and energy conservation. And the Uniform Building Code (one of the four proprietary model codes adopted by many cities now has a historic buildings amendment to its code. This allows local inspectors to provide waivers in cases of buildings the city considers historically significant.

3. Could an inspection program reasonably be conducted at three levels: first, to uncover conditions critical for health and safety; second, those which could become critical unless remedial steps are taken; and third, those which are not up to code but cause mostly minor discomfort to the occupant?

4. Should a more lenient enforcement yardstick be applied to owner-occupied houses than to rental properties?

5. Is the appointment of a receiver to manage a code-delinquent property any more than a stopgap solution, unrealistic in case of a widespread pattern of infractions?

Option
Perhaps it is time to try some major new policy approaches in code enforcement that would shift the initiative from the building department to the tenant. For example, by modifying landlord-tenant law, a tenant could go to court claiming infringement of a right to enjoy the use of his rented space, and request an order for compliance to a specific infraction. The landlord would be required to leave a security deposit with the court, and this would be tapped if the infraction were not corrected. Alternately, the tenant could make the correction himself and deduct the amount from his rent (see also discussion under the social issue *Tenant's rights*).

Where urban renewal has been successful from the standpoint of neighborhood conservation, how may such success be re-created elsewhere?

Re-creating success

Discussion

In medium-sized New Haven, the Wooster Square project of the 1960s managed to renew the housing stock, provide new public facilities and services, and build a stable, socially mixed community out of historic and new structures. In other words, it successfully achieved conservation through renewal.

But will such a renewal approach "travel"? For one thing, the conditions may not be present in other cities. At Wooster Square, there were ample renewal funds, creative urban design approaches, a high proportion of homeowners, and a politically savvy and committed mayor and redevelopment agency director. The effort was concentrated on a single district. In other New Haven districts, where activities were less focused, where the ratio of absentee landlords was higher, and where opposition to the alleged paternalism of the redevelopment agency began to emerge, the renewal approach fared less well.

The tools of urban renewal worked as limited, *physical* tools for conserving neighborhoods. They could not be expected to resolve major social and economic neighborhood problems—declining employment, crime, lagging quality of public schools. Moreover renewal always tended to come off best in commercial rather than residential districts.

Often it is the idea rather than the actual experience of an outstanding effort that carries over into other communities. Given the right climate, including a concerned leadership, a way will be found to make the seed grow.

Hudson
New Haven
Providence
St. Charles

National Register: time for a conservation category?

The presence of a local landmark or district on the National Register of Historic Places can have impact on local private and official attitudes towards such sites. Does the present wording (which focuses on architectural, historical, and cultural criteria) discriminate against important neighborhoods that do not seem to fit any of these criteria directly? Or is the present classification flexible enough to accommodate such neighborhoods?

Discussion

Many neighborhoods do not at first glance meet current criteria for listing on the National Register. The issue is between a narrow historic interpretation of *neighborhood* espoused by many preservationists and the broader one favored by urban planning groups. Developing quantifiable criteria for listing these more diverse neighborhoods is not easy, and partly for this reason the issue remains unsolved. Yet expanded listing criteria for the National Register along conservation lines would help such neighborhoods meet prerequisites for inclusion under environmental and legal protection statutes and funding sources, and would lead to greater recognition of conservation problems at the state level.

Cincinnati

Options

Expand the National Register to include a classification for conservation areas.

Introduce legislation at federal and state levels similar to Britain's Civic Amenities Act, giving local government broad powers to designate and protect neighborhood conservation areas. Many states are considering state land-use planning regulations, and conservation areas could become one of the critical environmental areas subject to scrutiny.

Legal

Preamble

Perhaps the single most important legal issue in the field of neighborhood conservation is the emergence and use of new types of zoning power to protect communities and sites.

Zoning in the form we have come to know it was upheld by the courts in 1926 when the U.S. Supreme Court, in Village of Euclid v. Ambler Realty Co., 272 US 365 (1926), validated a comprehensive zoning plan. In that decision the court held that a zoning ordinance must be "clearly arbitrary and unreasonable, having no substantial relation to the public health, safety, morals, or general welfare" to be overturned.

For years, Euclid was used to sanction zoning ordinances which tended to proscribe certain types of development in certain areas. Regulating such issues as density, setback, light and air, and access, zoning was seen as setting certain rules for development which would act to protect communities from unhealthy density and inappropriate uses.

During the 1960s, however, a series of advances in the field of zoning emerged, with important implications for making neighborhoods both attractive and economically viable. Moving beyond the use of zoning as a rather rigid set of rules, these advances sought to create in zoning a flexible tool that would meet, by means of incentives, a whole new set of priorities. The theory which underlay such an extension was stated by Donald H. Elliott, former chairman of the New York City Planning Commission, and Norman Marcus, counsel to the Commission, in an article for the *Hofstra Law Review* (Spring 1973):

"The concept of incentive zoning is based on the premise that certain uneconomic uses and physical amenities will not be provided in new development without an economic incentive. By amenity, we refer to a non-revenue producing building feature, be it plaza, park, covered pedestrian space, arcade, on-site subway access, etc. By incentive, we mean an economic advantage to a developer not present under traditional zoning, such as additional floor area beyond the district's stipulated maximum. . . ."

Incentive zoning became in essence a tool for negotiation in which density, with its economic rewards, was traded for development plans which offered needed services and physical amenities.

These plans included incentives to provide theaters in new buildings in a central business district, stores in a retail district, open space, housing renovation, community facilities, and other specific public amenities.

In due course, the concept of incentive zoning moved beyond such a specific focus to a broader set of options. A breakthrough was the special Clinton development district in New York City. The Clinton area is a neighborhood of low-income residential structures in fair to poor condition threatened by the spreading central business district of midtown Manhattan.

With planned development of certain parts of the Clinton area for a new convention center (later rescinded) and a passenger pier terminal on the waterfront, the threat of developmental pressures on the community became real and immediate. The City Planning Commission responded by adopting zoning which barred development in the interior of the Clinton area but permitted it on the fringe portions of the community which bordered on the central business district. But, more interestingly, the Commission adopted a perimeter zoning plan which offered a floor area bonus to developers who would renovate properties in the *interior* of the neighborhood or undertake other public improvements.

Thus, *zoning* was used to protect the character of a neighborhood. Elsewhere, communities have been barred from altering the facades of buildings in special zoning districts—action taken not under a separate landmark preservation statute, but under normal zoning powers deriving their legal foundation from *Euclid.*

Other special zoning districts have been established to protect scenic views and environmental quality.

Cincinnati
New York

Another significant departure from earlier zoning regulations is the concept of transfer of development rights. Though promising mainly in areas of strong development pressures, it is an attempt to cope with the economic squeeze on owners of landmark-designated buildings. It can be applied broadly by superimposing it over general or special zoning. It also aids those landmark owners who are tax-exempt and therefore cannot be helped through the tax abatement route.

Another innovative (but untried) zoning concept is that of "housing quality standards," an element of zoning reform developed for use in New York City, establishing a series of criteria of quality requiring compliance by builders. These criteria are divided into four categories: neighborhood impact; recreation space; security and safety; and design of the dwelling unit. This concept is deliberately geared as much to the tenants' needs as the landlord's interest.

And in December 1975, a U.S. Supreme Court decision allowed New York State communities to amend their zoning ordinances to permit high-density housing for the elderly even on land zoned for single-family houses on one acre or more. This decision extended the zoning power to regulate not only the use of the land—the traditional approach—but also the kind of user—in this case housing for the elderly—that could be allowed to occupy the property.

New zoning mechanisms such as these place within the reach of all communities a very extensive set of options under the zoning power. They do, however, raise certain key legal issues.

Designation vs. zoning

In several instances, the courts have held that the zoning power may take actions not normally permitted special landmark designation agencies. Such a ruling raises some legal doubts as to whether special district designation may be used as a preservation tool.

Discussion
The courts have increasingly held that zoning, which implies a regulation issued as a result of an overview of the needs of the locality as a whole, may take actions that are *not* within the power of commissions established to designate specific landmarks or historic areas. The charge of such commissions, in the opinion of several courts, is too specific to sanction so broad a use of regulatory powers.

The implications of such a distinction are substantial. They argue for a citywide planning and zoning approach to landmark and community conservation, rather than using the act of designation of specific sites or districts for these purposes. Courts will increasingly tend to look to the existence of an overall zoning plan and ask whether the needs of the entire community have been considered, rather than solely the needs of the designated area.

"Taking"

The "taking" issue has largely lain dormant as the result of a pattern of court decisions dating back many decades and generally upholding the right of states to regulate land use for the public benefit. But recent innovations in zoning power, especially that of incentive zoning, may revive the issue in a new light—not because incentive zoning can be interpreted as anything but a sufficient public purpose, but because it could be held as arbitrary and capricious.

Discussion
The taking issue says that if the use of private property is regulated too intensely, it is "taking" from the owner without just compensation. Until the late 19th century the courts tended to deny compensation to owners of business properties which had lost most or all of their value as a result of state regulation. (Taking up to that date had been interpreted as actual *physical* taking.) But Justice Oliver Wendell Holmes was shortly to state[5] that "the power of eminent domain and the police power differed only in degree and no clear line could be drawn between them;" and later:[6] "The general rule at least is,

that while property may be regulated to a certain extent, if regulation goes too far, it will be recognized as a taking."

The issue becomes most critical where development pressures are strong and/or where the environment is fragile. This is often so in urban neighborhoods at the edge of a booming central business district or in areas subjected to internal development pressures because of their intrinsic historic or cultural attractions.

Option
Develop model state enabling legislation authorizing local governments to establish a regulatory framework within which such tools as incentive zoning, economic subsidy, and transfer of development rights may be used to protect the integrity of designated neighborhoods. These could be accompanied, as in Britain, by the establishment of statutory standards for situations where compensation must be paid to property owners under the state's exercise of the police power.

Return on investment

With inflation and a growing cost-squeeze on building owners, the line between taking and regulation is likely to become much finer. The use of economic subsidy may become a key tool to sustain the legal basis of land-use controls.

Discussion
The line which the courts have drawn between taking of property without due process of law or compensation, and the regulation of a use under the police power relates in part to the question of economic return. Where a regulation prevents an owner from realizing a reasonable return on his investment, the regulation may become a taking of property for which compensation must be paid. The record of court decisions is inconclusive on this point.

New Orleans
Annapolis
New York

The issue arises especially in communities subjected to strong development pressures, such as in areas of outstanding historic or architectural value. Whether the remedy used is to buttress

designation with a mix of additional tools—including intensive code enforcement, a public revolving fund for restoring key buildings, major public improvements (e.g., parks, relief of traffic congestion, pedestrian amenities), and stronger zoning and administrative controls—or whether a blanket moratorium on demolition is imposed, the interests of the public in preserving a valuable public asset are pitted against the interests of owners and their right to develop their properties to obtain a fair return.

Compensating an owner for these kinds of restraints on the "highest and best use" of his property is generally too costly for local government to undertake. Some cities have established a number (such as 6%) as a measure of fair return if the building is designated as a landmark and the owner threatens to demolish it. Where cases have reached the courts, decisions have not shown any consistent pattern. A breakthrough for landmark preservation occurred in December 1975 when the appellate division of the New York State Supreme Court denied the Penn Central Railroad its wish to erect a 55-story office tower over the concourse of Grand Central Terminal, after a court battle that dated back to 1967.

A clash of interests can on occasion be settled well before it grows into a major confrontation, as in the case of proposed boundaries to a district to be subject to special regulation. Designation of the Putnam Heights historic district in Oklahoma City points up the legal links between historic designation and the exercise of property rights. Putnam Heights residents were prepared to forego potentially large short-term gains from the sale of their property for multifamily or commercial development, in return for the long-term benefit of protection of their present residential interests and overall neighborhood identity, as provided by historic designation. On the other hand, the owners of property on a major street just inside the district's proposed edge felt that designation would be an undesirable limitation on their ability to use their property. Including this street in the district would, they claimed,

Oklahoma City

constitute a táking by preventing them as investors from realizing the potential market value of converting their residential properties to commercial use. Eventually, this street was excluded from the historic district designation.

(For a specific discussion of development pressures, see the *Business/financial* section of this chapter.)

Too many variances?

The relative inflexibility of traditional zoning has caused property owners and developers to seek redress in cases of alleged hardship by requesting a variance. This has led to considerable abuse. Its impact can be especially pernicious in older neighborhoods where indiscriminate or insensitive disruption of the physical fabric can accelerate decay.

Discussion
Serious evidence of the trend to excessive resort to zoning variances is documented by Norman Williams, Jr.,[7] who notes that court involvement in zoning and planning is on the rise. This, he says, is in part because courts are suspicious of local boards that grant too many variances that end up negating the intent of local zoning ordinances. John J. Costonis, a pioneer of the development rights transfer concept, has said:

"A variance is supposed to be granted in the case of unnecessary hardship and practical difficulty. It is supposed to be a constitutional safety valve for zoning that is too restrictive. But . . . in many cities it is the running sore of zoning. It is the mechanism you use when you think that the bigger the building the better it is. . . ."

Nevertheless, one must recognize that variances which permit a higher floor-area ratio are often granted developers—even in specially zoned districts—because the municipality hopes this will help revive a stagnant neighborhood and attract an increased flow of capital. Residents who have lived in or been attracted to such neighborhoods because of their low density, small scale, and social ambience see the issue differently. The result is often a legal and political confrontation.

The intricate and often contradictory patterns of condemnation laws are seen as a legal issue affecting neighborhood conservation, as when a public authority announces it will condemn a property for a public purpose and then delays action.

Eminent domain (condemnation)

Discussion
The question of eminent domain, many lawyers, planners, and public officials feel, is ripe for reform. Most states have a hodgepodge of condemnation laws that are antiquated and contradictory. In New York State, according to a *New York Times* report,[8] 993 towns and cities, 556 villages, 777 school districts, 800 fire districts, and 5100 special districts that control sewage disposal and water supplies, plus the federal and state governments, are empowered to take property by condemnation.

The report describes the case of a Syracuse, New York, landlord of several rental buildings which the city had for 10 years planned to include in an urban renewal project. Eventually city officials changed their mind and decided not to take the properties. In the meantime nearby buildings had been demolished or boarded up, blight had set in, and crime had infested the area.

Compensation is available under such circumstances, but the procedures are haphazard at best; and a New Jersey Supreme Court decision in mid-1975 held that the *prospect* of demolition declared by an arm of government lowers property values and can be held a taking.

Options
Develop state model legislation establishing a simplified code to guide eminent domain procedures in all cases except those involving the federal government. It should cover public notices, public hearings, and a clear-cut procedure for appraisal, claims, and appeals.

To reinforce the rights of tenants in condemnation procedures, set aside funding at state and federal levels for compensating tenants for damages, including relocation expenses and compensation for lost business goodwill.

III/68

Business / Financial

Business / Financial

Preamble

There must be a proper combination of risk and profit incentives that stimulates businessmen, from small landlord to corporate executive, to invest assets in a neighborhood if conservation is to succeed without exorbitant public subsidies.

If such a financial climate is lacking (and public subsidies are limited) then it may be generated by an appropriate mix of direct and indirect financial incentive mechanisms, combined, if necessary, with stepped-up state regulation of lending sources and their business practices.

The process of trying to stimulate a healthy investment climate in actual or potential conservation areas has, in the past, raised a number of issues involving the attitudes of lending institutions, the limitations and potential of the property tax, the uses of certain new government subsidy programs, and the proper management of development pressures within or adjacent to target neighborhoods.

These economic issues cannot be isolated from other issues of an administrative, legal, social, or physical-design nature, and should be so viewed in the following discussion.

Redlining and disinvestment

Redlining and disinvestment are key links in a vicious circle which drains a neighborhood of the financial lifeblood it needs to survive.

Discussion
The terms *redlining* and *disinvestment* tend to be used interchangeably, but their meanings do not entirely overlap. *Redlining* refers specifically to the practice of lenders to deny, or to increase the cost of, loans to otherwise creditworthy borrowers because the property is in a specific neighborhood (sometimes marked on a map by a red line) where the lender does not wish to make loans.

In the lender's view, a real estate loan is more than a credit loan to a borrower. The security offered—the property—is important on its own merits because:

1. The property may later be sold on the basis of the buyer assuming the existing loan, with the lender given no opportunity to insist that the new buyer is creditworthy.

2. The borrower may encounter a financial reversal, and loss to the lender can only be avoided if the property's market value is greater than the outstanding loan balance at that time. If property values are declining in the neighborhood (based upon actual sales) the lender is alerted that a loss of this type is possible.

Property values in residential neighborhoods, historically, have declined for a variety of reasons including: change of use (from residential to commercial; from owner-occupied to tenant-occupied; from single-family to multifamily); a build-up of unperformed maintenance that gives the neighborhood the appearance of being "run down." An existing trend toward reduced values may also result in new residents having a lower average income than previously. Whether this income change involves racial change or not, the influx of lower-income residents often speeds up the decline in property values. To make a standard loan in a neighborhood undergoing change that could result in a continued decline in values is a greater risk than most lenders are willing to assume.

To reduce their risk, they may require higher down payments and/or a shorter loan maturity so that the loan balance will be lower if foreclosure occurs; or, they may charge a higher discount or a higher interest rate on the loan to increase their financial return to offset the risk; or, finally, they may use more stringent credit standards, or extra tough structural appraisal standards.

Quite often, prospective borrowers are simply denied a loan. At other times, rather than obtaining the standard 20- to 30-year self-liquidating type of mortgage (at the end of which, ownership is free and clear and the property may be resold or refinanced), the borrower receives a so-called five-year renewable "balloon" mortgage, which reduces the lender's risk, takes as much as twice as long to liquidate, and leads to a resulting jump in debt service.

Disinvestment has come to have a somewhat broader meaning than *redlining*. It covers the reluctant-to-invest attitude of insurers, landlords, shopkeepers, and businessmen in general, not only that of lenders. These individuals are what the 1975 HUD publication "The Dynamics of Neighborhood Change" calls the "intermediaries" of the disinvestment process, whose roles in the incipient stage of decline it goes on to describe in these ominous terms:[9]

"Intermediaries are those actors who play some role in the neighborhood, but who may not reside nor own property in the neighborhood. Such people as bankers, insurers, real estate brokers, public officials and private businessmen are intermediaries. These intermediaries make decisions that affect a neighborhood's desirability as a residential environment. After a neighborhood enters the 'incipient decline' stage, what these intermediaries do becomes very important.

"For example, when they think they detect an increase in the rate of decline, some banks will decrease mortgage terms, make credit requirements more strict, increase interest rates or points, increase down payments or limit home improvement loans. In doing this they are responding to what they think is an increased risk. Although the risk may not have increased, *their actions ensure that it does* [italics added]. In some cases, especially when an area is changing racially, real estate brokers often will 'steer.' Some neighborhoods are simply not mentioned to potential buyers. White families may be steered away from a neighborhood they are considering and black households may be shown *only* racially changing areas. It is sometimes claimed that 'steering' is a part of the broker's normal effort to match client to property. As opposed to 'block-busting,' it may not be a deliberate effort to manipulate neighborhood change but its *impact* may be no less devastating."

The implications are pernicious: landlords, for example, unable to obtain mortgages for purchase or renovation, cannot resell, refinance, or even depreciate (since a depreciation cycle can only be renewed by obtaining a new mortgage); and, in lieu of a long-term interest in the property, they treat it as a short-term, cash-flow, profit-making investment.

To make this pay, property owners exact the highest possible rent and reduce maintenance to a minimum, thereby accelerating the broad-scale cycle of physical, economic, and social deterioration and abandonment.

Disinvestment is often sharpened by local public policy, especially rent control, an inflexible property tax, and substandard delivery of city services.

Atlanta
Chicago
Louisville
Philadelphia
Sacramento

Options

Financial options designed to cope with disinvestment may be generally grouped as follows:

1. Indirect incentives:

- Municipal commitment of expanded funding for battery of neighborhood-focused infrastructure improvements.

- Make use of provisions of the Urban Property Protection and Reinsurance Act of 1968 to ensure an adequate flow of property insurance into marginal neighborhoods.

2. Direct incentives to lenders:

- Establishment of voluntary lending pools of private lenders to provide loans to high-risk borrowers.

- Enactment of federal and state legislation permitting thrift institutions expanded branching, lower reserve requirements, expanded services, and even a direct tax subsidy, in exchange for increased investments in marginal districts.

- Expanded state or municipal loan programs to thrift institutions and banks at below market interest rates.

- Offers to banks to become part of a low-risk,

high-profit development elsewhere, in return for investing in high-risk neighborhoods.

- A federal urban reinvestment fund—a revolving fund which could coinsure a high (up to 80%) portion of the risk of banks and thrift institutions making loans in marginal neighborhoods.

San Francisco

- Other expanded federal, state, and local mortgage insurance programs.

Seattle

- Make the deposit of city funds contingent upon issuance by the lending institution of a satisfactory social impact statement. Such a statement would need to show that the lender had complied with the city's policies.

3. Regulatory:

- Requirement for public disclosure of lenders' mortgage loan placements leading to public pressure through account withdrawals, etc. (In January 1976, President Ford signed a law that will require financial institutions with more than $10 million in assets—and situated in urban areas—to disclose information on the extending of mortgages.)

- Requirement to banks and thrift institutions to make a prescribed ratio of mortgage loans within the state (of benefit only to those states with net mortgage cash outflow).

4. Competitive:

   Establishment of a mortgage finance bank or state-owned bank for making high-risk mortgage and home improvement loans in marginal areas.

Nonfinancial options include use of a city's zoning power, code enforcement, campaigns to generate neighborhood enthusiasm for conservation, and miscellaneous tax mechanisms (described later in this section).

Property tax

Part and parcel of the issue of motivating private investment in neighborhood stability is the controversial impact of the local property tax.

Discussion

Panel members of a property tax workshop meeting at the 1975 Neighborhood Conservation Conference in New York felt that the threat of tax reassessment in the wake of property improvements was not a major deterrent to property rehabilitation. William Apgar of the National Bureau of Economic Research cited a limited study of 10 cities which showed that in only 10% of rehabilitation cases costing less than $10,000 did this lead to an upward reassessment. In renovations costing more than $10,000, reassessment came about 57% of the time. In many cases property owners were not aware of existing tax abatement programs.

Wilmington. Delaware

On the other hand, homeowners and landlords with marginal resources have been discouraged from investing in even basic improvements by a pattern of inflexible attitudes on the part of assessors.

As ordinances do not usually differentiate between a tax on land and a tax on improvements upon it, it is often to the advantage of the owner to keep land "fallow," and make his profit via a capital gain by selling off the land at the right price. (Pittsburgh did pass a graded tax before World War I, taxing land at twice the rate of improvements, but the point was to lure virgin land within city limits onto the market for development, and it had little or no impact once no such land remained.) In a suburban context, however, a stiff tax on underdeveloped land could accelerate sprawl.

Reinforcing the Apgar study, reference 10 likewise found that property tax concessions consistently ranked in perceived effectiveness behind such other neighborhood factors as zoning, condition of neighborhood, and change in assessed valuation of property.

An arsenal of tax forgiveness measures is available to local governments, and some have used them to advantage. But since all tax provisions are tied to promotion of the general welfare, the question may arise whether such incentives ac-

New York

tually benefit the public in some demonstrable way or whether they advance selected private interests.

Moreover, as stated in a working paper prepared for a 1972 task force:[11]

"Since taxes are paid only by private individuals or companies, use of tax incentives to accomplish certain social objectives necessarily means that we are looking to private enterprise to help carry out what are essentially public purpose objectives. Until the early 1960s, many people held to the view that public purposes are best achieved by government enterprise. Thus, in the case of low-income housing, the nation relied exclusively upon public housing financed under federal, state and city aided programs.

"But, in the past decade, it became increasingly evident that low- and moderate-income housing can also be provided by the private sector, functioning as non-profit organizations or limited dividend sponsors. Since the latter can also make use of the tax benefits available to private housing investors, there exist very powerful incentives to harness profit-oriented private enterprise to help meet our housing needs."

Options
Proposals to use the property tax to entice business into greater involvement in urban neighborhoods have included these:

1. Taxes on land:

    Proportionately increase the tax rate obligation on land as against improvements, to stimulate rehabilitation and discourage demolition.

● Deny capital gains tax treatment on proceeds of land sales to discourage speculation.

2. Tax abatements and credits:

New York

● Tax exemption on increased assessed valuation due to rehabilitation, with graduated increase to full tax after a specified number of years.

● Tax credit on all rehabilitation work up to a dollar ceiling.

● Informal preconstruction tax agreements between sponsor and assessor.

Boston

● A special tax abatement program to stimulate conversion of lofts, factories, warehouses, and office buildings to housing uses.

● Special conservation neighborhood tax assessment districts allowing for resulting revenues to be used to improve amenities within the neighborhood.

3. State programs:

● State grants to cities to compensate them for revenue losses due to tax abatement.

● Total state takeover of school financing, thereby freeing property tax revenues for other uses.

4. Miscellaneous:

● Special training programs and incentives for property assessors.

● Additional research programs on the effects of property taxes on conservation.

Are Federal real estate tax depreciation allowances a factor in the stabilization of neighborhoods?

Federal real estate tax depreciation

Discussion
Section 167K of the Internal Revenue Code permits a five-year tax write-off for rehabilitation expenditures in low- and moderate-income housing. In practice, the section benefits chiefly projects of high capital cost such as gut or total renovation, which in most neighborhood instances is neither possible nor desirable. If Section 167K were recast to allow moderate-income owners to participate, and make less-than-extensive renovation viable, its usefulness as a tax mechanism would increase.

Similarly, landlords could be obliged to recycle parts of the profits from 167K, using the funds to lower rents on a profit-sharing basis, as is done, for example, with tax rebates from New York City's J-51 tax abatement program.

Moreover, legislation has been introduced each year since 1972 under the title of the Environmental Protection Tax Act; this would in part deny accelerated depreciation benefits in cases of demolition of older buildings and replacement by new ones.

Rent controls

The pros and cons, as a stabilizing influence on neighborhoods, of municipal controls over rents continues to be a controversial topic.

Discussion
In the aftermath of World War II price and rent controls, many state and local governments chose to maintain such controls on rentals after they had been phased out at the federal level. In the decades since, these controls have caused controversy, with the real estate industry maintaining it cannot properly maintain or manage residential properties subject to limited rental income.

While controls are now limited in their effectiveness and scope, even in New York City, and most rental units are not subject to rent controls, the legacy of years of neglect and poor maintenance remains. In many areas, the scars of rent control are most deeply seen in the unwillingness of owners to treat their properties as long-term investments, as a result of years of deferred maintenance which sapped the vitality of the units.

Proponents of rent controls argue that such controls are not a prime cause of deterioration. They tend to believe that insofar as rental income is inadequate, it is due more to underlying market conditions than to legal rent controls.

Where rent control covers a large number of units in a conservation district, lifting such controls may well have the effect of dramatically increasing rents and driving cohesive and stable elements out of the neighborhood.

If historic preservation and conservation are to grow, they must take into account the private sector. One key issue is to uncover means to protect neighborhood resources within the framework of intelligent growth policy.

Growth controls with a viable tax base

Discussion
Until recently, preservationists have tended to confront with some reluctance the issue of growth and development needs of a neighborhood's economy. This in turn has influenced the direction of many programs. In cases of private, public, or institutional development pressure, some form of joint public-business sponsorship can reconcile the differing interests. In certain situations, the interests of preservation and those of the market economy will clearly have difficulty coexisting.

A major factor influencing the nature of development pressures is location of the neighborhood. If it is in or near the central business district, where competition for use of the land is strongest and development pressures greatest, conservation will encounter the highest resistance.

Austin
St. Joseph

In such areas, property holders, as well as tax-base-conscious local government, will seek or encourage new development and growth. Development will be measured not only by higher property values, but also by new jobs, retail sales, or desirable infrastructure improvements such as parking and enhanced highway access. Without strong zoning protection a conservation district will be hard put to preserve its amenities in the face of such an array of public and private forces. Indeed, if the development interests are powerful enough even a minimum ordinance may be hard to achieve.

Chicago

Portland, Maine

Albany

Certain amenities, such as open space, sound housing, or retail shops, may be preserved or provided by a private developer in exchange for a density bonus, as part of an incentive zoning program.

Many New England and other communities, as

Middlebury

Seattle
Savannah

they strive to conserve their small-scale neighborhood character, face a gradual loss of vitality as shopping and other key services move to larger markets on the outskirts. How can business be offered enough incentives to remain and to grow, *not* by demolition of sound buildings, but by their adaptive reuse? Some developers feel modern businesses will only rent in new, glass office buildings. Many bankers, on the other hand, believe good existing buildings can be economically renovated to accommodate most business demands.

Indeed, the idea that adaptive reuse can be sound financially is gaining. The May 1975 issue of *Fortune* contains many examples. So did the July 1975 Seattle conference on the economic benefits of recycling older buildings, cosponsored by the National Trust for Historic Preservation and the city of Seattle.

Charleston
New Orleans

Charleston

Savannah

Annapolis

In some neighborhoods historic restoration is big business. There's hearty cooperation from banks and realtors, as historic shells are bought, renovated, and resold at handsome profits (the social implications of this are discussed later). But the development pressures created by a combination of rise in land values, influx of tourists (in one southern city tourism is its third-largest source of income), and additional services required by a new, high-income residency, are becoming a severe test for many cities. Tensions have arisen over such issues as the construction of new, high-income rental housing in fringe areas bordering on designated districts. Facilities responding to consumer demands of the "one-day visitor" (taverns, fast-food operations, parking lots) have brought out the latent hostility between residents and business interests in many areas. It is hard to refute, for example, the president of the Annapolis Chamber of Commerce when he estimates that as much as 50% of the local economic base is tourism-dependent, and that the tourist dollar turns over eight times in the community. Therein lies the major dilemma faced by such neighborhoods: the overpopularity that detracts significantly from the residents' quality of life.

Furthermore (and concurrently), shopping and other convenience retail services needed by residents tend to close down in favor of specialty shops appealing to tourists.

San Francisco

In some cases a reaction sets in, in the form of "no-growth" restraints. Fast-rising land values in some cities that have an active business core trigger a wave of high-rise construction, leading to change in the visual scale of surrounding neighborhoods, blocking views and overloading city and retail services. Citizens in at least one major "tourist" city whose central business district is ringed by mostly stable neighborhoods took up the cause of an ordinance to impose a limit on building height. Citizen-sponsored height-limit initiatives were placed on the ballot. They were defeated—for two reasons: first, used alone, they were too simplistic as urban design tools; second, downtown business opposed them, claiming they would erode the city's tax base and its ability to provide services.

Yet the original questions remain: can cities with a high ratio of conservation areas economically survive on a no-growth tax base? What other revenue-generating sources can supplement a no-growth tax base for the delivery of city services?

Options

Develop a citywide plan integrating conservation neighborhoods into a comprehensive set of planning objectives and programs.

Investigate, compare, and select from a broad base of financial mechanisms, including:

1. High-risk revolving loan funds for rehabilitation of residential and business properties in conservation areas.

2. Neighborhood-based credit unions and consumer investment trusts to accumulate capital for loans to members.

3. Business loan insurance program and technical assistance to small business.

4. Formation of local development companies to

attract private investment to neighborhoods and serve as local conduits for small business administration loans to area business people.[12]

5. Broadened use of Section 223f of the 1974 Housing and Community Development Act, expanding mortgage insurance to existing multifamily projects in need of moderate renovation. By using 223f for refinancing existing indebtedness, landlords can extend the terms of their mortgage, thereby increasing the principal amount without a rise in debt service, thus providing capital for repairs and improvements[13] (p. 853 et seq.).

6. Formation of funds for acquisition and direct rehabilitation of properties.[12] These funds could take various forms, depending on whether rehabilitation is done directly by the prospective owner-occupant or through a developer.

7. Sale of general obligation bonds to underwrite a municipal rehabilitation loan and grant program for homeowners and small businessmen.

8. Expansion of the Neighborhood Housing Services program—private nonprofit organizations representing a partnership of neighborhood residents, business and financial institutions, and city government.

9. Clustering of Section 8 housing subsidies within designated neighborhoods.

10. Requiring contributions by developers to an infrastructure improvement fund or other physical or social amenities via incentive zoning or development easements.

11. Greater cooperation between HUD and neighborhood groups in reusing HUD-held properties, over and beyond those allocated to the Urban Homesteading Program.

12. Recapture surplus revenues from increased valuations and reinvest in the neighborhood.

13. Implement Section 802 of the Housing and Community Development Act of 1974. This section allows the federal government to guarantee taxable bonds issued by state housing and finance agencies, and to subsidize up to one-third of the interest payment on these bonds.

Berkeley
New York
Minneapolis
Baltimore
Pittsburgh
Dallas
Anacostia

The neighborhood rather than the city is often the best focus for any program of support by a private corporation.

Corporate involvement

Discussion
The corporation is in a good position to bridge the gap of uncertainty that deters banks and thrift institutions from helping marginal neighborhoods. The main reasons for corporate commitment are these:

1. The range of neighborhood problems requiring aid is usually wide, but at a scale possible for the corporation to conceive.

2. This same scale allows the corporation to do what it does best—to steer managerial and technical skills and initiative to a particular program, with well-defined limits.

3. It permits a direct, one-to-one relationship between the corporate representative and the neighborhood leadership, eliminating official red tape and delay.

Typical projects involving corporations could include establishment and/or support of job-training programs, day-care centers, sports and community activities, and vital nonmunicipal services such as reasonably priced food outlets.

Corporations will be reluctant to go into a neighborhood unless they are satisfied there is strong local leadership.

For their part, corporations must have a committed chief executive. They should start small, pick an easily definable project, be tough-minded enough to reject a proposal they do not like, and expect no immediate victories.

Social

Preamble

The social implications of neighborhood conservation are among its least well understood issues. Yet, while solutions are few, the problems themselves stand out clearly.

Among the key (some single this out as *the* key) problem areas are the social implications of poor housing management. The bulk of rental housing in target conservation neighborhoods is owned and managed by small landlords having little management experience and held back by the financial constraints of bank disinvestment, high operating costs and low-income tenants.

Into the same category falls the issue of self-help. One facet of this, urban homesteading, has not achieved to date its full potential as a way to conserve housing, because so many of the properties are run down, are in decayed neighborhoods, and require a greater investment than owners are equipped to make. Self-help of this type, often requiring a combination of cash, loans, and "sweat-equity," is an important national resource that should be tapped to greater advantage.

The issue of code enforcement also should be singled out. Although discussed earlier in the administrative section of this chapter, it is clearly a social issue as well in the impact it has on landlord and tenant alike. It is a frequent cause of abandonment. It controls the landlord's ability to sustain ownership of a dwelling and hence controls the life-style of the tenant. Presently, the initiative for compliance is a matter between the city's building department and the landlord. An idea (reviewed later) would give the initiative to the tenant, working through the courts.

As things are, the tenant's standing vis-à-vis the city is very weak from a legal viewpoint. His obligation is to the landlord—to pay his rent on time and not to wreck the premises. If, however, the concept of warranty of habitability were introduced into the lease, the tenant would be in a far stronger legal position to make repairs and deduct the cost from rent, and to be eligible, as he already is in some communities, for a share of tax abatement moneys returned to the landlord.

The second key issue is displacement. While it also affects owners, it is the tenant who, because of an upgraded building with a raised valuation and raised property tax, cannot afford the higher rent and must move, usually out of the neighborhood. There are at present few legal mechanisms to prevent private developers and owners using private funds from causing relocation. Even in renovation cases using public subsidies, such as Housing Act Sections 115 and 312, displacement has commonly not been avoided, despite some bright spots, such as Pittsburgh.

The goal of neighborhood conservation is not to conserve houses so much as to give people *the option* either to remain in their traditional community or to move away. Hence far greater concern is needed for the non-housing services available to residents—from city, state, and federal government agencies and from neighborhood businesses. A HUD-sponsored survey confirmed that residents will place schools, crime and clean streets above housing as causes for remaining in or leaving a neighborhood.

A further issue concerns the degree and caliber of participation among neighborhood groups. Racial, ethnic, income, political, and geographic factors all deeply control this aspect of conservation efforts, and much still needs to be done to channel the often opposing interests of groups divided along such lines into a more active measure of involvement.

New York

Pittsburgh

New York

The fate of entire transitional neighborhoods often hinges on the management experience of those who own the rental housing stock. This experience in most cases is very modest.

Housing management

Discussion
While the focus was still on renewal and new housing, the assumption was that new construction would alleviate some of the worst problems of deterioration. Except in cases of sharp and prolonged tenant hostility (viz the Pruitt-Igoe

project in St. Louis), this point of view persisted until the early 1970s when the focus shifted from the *new*, to preserving the *existing* stock in a neighborhood. It was then that the real nature and consequences of bad management began to show through. A 1972 HUD-supported survey of the Crown Heights area of Brooklyn, New York revealed that 15% of owners did not know what kind of mortgage they held, 23% had never heard of the city's municipal loan program, and 56% knew nothing of the maximum base rent law under which they operated.

The lack of expertise spread into virtually every aspect of management. A study of the New York University Real Estate Institute [14] showed serious management deficiencies being caused by the following:

1. Little or no involvement by professional management firms due to high risk and low fees.

2. Welfare occupancy, with higher than average misuse of dwellings and equipment.

3. Tight resources, forcing inexperienced *owners* to manage their properties rather than to engage *professionals.*

4. Difficulties with repair contractors.

5. Complexity of complying with government regulations.

6. Low productivity by superintendents due to faulty supervision.

7. Rent collection difficulties.

8. Absentee ownership.

9. Difficulty of evicting rent-owing or disorderly tenants.

Indeed, the problem is not limited to rental properties. A special task force of the public affairs committee of the Society of Real Estate Appraisers made an "Inner City Valuation Study" in 1972 which uncovered a pattern of abandonment and foreclosure resulting from inexperience with ownership and housing management. The study found that the

"new availability of special government-insured

financing created a market for transferring ownership of substandard properties to low-income families at a cost actually beyond their economic capacity. In a natural market, the property costs would have been depressed, but with the government's thirty-year financing terms, properties, with a natural remaining economic life of five to 10 years, were inflated.

"Many of the structures accepted for FHA insurance were substandard and in need of substantial, not cosmetic, repair.

"The tenant, upon taking title, had the extra expenses of utilities and maintenance. Maintenance costs in these structures were much higher than in new properties—thus requiring substantial expense which the new owners could not absorb.

"Further, while the landlord experienced declining real estate taxes as the values of the older properties declined, the new owner-occupant got increasing real estate taxes as sales continued at inflated prices.

"The new owners, on a generally limited income and knowing little about homeowner costs and responsibilities, just could not keep up with the increasing charges from taxes and maintenance."

Mechanisms must be found to respond to these problems if the decay of such neighborhoods is to be reversed.

Pittsburgh

Options
Community-based management companies in transitional areas would operate at a scale large enough for economies in staff, services, and material purchases. These companies would be attuned to the needs of the community. The companies would collect rents, process mortgage and bill payments, supervise building personnel, let repair contracts, rent apartments, and comply with regulations. To establish and fund such companies, a program should be created by state legislation [14] using loans to be paid back out of management fees.

HUD has sponsored a housing management trainee program at five universities. The first classes graduated in December 1975.

Self-help: urban homesteading

Urban homesteading, a promising approach for conserving the housing stock in declining neighborhoods, has encountered problems.

Discussion
Urban homesteading, under which a house is sold by the city for a nominal sum to an owner in return for a commitment to rehabilitate it to code standards and live in it for a set number of years before obtaining full title, has not proved to be the panacea it at first seemed.

Difficulties have arisen because most of the properties (often supplied by HUD from its inventory of foreclosed houses) were in highly decayed neighborhoods; were in bad condition; and required a substantial investment to make them livable (whereupon they often became targets for vandalism and theft because of their location). In some cases repair costs began to outstrip the unit's total estimated value, which was a paradox since the program sought to attract low-income families into the ranks of homeownership. Unless such families were able to invest substantial amount of "sweat equity," they could not carry the program.

Wilmington, Delaware

Milwaukee

Furthermore, it is hard for rehabilitation of dwellings scattered among many unconnected sites to reverse the downward trend in a neighborhood.

The challenge all along has been to steer properties to those for whom the program was designed, namely, modest-income families and individuals. On the other hand, as Ian Donald Terner, director of U-HAB of New York City, pointed out at the 1975 Neighborhood Conservation Conference, "what has gone on under the name of urban homesteading is the exact opposite of the idealism behind it." The successes have involved few poor people, few deteriorating neighborhoods, little self-help or "sweat-equity," little cooperative ownership.

There are bright spots. Professor Robert Kolodny of Columbia University notes that some 8,000 New York City properties abandoned by landlords have been taken over and managed by the tenants, some for as long as ten years. For most of them it was a last resort, and such groups are in constant need of capital and legal and technical advice. And while 8,000 is only a dent in an inventory of abandoned units that in New York, according to Ian Terner, has reached 200,000, it shows that where there is commitment a start is possible.

Options
Focus the urban homesteading program on "sounder" neighborhoods than has been the practice to date, and monitor closely the federal government's homesteading demonstration program, launched in 1975, under which 22 participating cities are provided with HUD-held properties of "positive" value, along with rehabilitation financing.

Integrate homesteading with other mechanisms applied by a city to a target neighborhood.

Baltimore

Tenants' rights

The rights and standing of tenants are of concern to neighborhood conservation because of the still largely impregnable standing of the property owner or landlord vis-à-vis local government and the courts.

Discussion
The issue of tenants' rights is part of the broader issue of tenants' standing. Common law tends to treat the tenant somewhat ambivalently, and when problems arise they are taken up between the owner and the city.

Must the landlord pass on to the tenant part of any property tax deduction? Can the tenant make repairs on the building and deduct them from his rent? To what extent is the tenant's consent necessary for co-oping a building? Can he initiate suits to reduce the tax assessment against the property?

According to basic landlord-tenant law, the tenant has one fundamental right—to occupy a physical space—and one basic obligation, which is to pay rent and take proper care of the rented space. The landlord's obligations, on the other hand, are largely to the city as a pre-condition of being permitted to own and operate a multiple dwelling. Tenants are becoming increasingly militant, however, and are raising such legal issues as implied covenant and warranty of habitability to justify intervention in activities traditionally in the landlord's province.

A proposed zoning reform, described earlier, under which a series of criteria of quality is established for builders of multifamily dwellings, would appear to be an important first step in going beyond the conventional criteria of health and safety to include the entire living environment of the occupants.

New York

In many cities requiring a neighborhood vote as a prerequisite to passing a district designation ordinance, it is usually specified that the vote be only by homeowners—whether resident or absentee—with virtual disenfranchisement of tenants in such circumstances.

Galveston

Options
According to Phillips and Agelasto,[13](pp. 858 and 859), in 19 states and the District of Columbia, courts have held that every residential tenancy includes a nonwaivable landlord warranty that the unit will be maintained in not less than minimum habitable conditions. Two state legislatures have so provided by statute. The warranty of habitability rule has been adopted by the Commissioners on Uniform State Laws in the Uniform Residential Landlord Tenant Act, adaptations of which have been enacted in Oregon, Arizona, Washington, Florida, Hawaii, Nebraska, Alaska, Kentucky, and Virginia.

Since the above article appeared, at least one additional state (New York) has passed a warranty of habitability statute.

Such statutes may be used either for a defense or in affirmative action. Thus a tenant may take his

landlord to court if his apartment has not been kept up to standards of habitability.

Services provided to residents by the city and other levels of government, and by the private sector, must be seen as key factors in the stability of neighborhoods. At stake are the issues of equity *(equal delivery of services to all neighborhoods), and* accountability *(of deliverers of services to citizens, and vice versa).*

Discussion
The long-term impact of housing rehabilitation programs on neighborhoods is tenuous unless an equal commitment is given to delivery of city services, to the protection of retail shopping and places of entertainment, and to proper incentives to keep and add to the job market in the neighborhood.

The quality of schools, a basic ingredient of city services, is a key element in attracting newcomers to a neighborhood. Indeed, as noted earlier, a survey of certain New York City neighborhoods (asking residents why they moved in and former residents why they left the neighborhood) found that schools, crime rate, and clean streets tended to outrank housing as an incentive to stay or move.

Similarly, the levels of fire protection, the provision of health care and day care, the maintenance of parks, access by public transit, the support level of the public library—all have been either neglected as factors in neighborhood conservation, or else largely uncoordinated with housing-oriented programs.

By combining the administration of city services such as fire protection, police, sanitation, and the public library in neighborhood-level "cabinets" equipped with considerable discretion, response to service shortcomings may be faster and better geared to local needs. But the requisite authority has been largely denied to local cabinet chiefs in the few cases to date.

Boston
New York

An often neglected nonhousing factor in stabilizing neighborhoods is the degree to which eligible residents fully avail themselves of benefits open to them *directly*, rather than *filtered* through state and local government. Such federal benefits as food stamps, social security, and Veterans Administration payments, seldom fully exploited, could go far to infuse additional funds into vital but often struggling neighborhood businesses. Any effort to enroll such people (which include a high proportion of elderly and handicapped) would yield immediate benefits to the level and quality of vital, private neighborhood "services," in the form of better stocked stores, a greater variety of entertainment, and more efficient convenience outlets.[15]

Option
Establish a Neighborhood Services Program, paralleling the public/private Neighborhood Housing Services programs of the Urban Reinvestment Task Force, to bring combined municipal resources to bear on the services problem. Such a program could provide legal services, subsidies for the provision of noncity services, coordination, and monitoring.

If commerce goes, so goes the neighborhood

There is a strong link between commercial decline and residential decline in a neighborhood.

Discussion
If people find everyday shopping convenient and pleasant this encourages them to stay in their neighborhood. Popular mechanisms for doing this include pedestrian malls, attention to street signs, tree planting, and a general upgrading of neglected areas.

Municipal government can help by putting local merchants in touch with banks, helping them through the maze of code provisions when they upgrade structures, and creating a favorable climate in general. In Boston, when the city decided it was important to shore up neighborhood merchants, CD block grant monies were made available to help defray costs of rehabilitating store fronts.

Seattle
Boston

The National Council for Equal Business Opportunities has provided advice to local merchants in Toledo, Philadelphia, Baltimore, Chicago, and Washington, D.C. This group tries to generate private investment. Local merchants are encouraged to create different, more intimate environments and types of service than are found in shopping centers.

Few of the consequences of successful neighborhood conservation have proved as resistant to treatment as the issue of displacement.

Discussion
Displacement of neighborhood residents stems from two causes: (a) nonconforming uses of structures; and (b) upgrading that leads to higher rents and replacement of poorer residents by more mobile and prosperous groups.

The first, forced relocation, occurs when certain kinds of residential occupancies, such as rooming houses, are proscribed as part of a neighborhood redevelopment plan. Displacement occurs as such structures are subjected to demolition or major renovation. Residents are forced to take up temporary quarters elsewhere, often outside the neighborhood, and in many cases never return. Some communities have sought deliberately to battle this kind of forced relocation.

Displacement due to upgrading is a far more pernicious and widespread phenomenon, and far less amenable to simple solutions. The difficulty lies in part in the economics of upgrading. This often makes the retention of an indigenous population unsound economically, however desirable it may be from a social viewpoint. Upgraded construction leads to higher valuation, higher taxes, higher rents—both the city and private developers stand to gain. In many cases this policy is consciously encouraged to retain middle-class families in the city.

On the other hand, displaced residents are forced to find other housing, as a rule in more deteriorated neighborhoods (often more remote

Displacement

New York

Galveston
Richmond
Wilmington,
North Carolina

from their places of work), adding to density and further overloading strained facilities and services.

An especially common cause of displacement is the kind of upgrading where large old mansions housing many families are converted to single-family use.

Part of the problem lies in the private nature of much renovation and restoration activity. In Richmond, for example, poorer families have been displaced as the result of successful preservation-type programs. Although the local historic foundation relocated them and paid their moving expenses, there were no regulatory standards governing the process, nor did the original residents have any legal safeguards beyond their leases. On the one hand, the foundation was operating as a private venture and had the legal right to regain property it had purchased for rehabilitation and reuse. At the same time it was, in effect, serving a public purpose as the organization sponsor for restoration of a designated historic district, raising the legal question as to whether, in the process, it acquired any quasi-public obligations.

To what degree individual owners gain from public subsidies raises serious questions of public benefit. In Atlanta, for example, newcomers seeking to upgrade the old Inman Park neighborhood not only accepted financial risks and social uncertainty, but they organized (e.g., to oppose a potentially disruptive interstate route) and had powers exercised on their behalf (in the form of historic district designation and rezoning) to help achieve their purposes.

From their point of view and that of the city, this kind of neighborhood recycling was highly desirable. But the beneficiaries were an almost entirely new economic and social class, and stabilization was achieved only at the cost of an almost total exchange of population. Should perhaps the wider public interest have been expressed when neighborhood change on such a scale was imminent? (Ironically, former residents would at least have received relocation payments had they been displaced by the highway; as it was, they had no legal protection from the new homeowners, and halting the highway made little difference to those who were eventually displaced.)

Options

Evolve standards governing relocation of families displaced by conservation or preservation. (Provisions: allocation of responsibility for relocation payments among the city; the historic foundation authorized to buy, renovate, resell; and the purchaser of the property.)

Establish a community development fund fed by designated "excess" capital gains due to increased valuation of properties caused by neighborhood upgrading. Use funds to subsidize rents of low-income families.

Establish a program for the city to purchase facade easements and to use its own or federal funds to restore these. Low- and middle-income families can then focus their modest resources on interior renovation and have easier access to loans due to the increased property value.

Apply the principle of the Uniform Relocation Assistance Act (which assists families displaced by federal action) to rehabilitation by private developers. According to Rep. Henry S. Reuss (D.-Wis.), who suggested such an approach, to obtain a local building permit for his redevelopment project, a developer would need to apply for and use HUD Section 8 funds to provide an alternative unit for any low- or moderate-income families to be displaced.

Citizen participation in neighborhood conservation is sometimes productive—and sometimes marked by difficulties of various kinds stemming from opposing interest groups, different values, duplication of effort, apathy, and ambivalent leadership.

Problems of citizen participation and leadership

Discussion

Although several groups concerned with conser-

Atlanta

Richmond
Wilmington,
North Carolina

Atlanta
Chicago
(Pullman)
Hoboken
Hudson

vation may coexist in a neighborhood or city, this may not only *not* guarantee a successful program but may even undermine activities. Groups with competing objectives often have difficulty uniting their interests, and programs suffer as a result.

Local, history-oriented preservation tends to originate among a loose cluster of *private* groups. Responsibility for advancing a program, after a settling of rivalries, eventually resides in a single group, sometimes with public or quasi-public status. Housing and conservation-oriented efforts, on the other hand, tend to have a more *political, public* basis, and sponsorship as well as leadership takes on this more public, socially oriented cast. When the two approaches coexist in the same neighborhood, confrontation can often delay and badly harm a program.

Over and above the neighborhood preservation vs. stabilization confrontation, there is superimposed a pattern along religious, racial, ethnic, income, political, and geographical lines.

Some typical manifestations of this are:

1. Religious. A small but well-organized religious minority with a strong record of voting may further its own goals out of all proportion to its strength.

2. Racial. A racial majority in a neighborhood may be apathetic but with a small activist nucleus. Programs may be approved in that district which are not necessarily appropriate for the majority who live there.

3. Ethnic. In many cities, white ethnic groups favor minimal government interference and demand the right to oppose any major shift in the demography of the neighborhood. They tend to occupy fair to good quality and well-preserved housing, often conveniently close to the central business district. Charges of "elitism" may arise when well-to-do outsiders, usually from higher income groups and different national origins, seek to buy into the neighborhood.

4. Political. On occasion an activist neighbor-

New York

Milwaukee
Boston

Providence

hood group, made up of middle-class intellectual whites, advocates reform programs; but having little contact with the grassroots, they will lose out wherever a local politican with a good grass-roots organization is opposed to their program.

5. Income. Higher-income groups in a neighborhood tend to be policy oriented, working through neighborhood association-type organizations. Lower-income groups tend to act through their religious, political, benevolent, and ethnic clubs. The lack of communication between the two models is often a serious barrier to effective joint participation.

6. Geographical. Overbalkanized block or sub-neighborhood associations can paralyze effective community input into a viable conservation planning process.[15]

An important ingredient of neighborhood stability is the attitude and participation of neighborhood institutions. Colleges, hospitals, museums, and churches in their way play critical roles as job markets, as facilities for community activity, as architectural symbols, as sources of financial support, and as focuses for moral leadership. On the other hand, they may be sources of friction whenever their expansion leads to displacement and relocation.

Options
Ad hoc mechanisms for channeling neighborhood participation into the municipal decision-making process have been established in most cities, often as a condition for the delivery of federal aid. Representatives of neighborhood groups nevertheless have had occasion to deplore the exclusion of such groups from the grant applications process, and the reluctance of city hall to hold hearings in the neighborhoods to uncover preferences.

Long-term solutions will result from city charter revision under consideration in several cities, typically designed to give neighborhoods a more formal voice in municipal deliberations without balkanizing city government.

Berkeley
Galveston
Providence

Austin
Baltimore
Cincinnati
Hartford
Minneapolis
Oklahoma City
Peekskill
Pittsburgh
Providence
Richmond
Savannah
Seattle
Wilmington,
North Carolina

Physical Design

Meanwhile, breakthroughs will still go to individuals (such as Councilwoman Sandra Graham of Cambridge, Massachusetts, or Chairwoman Antoinette Downing of the Rhode Island Historic Preservation Commission) who are able to rally a constituency. Ms. Graham, through intensive political effort, rallied enough support to attract a series of highly effective neighborhood stabilization and homeowner rehabilitation programs to her city and district. "The trouble with a lot of community efforts is that they're not political, and this is *a political situation*," maintains Ms. Graham.

Ms. Downing, even before her new appointment, was a resourceful and energetic organizer who pieced together what she frankly calls an "elitist" group of private individuals. These had the money and will to come into Providence's historic College Hill district, buy houses threatened by urban renewal, restore them, and live in them. "They not only saved the neighborhood," she told the 1975 Neighborhood Conservation Conference in New York, "they made *rehabilitation* into a word the city could accept without shuddering."

Conscious concern in public policy for a physical neighborhood setting that will retain residents, attract newcomers, stimulate investment, and encourage good maintenance of the fabric is a vital ingredient of success in any neighborhood conservation program.

The physical design or visual aspects of a neighborhood are in many ways the hardest to control because they are so largely the outcome of the social, political, economic, and legal forces operating in the city's neighborhoods.

Susan Southworth, the Cambridge, Massachusetts, city designer, has identified seven mechanisms to consider in the management of a neighborhood's appearance. These are:

1. Architectural review commissions. These mostly operate only in special districts.

2. Sign ordinances. These control the environmental impact of signs on neighborhoods.

3. Special design districts. These allow neighborhoods to control their appearance to conform to a theme each considers appropriate.

4. Historic district regulations.

5. City performance standards.

6. The building code, its provisions and enforcement.

7. Tax incentives. These are an effective means of eliminating or discouraging negative visual elements.

Concern for appearance, in terms of overall municipal policy, has its roots in the landmarks preservation movement. This pressed for and obtained ordinances designating specific structures and districts, requiring conformance with certain guidelines subject to interpretation by a publicly appointed review board or commission. Concurrently, buildings and sites were surveyed and nominated for listing on the National Register of Historic Places or state or local registers.

Such measures served up to a point in preserving

key physical features of designated districts. They were, however, imbued with certain aspects which limited their effectiveness in the broader context of neighborhood conservation. For example, how can they be made to accommodate the vital, cohesive neighborhood that is devoid of any clear-cut historic or architectural character?

In such neighborhoods the issue of housing renovation becomes very important. In some neighborhoods the structural quality of housing was *never* high, and seeking to preserve it may do no more than buy time at exorbitant cost. Other neighborhoods in decline have stocks of sturdy, attractive housing that give the area a distinctive flavor; there, limited interior and cosmetic renovation are appropriate.

In many cases where demolition is the only reasonable approach, there arises the question of new construction. Should it conform in style to the existing physical context? This makes sense where this context can be fairly simply defined or spelled out. But where the attraction of the neighborhood is based more on lively street life or location near a natural feature such as a hill or a waterfront, guidelines for new construction become harder to establish.

In well-established landmark districts excessively strict or specific guidelines can have several kinds of consequences:

1. They can put a severe cost burden on property owners of limited resources who have nonconforming facades. Many landmarks commissions lack the means or powers to subsidize such owners.

2. Strict guidelines tend to reflect the aesthetic biases of their creators—this can jeopardize what may be a vital visual ingredient of a district, such as Victorian additions to a colonial housing stock.

3. Tight guidelines can cause economic stagnation through restraint on development, causing businesses to leave the area.

Finally, physical design policy necessarily must recognize the broader question of open space. Special zoning districts are able through incentives to require developers to provide open space such as parks, playgrounds, and pedestrian areas and to protect scenic views and vistas. But such mechanisms work best in a climate of active and large-scale development. Workable tools still remain to be forged that will protect and enhance open space in the kind of neighborhood that lacks easy-to-define features and is not the target of development pressures.

Especially insidious in such cases is the incremental impact on neighborhood character of new small buildings—a gas station here, a fast-food shop there—if these do not respect the character of the street.

The street in a viable neighborhood is like an outdoor room. Planner John A. Gallery has noted that up to 40% of the land area of most cities is made up of publicly owned streets. What attracts people to streets, in the long run, is other people. Thus it is vital for a municipality's physical design policy to concern itself with these issues.

The following section lists and discusses some of these issues in greater depth and reviews options.

To what style or period should a district or individual building which has gone through several styles and periods be restored?

Conformance: structure in search of a style

Discussion
The issue is serious because biases may be incorporated into official standards governing restoration. For example, a city's planning commission or urban renewal agency may disagree with the state historic trust as to the extent to which historic restoration should seek to retain ornate Victorian additions to the colonial character and style of original buildings. If the city's preservation ordinance or renewal plan uses language such as: "Emphasis should be on correct period,

Hudson

sash, doors, cornices, siding and other exterior details, and the removal of present day anachronisms, such as aluminum awnings, and of *defacing Victorian features or additions* to pre-1850 buildings" (italics added), a bias has clearly been built in which may eventually erase important segments of the community's heritage.

Charleston
New York

Sometimes outstanding structures, such as warehouses and industrial plants, are threatened because traditional preservationist forces shaping a city ordinance did not consider them important enough in terms of style or function to protect. (In an enlightened move, a city law was passed in late 1975 that would expand New York City's so-called J-51 tax abatement provisions to encourage conversion of existing hotels, lofts, and other commercial property to residential use.)

A flexible, common approach is to write into ordinances and guidelines the requirements that alterations conform to a district's contours in terms of such requirements as height and setback, material colors and textures.

New York

However, this requirement can often put a burden on the property owners. If the owner of a newly acquired corner drug store is of a mind to remodel it and must therefore replace a sleazy metal storefront with brick, he may balk at the increased cost when he finds that the city agency responsible has no funds to help him.

As for new construction in historic districts, what is the ideal point, in the range between unalloyed imitation and unabridged design freedom, which design guidelines should stress? Faithful copying will quickly embalm an entire district; a total absence of guidelines will overload the design review board with cases until it builds up a good inventory of precedents.

An additional concern is the growing problem of controls over areas just outside the boundaries of historic districts and subject to development. The scale and fabric of such districts need to be adequately safeguarded at their fringes by buf-fer zones whose scale and land use do not disrupt their character.

Charleston
Savannah

The specter of economic and design stagnation stalks districts with overly strict design controls.

Super-preservation or stagnation

Discussion
This specter can come to haunt a city that sincerely feels it is preserving historic character or flavor. The problem can arise as easily in a Western city with a Spanish or Indian architectural tradition as in Eastern cities with their colonial, neogothic, classical, or Victorian fabrics. The consequences of inflexibly literal design guidelines include:

Sante Fe

1. Visual harmony between original and new imitative buildings is usually more superficial than real, since the two kinds use different materials (concrete, in lieu of adobe) which age at different rates and (due to the improved quality of modern materials) outlast the historic buildings.

2. A mixed pattern of conforming buildings in a district—some authentic, some imitative—dilutes the impact of the true historic examples, especially as the copies begin to outnumber the authentic.

3. The severe style regulations tend to place an extra burden on small homeowners and businessmen obliged to invest extraordinary sums when altering their properties, encouraging businessmen to leave the district for a less restrictive marketplace.

In areas with strong development pressures, owners are often faced with the choice of rehabilitating a property with current tenants in occupancy, or of renovating it so as to create essentially a new, upper-income building. (The visual implications are discussed here. The social implications were discussed under "Displacement.")

Plain rehab or "upward" conversion?

Discussion
A surge of developmental pressure confronts owners with difficult choices. An owner may

convert a low-, or middle-income property into an upper/middle or upper-income building, and where the market will support such conversion it is a difficult alternative to resist.

Galveston
Atlanta

Federal tax laws permit an accelerated depreciation over five years of the capital cost of renovation in certain areas. In case of substantial remodeling, such a tax shelter can be substantial—usually averaging about $5,000 per unit per year for five years. Cash flow would be improved by attracting a more wealthy group of tenants, and financing is often available from municipal government.

On the other hand, such "upward" conversions pose a serious problem for neighborhood conservation, since it tends to destroy the stock of good housing for the less-well-to-do and tends to alter the character of a community. In a nondesignated district it can easily disrupt the architectural harmony of the area, unless held under control by a combination of zoning regulations, constraints on the granting of tax abatement and government loans, curbs on relocation and eviction procedures, and requirements that the renovated structure conform to the contours of the community.

**Renovation:
gut or
moderate?**

Two schools of thought have emerged concerning renovation in conservation areas: one advocates large capital expenditures to remake a building; the other urges a more muted approach. When should renovation be used to stem decay and when merely to buy time?

Discussion
Except in cases of deliberate upgrading to attract high-income tenants or buyers, or in cases where the physical condition of the structure precludes any other option, the issue of *how much* to renovate is of great importance. Many feel that extensive physical renovation is important from a long-term viewpoint, and urge virtual demolition and reconstruction, despite the high capital costs and forced tenant relocation.

Advocates of more moderate renovation point to the high rent rolls and dislocation brought about by total renovation, to the dangers of disruption of community character and cohesion, and to doubts about the marketability of the resulting units.

The other side sees this as a Band-Aid approach, doing little more than preventive maintenance, the outcome of which may not outlast the term of the loan. They argue that the investment of money in an unsound physical structure is only supportable if thereby the structure is made fully sound physically.

The availability of Section 8 funds to subsidize rentals in total renovation or adaptive reuse efforts is a key variable in this issue.

Detroit

The possibility of adaptive reuse of a landmark structure is an element to consider in this context. There is a residual bias against reuse, despite an expanding record of successful cases varying from modest cosmetic changes to a total gutting. Yet developers are often hard to find, and institutional owners sometimes give in too easily before what they see as uncertain financing and a cloudy future for the neighborhood. Commitment by a public agency to lease space in such a building—as sought in Senate Bill S865 (the Public Buildings Cooperative Use Act) sponsored by Sen. James Buckley (C.-R., N.Y.) and passed by the Senate in 1975—would help attract financing and a developer to such landmark neighborhood structures.

Conclusion
The street in a viable neighborhood is like an outdoor room. Planner John A. Gallery has noted that up to 40% of the land area of most cities is made up of publicly owned streets. What attracts people to streets, in the long run, is other people. Thus it is vital for a municipality's physical design policy to concern itself with these issues.

Notes to Chapter III

1. "From Euclid to Ramapo: new directions in land development controls," by Donald H. Elliott and Norman Marcus. *Hofstra Law Review*, Spring 1973.

2. *Street-level governments: assessing decentralization and urban services*, by Robert Yin and Douglas Yates. Washington, D.C.: The Rand Corporation, 1974. $5.

3. "Municipal housing code enforcement and low-income tenants" by Chester W. Hartman, Richard P. Kessler, Richard F. LeGates, *AIP Journal*, March 1974.

4. McNulty, Robert H., in recommendations for the community conservation section in the Final Report of the Task Force on Land Utilization and Urban Growth, September 1972. Published in part in "The Use of Land" by William K. Reilly, Rockefeller Brothers Task Force.

5. Rideout vs. Knox, 148 Mass. 368, 19 N.E. 390 (1889).

6. Pennsylvania Coal Company vs. Mahon, 260 U.S. at 415.

7. *American Land Planning Law* by Norman Williams, Jr. 5 vols. Rutgers University Press, 1975.

8. *New York Times*, 27 April 1975.

9. Mitchell, James, Public Affairs Counseling. *The Dynamics of Neighborhood Change*. U.S. Dept. of Housing and Urban Development, Office of Policy Development and Research, 1975.

10. *A study of the effects of real estate property tax incentive programs upon property rehabilitation and new construction.* Prepared by Price Waterhouse & Co. for HUD Contract #H-1300, 1973. Supt. of Documents, Washington, D.C. 20402. Stock No. 2300-00238. Unnumbered pages. $3.70.

11. From a working paper prepared for the 1972 Task Force on Land Utilization and Urban Growth, Laurance S. Rockefeller, chairman. Work of task force led to publication of "The Use of Land."

12 Andrea, Matt, *Draft operational plan, Neighborhood Improvement Program*, Washington, D.C., June 1975. Unpublished.

13. Phillips, Kenneth F. and Agelasto, Michael A., II. "Housing and Central Cities: The Conservation Approach." *Ecology Law Quarterly.* Vol. 4, No. 4, Berkeley, Calif., 1975.

14. *Saving New York's Neighborhoods*, Vol. 1, prepared by New York University Real Estate Institute, Richard Morris, Project Director, 1975.

15. Analysis developed by Richard Morris, New York City economist.

Chapter IV

The States' Role in Neighborhood Conservation

The States' Role in Neighborhood Conservation

On the surface, it would appear that neighborhood conservation efforts to date have found their main source of public-sector strength in local government. Furthermore, few governors could now claim a coordinated statewide program dealing with the subject. On the other hand, state-level policies and programs have had a profound effect, for good and for ill, on the health and vitality of urban neighborhoods.

Contributions to neighborhood quality by the states have largely been by default. Much of the time state influence has surfaced in the form of improper coordination, unimaginative programming, and outdated policies which have often promoted, rather than slowed, the process of neighborhood decay. In short, the untapped potential for a state role in neighborhood conservation remains enormous.

This perhaps gloomy picture is modified by sizable variations among the states in terms of policy emphasis (urban, suburban, or rural), staff size and expertise, and historical tradition. Nor can one ignore the sweeping fluctuations brought on by changing governorships, appointive office holders, and legislators.

Yet every state shares the opportunity—and the responsibility—to assist in neighborhood conservation efforts, both through direct action in the form of economic support, tax incentives, technical assistance and regulation, and through the range of powers it may delegate to localities within its borders.

Delegation of powers

While direct state action can do much to help revitalize neighborhoods, the promise of what the states can do through enabling legislation is much greater. Central to this fact is the concept of home rule, whereby a state delegates a cluster of basic self-governing authorities to certain cities and counties. Historically the states have varied in the degree to which they have granted home rule charters. In most states a tradition of paternalism has not only placed limits on the ability of localities to generate revenue, but has also weakened local efforts to provide needed public services.

Home rule

Put simply, the states possess an absolute constitutional control over the structure and legal powers of local government. Without home rule a commmunity must go to the state legislature for permission to undertake a wide range of activities, and is prevented from forging solutions to its problems at the level of city hall.

Home rule, or a lack thereof, has been the source of both opportunities and constraints in neighborhood conservation. In its broadest sense home rule simplifies, or at least cuts short, the process of initiating conservation schemes, by deleting the otherwise necessary state legislative approval stage. In a more specific sense home rule makes easier the various forms of taxation needed to make possible the services and other programs for upgrading neighborhoods. The power to tax, however, has been accompanied by debatable side effects whenever it has permitted a local property tax to rise to excessive rates, thereby contributing to deterioration or abandonment. In Pennsylvania local governments have been granted the right to tax while the state reserves the right to establish the subjects of taxation.

Pennsylvania

The home rule question has other, broader implications. An anti home rule bias in some states (Ohio for instance) has prevented localities from decentralizing decision-making authority to neighborhood councils or review boards.

Ohio

The related state-delegated powers of incorporation and annexation have had a substantial impact on the survival of urban neighborhoods. Remnants of 19th century rural dominance in state legislatures still make annexation difficult for many municipalities and hinder expansion of the community's tax base. At the same time, state regulations governing suburban incorporation have by and large tended to promote incorporation, thus worsening the drain on city services due to increased numbers of non-property-tax-paying commuters. (In Ohio, townships may not incorporate but may annex to a city if the city wants it. Often the township's tax base is not enough to offset the extra services the city would have to provide.)

These trends have tended to hurt local ability to undertake physical improvements and provide municipal services in center city neighborhoods.

Police power
Beyond these most basic of delegated powers is a whole package of powers which a locality may exercise only if so authorized by provisions of state constitution or statute. Uppermost among these are the police power and the power of eminent domain, both of which are in turn tempered by due process provisions in the federal and most state constitutions. The potential impact of these powers on community development in general and urban neighborhoods in particular has been shown to be very great.

The police power is a rather broad power of uncompensated regulation justified on the basis of promoting the public health, safety, morals, and general welfare. Eminent domain, on the other hand, is the power whereby a governmental entity may acquire the title to private property or an interest in it without the owner's consent so long as the owner receives fair compensation. Both powers may be exercised only for an appropriate governmental objective.

Zoning
Local regulation of land use in the United States did not become firmly fixed until a 1926 Supreme Court decision upheld municipal zoning as a legitimate exercise of the police power. Since that time, court cases have largely focused on the issue of ensuring property owners a "reasonable return" when property is regulated through the police power, i.e., to preclude regulation from constituting a "taking." The legitimacy of zoning as a local police power exercise has long been beyond dispute. Questions remain of course, in the matter of actual administration of this power—that is, the issue of exceptions and variances which serve to alter the law. (These issues are further discussed in Chapter III.)

Local zoning ordinances are now widespread, either as a result of specific delegation by the states or, in the case of localities with home rule charters, pursuant to more general powers of self-government. Yet even in those states where some or all localities are authorized to establish zoning ordinances, problems arise because so many state enabling statutes are out of date.

Most states still rely on general zoning statutes derived from a model developed under Herbert Hoover's tenure as Secretary of Commerce. A few, including New York, Illinois, and California, have facilitated a comprehensive revision of their zoning enabling legislation. Other states, notably Wisconsin, have brought about significant changes in local zoning through minimal changes in the language of state enabling laws. Most legislatures, however, have found an excuse for delay by awaiting the long pending Model Land Development Code now nearing completion by the American Law Institute.

California

Illinois
New York
Wisconsin

In some cases, legislative intent must be reexamined to see that it corresponds to present-day concerns and to supply localities with powers broad enough to fit changing circumstances. In about a dozen states, language in enabling statues which promotes the rigid separation of functions in communities (industrial, residential, etc.) has been reevaluated in light of the growing enthusiasm for diversity of use in urban neighborhoods. This lead should be formed elsewhere.

Eminent domain
The exercise of the power of eminent domain by a state and, if so authorized, by its subdivisions is more direct on the surface than is the police power, but is characterized by similar subtleties of interpretation and difficulties in application. In fact the equitable exercise of eminent domain has been the focus of recent reform efforts by the National Conference of Commissioners on Uniform State Laws and the New York State Legis-

lature. A model code developed by the NCCUSL seeks to: (1) simplify legal proceedings if they arise from a condemnation action; (2) require both technical and financial assistance when relocation is necessary; and (3) clarify definitions of "just compensation."

In addition to addressing some of the inconsistencies dealt with in the NCCUSL model code, the New York legislation would expand public notice requirements for all condemnation actions including those undertaken by authorized cities, counties, fire districts, and quasi-public institutions within the state. Two related bills, The Uniform Relocation Assistance Act and The Uniform Change of Grade Act seek, respectively, to expand relocation assistance for businessmen and to ensure compensation for certain types of property damage in unincorporated areas.

Historically, the effects of condemnation actions by states and their subdivisions have hamstrung efforts to maintain neighborhood identity and integrity. This impact reached its zenith during the height of urban renewal activity and interstate highway construction. Elimination of abuse through statutory revisions at the state level should be a matter of high priority.

Bonding authority
The ability to issue bonds is another useful tool to communities wishing to initiate or encourage physical improvements in target neighborhoods. For instance, the issuance of tax-exempt bonds with relatively low interest rates makes it possible for communities to pass on their savings in the form of low-interest loans to property owners. The states of Maryland and California, among others, have permitted certain cities to issue bonds to finance such loans for rehabilitation. In most cases, communities are not permitted to exceed a specified limit of indebtedness in their use of bond financing.

California
Maryland

Lending authority can also be a major issue in local efforts to conserve neighborhoods. Many

states have permitted certain localities to provide property and/or credit to entities in the private sector. In a number of midwestern and western states, however, such authorizations are restricted or even prohibited. In a mood representative of several states, Utah legislators recently refused to permit the state's new housing finance agency to make direct loans because of what they saw as a "moral problem" of competing with private lenders.

Ohio
Utah

In other states, where statutes prohibit credit to private individuals or corporations, localities are unable to subsidize property write-downs including the sale of abandoned structures to homesteaders for nominal amounts. In the state of Washington, preservation-directed revolving funds proposed in Seattle are encountering problems involving the city's authority to co-mingle public and private funds.

Washington

This same issue has in the past impaired the ability of certain states and localities to carry out rehabilitation loan programs that would replace HUD Section 312 funding. Although such loan programs are an eligible cost under CD block grants, many communities are barred by state law from pursuing it. Now a bill extending Section 312 has been passed, however (with funding through August 1976); it permits Section 312 loans to be combined with CD block grants, especially to foster urban homesteading. In those states where authority to lend is delegated, the tool has proved useful for neighborhood conservation. The delegation of this power in New York State, for example, made possible New York City's municipal loan program which, after a slow start, has proved a useful resource for low-cost lending to upgrade city neighborhoods.

New York

The public benefit corporation
Another tool which may be fruitfully applied to neighborhood objectives is the special public benefit corporation. Created either directly for a statewide purpose, or indirectly by giving a locality the authority to create one, these corporations can acquire the necessary powers for property ownership, bond financing, lending, and

condemnation, while maintaining a high degree of independence. With prior authorization from the state, the city of Seattle has used this power to establish the Historic Seattle Preservation and Development Authority and the Pike Place Development Authority to promote renewal through rehabilitation and adaptive reuse. Since its establishment by the state of California, the San Francisco Bay Conservation and Development Commission has guided the growth of waterfront neighborhoods in the Bay area.

Washington

California

Historic preservation powers

A growing number of states have enacted enabling statutes geared specifically to historic preservation. These statutes are narrow in approach, but they have proved helpful in maintaining the character of many urban neighborhoods and they offer considerable potential for expansion. While some cities derive their ability to regulate historic districts from general state zoning laws, most stem from enabling statutes dealing specifically with historic district zoning. Since 1931, when the city of Charleston, South Carolina, promulgated the first historic district ordinance, well over half the states have enacted enabling legislation for this purpose.

South Carolina

Nevertheless, the concept requires broadening before it achieves its full potential for urban neighborhoods. A Vermont enabling law permits the establishment of special zoning districts. In North Carolina, one community has been authorized by the State legislature to establish special zoning for areas of visual distinction referred to as "appearance districts." Another North Carolina statute authorizes local appearance commissions; these do not actually have zoning power, but may recommend that certain aesthetic conditions be placed upon the issuance of special or conditional use permits.

Vermont

North Carolina

Regulation of this kind, generally contained under the rubric of aesthetic zoning, is still being tested in some state courts on the issue of whether or not such regulation constitutes an appropriate exercise of the police power.

Historic district regulation and other forms of aesthetic zoning increasingly have been seen by state courts as promoting the general welfare by enhancing community pride and identity and encouraging orderly growth. Most often, however, the courts have tied these forms of regulation to the police power by means of their *economic* impact—e.g., promotion of tourism or enhancement of property values. In other words, the courts have historically held that aesthetic values alone are not enough to justify use of the police power.

In the last several years, however, this doctrine has been altered substantially by decisions in the courts of such states as Massachusetts, Oregon, New York, and California. In these states, the courts have confirmed the constitutionality of ordinances enacted purely on the grounds of preserving aesthetic character. Generally speaking, architectural or historic significance is easier to define than visual quality and thus is easier to prove in court.

Massachusetts
Oregon
New York
California

Accompanying this favorable trend in state courts is a string of inconsistent decisions involving the taking issue, i.e., the question of whether certain forms of regulation, including aesthetic zoning, constitute an abridgement of private property rights requiring compensation. It has generally been more difficult to defend regulation of individual landmarks than of structures within designated districts.

Easements

States may also advance neighborhood conservation by permitting localities to obtain less-than-fee property interests or easements. Through state law, localities are enabled to acquire such interests through purchase, condemnation, bequest, or donation.

Statutes authorizing historic or scenic easement programs are often accompanied by tax incentives for the donation and sale of less-than-fee interests, such as income tax deductions, capital gains treatment of proceeds, and property tax

Tennessee
Oregon
Virginia

relief. Tennessee, Virginia, and Oregon, for example, provide for reduced property tax assessments when real property is subject to an easement.

Taxation

The entire subject of taxation is critical to the success of neighborhood conservation efforts. Despite growing skepticism about the use of the taxing power to determine public policy, a large number of states continue to use both income tax and property tax policies to promote property enhancement, long-term owner occupancy, and commercial vitality. Provisions under which the state allows localities to give a credit against the property tax for the value of a specific improvement are by and large preferable to provisions which call for across-the-board abatements for *all* historic properties. Whereas the specific credit acts as a direct incentive to improve a property, the across-the-board abatement merely lessens the burden of owning historic property but doesn't directly encourage specific improvements.

Wisconsin

Following Wisconsin's lead in 1964, several states have enacted so-called "circuit breaker" legislation to provide relief for low-income individuals from excessive property tax burdens. This permits homeowners to deduct most of their property tax payments from state income tax. The states of New Mexico and Maryland take a slightly different approach and permit counties and/or municipalities to accept all or part of the costs of rehabilitating historic buildings as a credit against property taxes. This concept is promising for less "historic" buildings in special neighborhoods.

New Mexico
Maryland

Property tax abatements and exemptions have been used effectively in a few states to promote maintenance or revival of older buildings and neighborhoods. The flexibility of this approach, however, is inhibited by the requirement in almost all the states that "ad valorem" taxes on real, personal, and intangible property be levied uniformly throughout the state. In Connecticut, municipalities may abate all or part of the prop-

Connecticut

erty taxes on buildings of architectural or historic merit. Eligibility is decided by the municipalities or delegated to private groups with the proper expertise. Some states also have schemes to exempt registered buildings and districts from property taxes for specified time periods.

New Jersey
New York
Puerto Rico

North Carolina has recently passed legislation providing for a five-year rollback of property taxes in which the owner of a certified property is required to pay only 50% of his assessment until after the fifth year. There may be problems because of the heavy burden of interest payments due at the end of the deferral period, or in the event that through fire, vandalism, or other damage the property loses the characteristics which made it eligible for deferral.

North Carolina

Another delegated power worth investigation gives localities the authority to use tax increment financing to pay for public investment in urban neighborhoods. Following the lead of California, which in 1952 authorized tax allocation financing through constitutional amendment, a growing number of states have passed enabling legislation.

Put simply, tax increment financing sets aside projected increases in tax revenues due to new development in order to pay for public improvements serving the new development or to repay bonds used to finance such improvements.

While this approach has been used with much success in several states, notably California and Minnesota, to promote important redevelopment, many pitfalls remain. In addition to the uncertainty of projected increases in tax revenues, disadvantages include the tendency of the system to intensify development in pleasant low-density areas and, if abused, to freeze the tax base of a city for lengthy periods.

In 1968 a report of the National Commission on Urban Problems observed that "beyond passing enabling legislation which allowed local authorities to act, or which delegated stated police powers over zoning regulations and building and

**Direct
state
support**

housing codes to the cities, most states have played a minor and passive role in housing American people, especially those with low incomes." Since then, the states have made modest but mixed progress in their attempts to actively increase the supply of housing and to support such vital nonhousing components of neighborhood quality as social services, commercial vitality, law enforcement, and pedestrian amenities.

Since the Commission's report, the number of states with housing finance agencies has grown to the point where 32 states now have one or more such agencies. On the other hand, the movement to establish state community affairs agencies, which peaked in the years immediately following the riots, has leveled off. The offices in each state with responsibility for encouraging historic preservation vary widely in size, focus, and impact. State arts agencies are gradually increasing their grants and technical assistance in architecture, preservation, outdoor sculpture, and other cultural activities with potential for neighborhood enhancement.

And, finally, state agencies which support programs in health, education, law enforcement, open space and recreation, and transportation have continued to assist urban areas with varying degrees of success.

Direct support by these state agencies takes many forms including grants, loans, and subsidies as well as technical assistance through publications, site visits, and advocacy work.

State housing finance agencies

Among the most promising of state-based efforts to date are the state housing finance agencies (HFAs). Since the first housing credit agencies of Hawaii and California, dating to the early 1920s, HFAs have arisen in the states in varying forms and with a wide range of power and responsibility. Several states established farm and home loan programs for veterans following World War II, and Connecticut and New York began programs to assist middle- and low-income families soon thereafter. It was not until

1960, however, with the New York State Housing Finance Agency Law, that the HFA took the form it has in most states today.

Encouraged by the success of New York's HFA, Massachusetts and Michigan established their own in 1966. The greatest increase followed enactment of the Housing Act of 1968 which made possible the "piggybacking" of state assistance with federal Section 236 subsidies.

By and large, HFAs are independent components of state government which seek to encourage private housing enterprise by providing low-interest loans, second mortgage financing, loans to lenders, start-up money, and technical assistance. In New York, the Urban Development Corporation had additional responsibilities in the area of acquisition, development, and management of real estate.

Designed to be financially self-sufficient, the HFAs have been authorized to issue their own tax-exempt revenue bonds. Although these bonds are usually not backed by the "full faith and credit" of the state (as are referenda-approved issues), their security (and thus their appeal to investors) is enhanced by a "moral obligation clause" requiring the HFA to maintain adequate reserve funds, and indicating the willingness of legislatures to make up deficiencies. Limits on indebtedness of HFAs range from under $25 million in some states to no limit at all.

HFA staffs tend to be small and are afforded wide flexibility, since most HFAs are exempt from direct state fiscal controls, civil service requirements, and competitive bidding procedures.

In recent years, HFAs have turned to special issues in housing involving the elderly, the handicapped, and the integration of mixed racial or income groups. They have also begun to focus on rehabilitation of individual homes, multifamily dwellings and, in some cases, whole neighborhoods. In general HFAs have shown a willingness to take risks beyond those assumed

Hawaii
California

Connecticut
New York

Massachusetts
Michigan

New York

by private lenders. In Detroit, for instance, the Michigan Housing Finance Agency is working closely with HUD to repair deteriorated housing stock now owned by the federal government due to defaults on FHA loans. Yet few have developed really significant programs in rehabilitation.

In predicting the potential of HFAs in neighborhood conservation and community development generally, one can with profit review the different methods used by HFAs to achieve their objectives to date. The lion's share has involved direct mortgage loans to developers for the construction or rehabilitation of privately owned and operated multifamily development. Since 1968 over 200,000 housing units have been financed in this fashion, of which some 117,000 involved Section 236 rental subsidies. Of all the HFAs, 23 have undertaken this kind of direct financing; some other states have the authority but have not yet used it.

Example: Massachusetts
A look at the Massachusetts Housing Finance Agency (MHFA) shows how neighborhood vitality can be achieved through direct loans to developers. Created in 1966, MHFA closed its first loan in 1970 and began financing housing projects throughout the state. Required by statute to set aside at least 25% of each development for low-income persons MHFA has managed to create mixed-income developments with reportedly high standards of design, construction, and management.

A growing number of projects have involved the rehabilitation of aging housing or the conversion of older factories and other commercial buildings. In these projects MHFA sees to the relocation of residents in buildings scheduled for rehabilitation, and requires that rehab projects include units of a size which can accommodate original tenants at affordable rents. In addition, MHFA staff makes post-completion inspections of rehabilitation projects to help ensure proper maintenance. MHFA also is authorized to replace management agents for developments if necessary.

As of March 1975, MHFA had provided permanent financing for 20,801 housing units in 151 developments, of which 14.5% involved rehabilitation and 15.7% were located in Boston neighborhoods.

The agency's use of direct financing of adaptive reuse building projects goes a step beyond the tradition of financing new construction almost exclusively.

Many HFAs are also working to increase the amount of mortgage capital available in the market through mortgage purchase and loans-to-lenders programs. These are especially important during tight credit periods.

Under mortgage purchase programs, the HFA buys up existing or newly initiated mortgages from conventional lenders, enabling the lender to reloan the proceeds at a reduced interest rate to low- and moderate-income borrowers according to HFA requirements. In several states, only federally insured or guaranteed mortgages may be purchased in such programs. In Minnesota, a mortgage purchase approach has been developed and subsequently adopted by several other states. In the Minnesota Homeownership Loan Program, the HFA invites lenders to apply for an advance commitment to buy mortgages in specified geographic areas. Following approval, the lender has six to 12 months to originate the loans and deliver them to HFA. A similar program pending in Utah will stress the upgrading of urban neighborhoods.

In their loans-to-lenders program, HFAs make below market interest rate loans to mortgage lending institutions. These in turn make new residential loans. In many states this approach is accompanied by controls over the lender involving interest rate, income level of recipients, and type and location of housing.

New Jersey has taken this approach in its center city neighborhoods, having made special low-interest loans to institutions willing to relend in 24 specified urban areas, thereby permitting the banks a greater yield spread than available elsewhere.

New Jersey
Illinois
Michigan

Several other mechanisms have been used by HFA's in getting more houses built. New Jersey, Illinois, and Michigan have instituted revolving funds for low-interest (or interest free) loans to developers to cover start-up costs such as design fees and appraisals. Several HFAs offer technical assistance to developers on financial, legal, management, and design matters. The new Utah HFA wants to encourage realtors to engage in "reverse blockbusting" and to stimulate private lending in formerly redlined areas.

In some states the HFAs have been made better through coordination with state and regional planning bodies.

New York

Despite successes, many problems remain for the HFAs. Some 80% of HFA activity is still in suburban housing. Disregard of urban neighborhoods is made worse by administrative and statutory limitations which prevent many states from financing rehabilitation and recycling. Furthermore, the problems of New York's UDC and questions over use of the Section 8 federal subsidy program in high-cost areas have tended to impair the ability of HFAs to market their bonds. On the other hand, the appeal of state housing bonds appears to vastly exceed that of bonds issued by local housing authorities, many of which have been unable even to obtain a rating for their bonds.

State community affairs agencies

Another state-level tool that appears in some form in a majority of states is the state community affairs agency (CAA). Referred to in some states as the Department of Community Affairs (Pennsylvania), in others as the Division of Housing and Community Renewal (New York), the scope and functions of these agencies vary greatly. In general, their responsibilities include state and regional planning, urban renewal, and housing. In some states these agencies are closely tied with the HFA. Other concerns cover property, relocation, economic development,

health, and the environment. CAAs also administer many federal grants and contracts in these subject areas, provide technical assistance to communities, and often act as a coordinating mechanism within state government.

The existence of a CAA type of cabinet- or sub-cabinet-level agency concerned with urban affairs is, at minimum, a sign of state attention and a source of urban expertise within state government. Yet few states have provided their CAAs with sufficient funds or authority to help bring about true change in the inner city.

Massachusetts

Rhode Island

Pennsylvania

New Jersey

There are some successes. In 1974 and 1975 the Massachusetts Department of Community Affairs focused its technical assistance to smaller communities on identifying housing and commercial structures with adaptive use potential. Local planners from the Rhode Island Department of Community Affairs work closely with state historic preservation staff when preparing statewide land use plans. In Pennsylvania the Department of Community Affairs makes grants to municipalities and redevelopment authorities so they can make rehabilitation loans similar to those available hitherto under the federal Section 312 program. The Demonstration Grant Program administered by the New Jersey Department of Community Affairs provides grants to borrowers to reduce interest costs on conventional home improvement loans. Eligibility is limited to cities with federally assisted renewal areas.

State historic preservation offices

Another source of direct state support for neighborhood conservation, only partially tapped, lies in those offices in each state responsible for historic preservation. While eleven states now have independent agencies whose chief function is historic preservation, most state preservation offices are still found within agencies whose responsibilities also cover cultural matters, natural resources, or parks and recreation.

Indeed, a major weakness of state historic preservation efforts to date has been conflicts in policy, staffing, and funding that come up when preservation concerns are housed in competing or even unsympathetic agencies.

Following the passage of the 1966 Historic Preservation Act, the governors of each state were asked to appoint a state historic preservation officer to oversee preservation policy and programs and to administer grants-in-aid available from the U.S. Department of Interior. Although Interior would like to formulate criteria to guide selection of SHPOs, these officers have often been individuals with either little background in preservation or else a narrow archival view of the field.

In addition to administering federal grants, state preservation offices5 make surveys of historic resources, oversee the certification of valuable properties through the National Register of Historic Places or similar state registers, review federally required environmental impact statements, and carry out various planning, technical assistance, and education functions.

In many states, state funding is scarce for preservation planning other than that required to match Interior Department grants. Thus, much of this support takes the form of technical assistance and education. And in some cases this has worked very well, such as Rhode Island's public awareness efforts and Massachusetts' statewide preservation workshops.

Rhode Island
Massachusetts

State historical commissions and similar agencies could go much further, however, in working with lending institutions, legislators, federal area offices, and other decision makers to acquaint them with neighborhood conservation objectives. For example, greater heed could be paid to such items as compatibility of new construction in older areas and development of design criteria to guide the same.

Some states, encouraged by the Interior Department, are now exploring ways to multiply the impact of available dollars by setting up easement programs and by establishing revolving funds to provide loans for restoration, rehabilitation, and adaptive reuse. (Only National Register properties are eligible for such loans.)

In implementing their own regulatory policies and those mandated by a variety of federal programs, the states influence neighborhoods by establishing controls relating to historic preservation, land use, the natural environment, housing, and banking.

Regulation

Preservation planning
In addition to participating in federally required review procedures, a number of state historic preservation programs, notably North Carolina, have advisory councils to review state-sponsored projects that will affect historic resources. These procedures rest on registration systems that attest to the federal, state, or local significance of certain properties or areas, and they have served to delay or prevent adverse action.

North Carolina

Review responsibilities assigned to states under Section 102 of the National Environmental Policy Act, Section 106 of the National Historic Preservation Act, and Section 4 (f) of the Department of Transportation Act have on occasion helped to divert threats, but at major cost in staff time.

Preservation planning in each state grows out of surveys and inventories (usually carried on with federal aid). The information gathered by these surveys offers a chance for early planning, but few states have actively sought to coordinate preservation planning with statewide planning in transporation, recreation, or land use. About one state in three makes survey information available only on request to federal, state and regional agencies with planning responsibilities. The Rhode Island Historical Preservation Commission, in cooperation with its Statewide Planning Office, decided to computerize its survey information, with a computer terminal to be placed in appropriate state agencies. Illinois, New York, and several other states are trying to improve their preservation inventory retrieval systems.

Rhode Island

New York
Illinois

Land use and environment

Reviving the notion of state-based land use control after many years of local emphasis, more states than not have taken some recent action to promote wise land use. In most cases, the approach has been piecemeal, but a few states have pursued comprehensive land use and regulation policies. These states mostly require some form of environmental impact assessment. Regulation can generally be broken down into four categories: statewide consideration of "major" public and/or private actions requiring state funding or approval; statewide regulation of specific types of development; regulation of "critical environmental areas"; regulation and programming of selected public facilities and private utilities.

In most states, land use policies have been oriented toward non urban natural areas, the neighborhood scale being a level of refinement not yet addressed. Fortunately for urban neighborhoods, most states that use the "critical environmental area" approach take historically valuable areas into their definitions. Hawaii requires localities to prepare urban design plans.

Vermont's Act 250, passed in 1970, and the Land Capability and Development Plan, show how historic and visible assets can be integrated into a state's framework for land use regulation. Although the Vermont program has been criticized by some as underenforced and underfunded, it—and those of a handful of other states—are said to be about the most innovative the states have to offer to date in terms of meshing land use and preservation concerns. The next step, in these states and elsewhere, is to guide land use in older urban neighborhoods.

Federally assisted planning programs

Another opportunity for state leadership lies in the federally assisted and/or required planning programs. These programs, responsibility for which is largely in the lap of the states, include those assisted by the Environmental Protection Agency (air and water quality), National Oceanic and Atmospheric Administration (coastal zone management), the Economic De-

velopment Administration, HUD's Section 701 Comprehensive Planning Assistance Program, the Federal Highway Administration (state and metropolitan planning), the Urban Mass Transit Administration, the Federal Aviation Administration (airport planning related to noise and safety), the Bureau of Outdoor Recreation, and the National Park Service—in all a very broad spectrum indeed.

What is the potential effect of these federally assisted planning programs on neighborhoods and their conservation? First, most of them require citizen involvement in the formulation of state plans, providing a forum for citizen input involving neighborhood concerns. Second, these programs allow for early identification of significant neighborhoods and, as a first step to protection or stabilization, permit inclusion of these places in statewide plans.

Many states now have independent programs in such areas as solid waste, noise pollution, strip-mining, wetlands conservation, highway beautification, and air and water quality. Hawaii and Maryland regulate noise pollution, Oregon's famous "bottle bill" outlaws disposable bottles, one state in three has laws relating to resource recovery, and California has created a regional agency to fight air pollution in the Los Angeles–San Diego area. The time is certainly ripe for states to include conservation of urban neighborhoods among their regulatory programs to cover gaps unfilled by municipal initiatives.

Housing and building codes

In a growing number of states, public officials and advisory commissions have been working toward uniform statewide codes. Massachusetts adopted such a building code in 1974.

The benefits of uniformity notwithstanding, statewide building codes have proved on occasion to be rigid and insensitive to the special problems of adapting older building to contemporary use. They are written in terms of new construction rather than rehabilitation. In Oregon public pressure brought about changes in

Hawaii
Vermont
Florida
Oregon

Hawaii

Vermont

Georgia
New York
Minnesota

Hawaii
Maryland
Oregon

California

Kansas
Tennessee
Rhode Island

Oregon

Connecticut
Massachusetts

the Oregon Structural Specialty Code to permit greater flexibility when applied to designated historic structures. Connecticut and Massachusetts architects are working with state building code officials to remove roadblocks to adaptive use without impairing health and safety standards.

Another code issue, that of enforcement, surfaces on the state level as a matter of financial support as well as a matter of regulation. To provide a carrot to complement the stick of state and local housing codes, several states have funded communities and property owners in return for attempts to upgrade housing in certain neighborhoods. These state programs were mostly formulated following cutbacks in 1973 of Federally Assisted Code Enforcement (FACE) programs assisted in part by Section 312 rehabilitation loans. In Connecticut the Department of Community Affairs set up a program several years ago to provide grants to communities to bolster their code enforcement programs.

Connecticut

New Jersey

New Jersey's Demonstration Grant Program was used in several communities to advance code enforcement, working through local lenders, public officials, and citizen advisors; the Department of Community Affairs has helped over 650 property owners in two wards of a township near Newark: of 2,000 structures in the area over 80% were built before 1940, and as a result of the state's efforts only 4% now violate code standards.

Banking

The phenomenon of redlining, or the refusal of banks to loan in areas of seemingly high risk, has been amply documented. Recognizing the practice as a severe threat to the health of older urban neighborhoods, some states and localities have begun to investigate methods of reversing the trend. These methods include efforts to obtain documentation on restrictive lending policies, requiring lending institutions to disclose information on the geographical sources of their deposits and their loans. In 1974 the governor of Massachusetts adopted the views of a special task force requiring a limited form of mortgage disclosure and a review board would oversee this

Massachusetts

beginning in 1976. In 1975 the District of Columbia considered withdrawing the District's deposits from institutions with a poor record on center city lending. Several bills debated (but later defeated) in the 1975 New York State legislature would have increased the total number of dollars for mortgage lending in center cities.

District of
Columbia

New York

Late in 1975 the California Business and Transportation Agency proposed regulations aimed at reducing redlining. In addition to requiring that lending institutions disclose by census tract the dollar amounts of mortgage loans and deposits made in these areas, the regulations would prohibit lenders from considering neighborhood decline (as opposed to the mortgageability of a given property or the credit worthiness of the borrower) in assessing a potential loan. A related proposal would set up regional boards of inquiry around the state to hear complaints involving wrongful denials of mortgage loans. (For additional discussion on local redlining practices see Chapter III.)

California

State banking commissioners see the protection of depositors as their main objective, and this has tended to limit their interest in the secondary impacts of state banking policy on community development and conservation efforts.

Much is possible that is not being done. Increased state funding for neighborhood-based programs is an obvious need, but so are innovations in state policy. These would require realignment of legislative and administrative priorities but little new funding. In fact some programs designed to enhance neighborhoods would also permit cost savings. For example, economic reuse of older buildings for state office space is being carried on in New Hampshire, Missouri, and Vermont as a way to maintain scale and identity in neighborhoods.

Prospects

New Hampshire
Missouri
Vermont

The National Governors Conference, with neighborhood conversation included in a recent study on state-local relations, raises hopes that governors, legislators, and other state officials will shortly see neighborhood conservation as a major state objective.

Neighborhood Conservation: A Look at the Record

Albany
Anacostia
Annapolis
Atlanta
Austin
Baltimore
Berkeley
Boston
Charleston
Chicago
Dallas
Detroit
Galveston
Hartford

Hoboken

Hudson

Louisville

Madison

Middlebury

Milwaukee

Minneapolis

New Haven

New Orleans

North Adams

Oklahoma City

Paterson

Peekskill

Philadelphia

Pittsburgh

Portland

Providence

Richmond

Sacramento

St. Charles

St. Joseph

St. Paul

San Francisco

Santa Fe

Savannah

Troy

Wilmington, Del.

Wilmington, N.C.

Neighborhood Conservation: A Look at the Record

Albany
New York
Population: c. 116,000

In this chapter and the next, the experiences of over 40 cities are described. The presentations are intended to be factual—no effort has been made to judge the appropriateness of policies or programs. Where there is an assessment, it reflects a consensus of those interviewed in that city.

Cities were selected in part because they offer an insight into a particular conservation approach or attitude, in part to obtain a reasonable cross-section of cities by size, composition, and age.

Although some cases are preservation rather than conservation-oriented, they are included because they point up certain principles and issues that apply beyond their own confines; in the case of cities like Charleston, S.C. and Savannah, Ga., preservation programs have been in action long enough so that their impact on conservation may be gauged.

Each case study is arranged roughly according to how and why the conservation effort started, where and how it obtained support, how the effort was managed, and what principal tools and tactics were used to carry it out. Population figures are drawn from the 1970 census, except for Anacostia, which the census listed only as a part of Washington, D.C.

A shorthand style has been used throughout this chapter for the sake of brevity and convenience.

Key abbreviations are included in the Index. Additional sources of information on each city are listed in Resources, page 257.

Synopsis

Albany's inner core in state of social and economic flux due to massive rebuilding, chiefly around huge new governmental center ("South Mall") and mixed but predominantly black South End. City neighborhoods on brink of extensive conservation. City faces difficult choices over renewal versus conservation.

High rate of abandonment. Inner city around South Mall has about 25,000 people; 30% of housing owner-occupied. In South End, rate is 5%. Center Square and Hudson Park have fine 19th-century architecture. Center Square largely restored and population expected to remain middle class, professional white.

Hudson Park is racially mixed, predominantly white and blue collar. Black poor are entering as are many students from State University (SUNY). Housing stock is largely 19th-century masonry. Owner occupancy 30%.

South End has oldest surviving concentration of 19th-century housing in city—masonry rowhouses and freestanding frame structures dating from 1815 to 1895.

Initiation

The giant South Mall, which was created to house state government, galvanized neighborhood groups into action. In 1974 a small group of residents founded Historic Albany Foundation (HAF) to promote citywide preservation and to acquire, hold, and restore buildings of historic or architectural interest. Funds from membership, NTHP, plus $25,000 from National Endowment for the Arts. Key triggers were two men who jointly owned 75 houses in area and who planned large-scale demolition for new project. After year's negotiations with HAF, these owners have agreed to a program of total preservation and adaptive reuse. Plan to donate facade easements to HAF.

Attitudes to conservation range from disbelief (real estate, construction groups) to benign neglect (by city). Mayor Erastus Corning, in office 34 years, exerts major control over events.

Construction of South Mall, SUNY campus, brought many newcomers to inner city (22,000 new state employees anticipated in next few years). Pressures on housing market in areas around South Mall.

publicly financed preservation effort. Mixes preservation with urban renewal. Exterior renovation paid for by city, interiors by developer. One hundred buildings in South End architecturally and historically significant; 100 new buildings to be erected at similar scale.

Authority and commitment

Report of the Committee on South Mall Environs (by a joint city-state committee) urges Albany Zoning Ordinance be amended to establish:

1. Special historic preservation areas and development areas as overlay zoning districts in neighborhoods adjacent to South Mall.

2. Special zoning regulations for these areas.

Design controls for inserted new structures set minimum and maximum heights, setbacks, and projections. HAF critical of zoning which restricts multifamily residential use in most of historic district.

City established Capitol Hill Architectural Review Commission in 1974: four members appointed by mayor, four by governor. Mayor names chairman. Commission still in formative stages; effect not yet felt.

Management of programs/ tools and tactics

Community Development Program (1975) directed toward four target areas, three residential neighborhoods and downtown. $1 to $1.5 million to be spent on rehabilitation activities in those areas each year through 1978 via interest subsidy grants, acquisition, and public improvements.

Program will be cooperative. Housing services offered through neighborhood centers. In South Mall target area, neighborhood coproration expected to administer preservation loans; city retains final say. Tax abatement unlikely. Improved buildings not assessed upward, but city under pressure from state to do so. Using 701 planning funds, citywide survey to identify properties of special architectural, historic value.

South End "Pastures Project" is city's first major

Anacostia

District of Columbia
Population: c.22,000
(Not a census figure)

Synopsis

Anacostia, in Washington, D.C.'s far Southeast quadrant, is a 2.2-square-mile neighborhood (3.2% of District area) trying to reverse decline in housing and neighborhood conditions dating to early 1960s. Influx of lower-income families due to urban renewal displacement elsewhere in city, and failure of city services to keep pace with rise in population, started downslide.

Within Anacostia area is Uniontown district, a working class neighborhood built after Civil War, under consideration for historic district designation. There has been a 39% population rise since 1960. Black population in 1960, 60%; in 1970, 69%. Other characteristics: 46% of population less than 18; median age 23; female-headed households are 25% of total; 21% of population receive some form of public assistance. Owner-occupied: 1960, 24%; 1970, 13%. No architectural style predominates.

Initiation

Late 1950s–early 1960s saw middle-income families leave; replaced by lower-income problem families displaced from other areas of city. City attention and services did not keep pace. Old housing stock overstressed. All social problems evident; commercial disinvestment. D.C.'s first elected mayor sensitive to problems of Anacostia, directed city departments to increase services. Lawsuit brought by community groups on gap in city services still in progress, but forced issue to the front in City Council's mind.

As for historic district in Uniontown, Frederick Douglass home was designated landmark in 1962, restoration effort lasted 10 years, opened in 1972. Interest among members of D.C. Joint Commission on Landmarks in expanding area to include surrounding homes and area.

Strong sense of community identity; small number of key individuals in many groups keeps participation and community spirit alive.

Authority and commitment

Neighborhood Housing Services program (NHS) is outgrowth of Federal Home Loan Bank Board effort to involve Savings and Loan Associations (S & Ls) in urban revitalization.

Many S & Ls criticized for redlining. Borrowed successful Pittsburgh program started by community people and local banks in 1968. Two pilots projects started by FHLBB in 1972 in Anacostia and Oakland, California.

Specific objective of NHS program is to arrest housing decline in neighborhood by providing financing for home improvement efforts. Also to increase involvement of lending institutions in Anacostia; to advise residents on home financing, budgeting, etc.; to provide other technical assistance to area homeowners; to encourage other agencies to improve services.

Management of program

NHS is nonprofit, has paid, full-time executive director, and small staff. NHS has access to city inspectors who survey for code problems and supervise contractors' rehabilitation work. Once problems identified and costs estimated, NHS works with homeowner to secure funding. Under NHS program in other cities, S & L's have agreed not to "redline," i.e., S & L's will not refuse to fund home improvement loans to households that meet normal loan criteria in neighborhoods previously considered "high risk"; important part of concept, since no bank is asked to take out of the ordinary risk. If household is below bank's income criteria, then arrangements made out of "high risk"/low interest revolving fund; generally, part of loan funded by bank, part from fund. Flexible arrangements on interest rates, terms tied to household's needs. (Average loan: $4,500. Range from $300 to over $8,000. Thirty loans made through early 1975.)

Operating tools and tactics

Land use and development controls
Historic preservation survey conducted of Uniontown areas as part of City Options grant from National Endowment for the Arts to Washington Planning and Housing Association, introduces options for community consideration, but will not recommend strict architectural standards because impractical in low-moderate income area. Concern that historic district designation of Uniontown might lead to residents being displaced by rising property values.

Tax policy
Some fear rehabilitation can lead to higher property taxes. But Anacostia generally under-assessed, so not yet a widespread problem. Bill passed in late 1974 advises tax assessment procedures in city. Authorizes assessment at market values, but tax at lower rates than now assessed; provides for differential rates depending on kind of property and says district must adopt tax incentives for housing rehabilitation. Several incentives under study, mostly involve tax credit and tax abatement concepts.

Financial mechanisms
District of Columbia earmarking major portion of CD block grant for conservation-related activities, including acquisition and/or rehabilitation of public and private housing units now off market (total about 80 in Anacostia) and $3,000,000 to citywide revolving rehabilitation loan and grant fund.

NHS has operating budget of some $50,000 per year (generally from S & L contributions). In Anacostia, three local foundations and Ford Foundation contributed to establish revolving fund. Additional $750,000 is earmarked from city's CD block grant (see below).

DC housing and community development policy
City Council shift of CD block grant money from scheduled urban renewal to neighborhood conservation indicates major focus on rehabilitation use of existing stock. Anacostia one of two action areas (other Capitol East) selected for first year neighborhood improvement program. Conservation activities will be partnership between new city departments of housing and community development and NHS. Program scheduled for implementation late 1975.

Displacement/relocation policy
Under tax incentives for rehabilitation, one idea is to give it only to rental unit owners who retain existing rent structure (i.e., given tax credit to offset rent rise that ordinarily would result from rehabilitation). One mechanism is community controlled organization to buy homes as they come on market before prices get too high.

Annapolis
Maryland
Population: c. 30,000

City's historic district meets waters of Chesapeake Bay at Annapolis dock, site of maritime activity for 300 years. Water is dominant: it complements network of narrow streets, brick-paved sidewalks, and houses of 17 distinct styles. District registered as National Historic Landmark District (1965). Covers 284 acres, 7% of city's area.

City is site of State Capital, county seat, and home of U.S. Naval Academy. Historic District Commission dates to 1969. Historic Annapolis, Inc., private nonprofit preservation group with 3,000 members, established in 1952.

In early 1960s, half of shops on main shopping street of Historic District stood empty. Historic two- and three-story houses showed age. Now many are restored by increasingly affluent residents. Main shipping street now prosperous. Problems of success: conflicting demands from merchants, residents, and government. Residents object to tourist traffic, parking problems, exit of convience stores in favor of tourist shops. Four levels of government coexist. Their buildings abut historic district, threaten expansion.

Historic Annapolis, Inc. (HA), nonprofit membership group, began effort in 1952, led by Mrs. J.M.P. Wright. Knows how to wield power and influence. Homes, stores, dock area deteriorated. HA focus on saving buildings, e.g., Charles Carroll's house, Barrister, Brice house, Slicer-Shiplap house. Also 140 street signs with original 17th- and 18th-century names erected. Highly visible early efforts valuable. HA then began to identify views and vistas, to survey paving, complete streetscape drawings. Clear record of historic district is resource, as well as idea of opportunities. Record has served as evidence in court and support for applications before Historic District Commission.

HA drew up "obstacle chart." Included lack of legal tools, lack of awareness on part of community, lack of awareness on part of businessmen. Devised strategies to overcome these. In early 1960s, Annapolis was discovered partly due to easier road access. First affluent families began to buy and restore.

Community attention focused on threat to historic area by some large planned projects—eight-story Hilton Inn (mid-1960s) on the dock; C and P Telephone Co. Bldg. Community was galvanized to support historic district ordinance and Commission (see Authority and Commitment). Business community supported Hilton. So did some councilmen due to half-million-dollar local payroll.

HA keeps scrutiny over all activities in historic district. Relations between HA and state, Naval Academy, federal officials good; also between leaders of HA and current city fathers. As to businessmen, HA comfortable only with those who share its vision. Same people have headed HA since founding; Critics call for new blood.

Historic District Commission (HDC) is official body approving all physical changes in district visible from public right of way. A vice president of HA also chairs the Commission. Improved relationships with minority groups, in part because of HDC's efforts to save historic Mt. Moriah Church, important to black people.

From 1958 through 1973, HA lists the following: $1.3 million in foundation grants; $1.634 million in private donations; $2.046 million in public grants. The money went for two major efforts: a revolving fund and easement program, and restoration of a house and gardens.

Revolving fund started in mid-1960s with $68,000. Enabled HA to buy and resell with protective easements $2.25 million worth of real estate. Program has bought about 30 easements (at average cost of 10% of market value). Revolving fund and easement program saved about 250 buildings, says HA.

Authority and commitment

Historic District Commission (HDC) established by 1969 City Ordinance. Ordinance follows the state enabling legislation, codified in 1963. Approval from HDC mandatory for construction, moving, demolition, or alteration of any structure affecting exterior appearance, if changes visible from adjacent public way in historic district. Interior changes outside jurisdiction. HDC required to "be lenient in judgment of plans for structures of little historic value, strict for those of value." Violators guilty of a misdemeanor. Business community, bankers, real estate men, city government, each for own reason, pleased with ordinance as means of upgrading area, realizing greater tax base as housing values increase without adding to service burdens. Preservationists pleased too, but see need for constant monitoring lest merchants/ realtors/bankers overexploit district. Residents pleased but concerned over parking and traffic, tourists, decline of convenience shopping. Local bankers last on board: most pre-1970 loans from Baltimore banks.

Management of program

Five-member HDC meets monthly. Historic Annapolis always present and comments on applications. HDC criticized for insufficient professional staff expertise. No funds provided for this purpose. Major controversies usually have to do with new development projects. By and large, applications in Commission's purview are approved. State complex nearby not subject to HDC review, hence chance of problems in future as complex expands. HDC meetings open; anyone may attend and testify. But involvement modest unless individual's property or home is at issue.

Some see preservation leadership in Annapolis as elitist, though individuals of all races and incomes worked to save Old Market House. However, few low-income residents active. Relocation officer for urban renewal authority concerned for decent homes for the poor, jobs, etc. Still, referendum establishing ordinanace and HDC passed 2-1 in every ward, including lower-income ones. Also, HA's 25-year efforts to raise community consciousness acknowledged by all.

Operating tools and tactics

Tax policy
Buildings in historic district not taxed at value accrued due to historic value, but at replacement value outside district for structure of like utility (i.e., without regard for value of special carpentry). Hence, buildings in historic district get tax break. Some suggest city is not recovering the revenues it could if buildings assessed at fair market value (including historic district value); favorable assessment should be applied selectively, they say. Current arrangement popular among property owners; few politicians would want to change ground rules at this time.

In 1969, property values in district at $38.4 million, 112% increase from 1961 level. Tax base growth said to be substantial function of historic character of old city. Typical of experience in other historic areas.

With 7% of city's land area, historic district has about 19% of the city's assessable base. Historic area's tax base seen as windfall for city, since cost of rendering services to district remained about the same in relation to normal citywide cost increases. (Economic analysis by Robert Gladstone and Assoc.)

Financial mechanisms
Maryland State Historical Trust acquires easements and restores structures. In exchange for financial assistance on the restoration, city gives the Trust an easement. The Trust also aids Historic Annapolis, Inc. with financial grants for restoration.

Private: see above for discussion of Historic Annapolis' funding ($5 million in grants from 1958–1973). No major bank investment programs. Major investments by individual property owners, with local bank mortgages. Existence of easement on residential unit has little effect on securing mortgage; on commercial property it does, due to constraints on potential reuse or conversion of structure.

Displacement/relocation policy
Some low-income families displaced in historic district. Homeowners sometimes given money and opportunity to leave district for larger residence in outlying area. For renters, no alternative except subsidized housing, for which there is no money.

Public services
Parking and traffic are a constant headache to neighborhood residents and inconvenience to tourists. Historic district often congested to maximum. City has bus system composed of converted school buses; too bulky for historic district.

Atlanta

Georgia
Population: c. 497,000

Focus of neighborhood conservation efforts in Inman Park Historic District. Covers 25 city blocks, 375 buildings, 1½ miles from CBD. Developed as one of first garden suburbs in 1880s, area has ornate, spacious wood frame mansions on large lots.

Before restoration, area was becoming a slum. Houses subdivided into apartments. Overcrowding—converted single-family houses held up to 35 people. Absentee landlords rented apartments by the week to transients. Much abandonment. Owner-occupancy dropped to 25%.

Initiation

Starting in 1969, outsiders begin to buy subdivided houses in Inman Park, restore and reconvert single-family dwellings. Growing homeowner population organizes around issue of opposition to highway. As result of court-ordered environmental impact statement, highway finally rejected by Secretary of Transportation and City Council. City decided to negotiate to create city park on cleared right-of-way.

Authority and commitment

Inman Park Restoration Inc. (IPR) formed 1970 by small group of new and old residents "to fight the battle for inner city living." IPR manages to have area placed on National Register (1973).

In 1974, designated as a local Historic District. Impact weak, mostly protection from spot commercial rezoning. Does not prescribe preservation treatment; depends on good taste and voluntary cooperation to preserve, restore buildings. IPR offers technical consultation.

Also IPR wins rezoning from commercial (as mapped in city's 1954 zoning ordinance) to residential. Rezoning helps stabilize residential uses, reassure newcomers.

New neighborhood transit station with parking facilities planned. Fearing adverse effect, IPR presently using legal and political means to persuade subway authority that station design must minimize traffic, noise, and air pollution.

IPR is private civic organization, initially incorporated in 1968. Meets monthly, committees more often, to contend with neighborhood problems such as zoning, transporation, improved public services. Most members are young professionals, many of whom provide volunteer services. IPR activities: newsletter, spring festival, articles.

Management of program

Purchase and renovation loans scarce. Some relief comes from credit union formed (1973) by Inman Park and four nearby neighborhoods to provide second mortgages and home improvement loans to residents of the five areas. Union now has fund of $125,000.

Operating tools and tactics

Much restoration work done by homeowners themselves, due to scarce loan money. Even so, property values zoom. City has no tax incentives to encourage restoration, but code enforcement aids restoration, homeownership by applying codes less strictly to new owner-occupants than to old rental properties.

Owner-occupancy has risen from 25% to 70%; dramatic change in socioeconomic character of population. White population stabilized; area now interracial (about 10% black). Some displacement of previous residents.

Self-promotion important source of revenue (annual spring festival, walking tours to restored houses, guide book). Income used for tree planting and landscaping of neighborhood parks, challenges to highway construction and negative effects of transit station, and for support of two daycare centers.

To date, no federal funds used. However, city will use some CD block grant funds to upgrade neighborhood.

Austin

Texas
Population: c. 252,000

Synopsis

Austin's major public conservation activity is city's Community Development Program; $21 million committed through 1979 to upgrading municipal facilities in residential neighborhoods. Program will cover relocated water and sewer lines, street lighting, street and sidewalk paving, bus shelters, modernized intersections, etc. Work underway in East Austin, a black community, one of most deteriorated areas in city.

Private rehabilitation activities focus on East Sixth Street in downtown Austin. Commercial street, developed in 1870s. There are 25 buildings historically significant. Area marked by mixture of smaller businesses owned by different ethnic groups, patronized by various races, nationalities, and income groups. Some 200 businesses, mostly in two-story buildings along seven-block stretch of East Sixth Street.

Initiation

Over past few years, business premises along East Sixth Street renovated by new, more prosperous owners catering to middle-class white clientele, many of whom worked downtown. Heritage Society of Austin (HSA), citywide preservation group; East Sixth Street Conservation Society, a merchant's association; City Planning Department join other concerned individuals to find ways to save original character of street.

Earlier loss of Victorian mansions near state capitol had aroused architects and historic preservationists. Combination of citizen and professional interests cleared way for adoption of city Landmarks Ordinance.

Authority and commitment

Landmarks Ordinance passed 1974; Landmarks Commission created. Plans for changes to or demolition of designated historic properties reviewed by Landmarks Commission. Demolition can only be delayed, allowing time for purchase by preservation groups or others. By mid-1975, no historic designation imposed on property without agreement by owner.

Designation must go through Planning Com-

mission; subject to public hearing. For fear a court test of Ordinance on a "weak" designation might jeopardize entire Ordinance, only buildings of obvious significance designated to date. East Sixth Street still not designated a local historic district, but effort to do so is underway.

"Outside" professionals, university people, and others spearhead organized preservation efforts in East Sixth Street (and other areas) through HSA, its subsidiary, Austin Heritage Foundation, and Austin Tomorrow. Business participation individual rather than merchant's association.

Management of program

Austin Heritage Foundation has revolving fund (patterned after Historic Savannah Foundation) supported by low-interest bank loans, to buy properties threatened with demolition and to provide loans for restoration. Of $200,000 now in fund, over $50,000 loaned for six buildings on East Sixth Street. Loans enabled owner-occupants to restore properties, resist pressures for acquisition, changes in use, major renovation.

Operating tools and tactics

Seeing need for improved public services: East Sixth Street program includes proposals by merchants and allies for lighting for night shopping, diagonal parking, two-way traffic to encourage additional shoppers.

Baltimore

Maryland
Population: c. 905,000

Editors' note: The Baltimore story is in two parts. Part One describes Fells Point, an old waterfront neighborhood. Part Two reviews the city's neighborhood-oriented housing programs and their use in the West Baltimore neighborhoods.

1
Fells Point

Synopsis

Fells Point began as a seaport, and in the early 18th century became one of the major ports of the east coast. It was developed by the Fell family as a community separate from Baltimore Town—and at one time was larger than the town that eventually swallowed it. Today, Fells Point centers on foot of Broadway on waterfront in southeast Baltimore. Central portion designated historic district in 1969. Real Fells Point spreads beyond these strict boundaries. Dominant land uses are residential/commercial, with heavy commercial and industrial at edges. Broadway is most developed commercial area, lined with shops, taverns, bars; there is a city-owned seafood, meat, and produce market in mid-Broadway. Taverns, bars spotted throughout neighborhood. Houses generally two- to three-and-a-half-story row or town houses. Largest institution is block-square St. Stanislaus Roman Catholic Church.

Population diverse: Polish, Russian, Greek, Lithuanian, German, Italian, Hungarian. Blue-collar, but recent influx of artists, students, professionals.

Initiation

Population diversity is both one of neighborhood's virtues and source of problems. A sociological study of area groups population according to interest in neighborhood: about 10 to 15% classified as preservationists; another 10 to 15% as "hippies"; rest are merchants, bar owners, old-time residents. Very few blacks. Each group sees different future for neighborhood.

Neighborhood has big collection of historic structures. Society for Preservation of Federal Hill, Montgomery Street, and Fells Point (SPFP) concerned with houses as well as with many large commercial buildings of historic interest. These are linked with waterfront: wharf buildings, warehouses—could be developed for residential use. Waterfront structures no more than 50% occupied. Fells Point has a *working* waterfront, dealing in repairs and ancillary businesses such as tugboat base. (The waterfront and commercial buildings are the subject of study by Edward Jakmauh, funded by National Endowment for the Arts.) As entertainment center, Fells Point attracts visitors to taverns, restaurants.

Real estate speculation takes place in two ways: (1) developers and landlords determined to buy into, rehabilitate, and improve neighborhood; and (2) typical absentee landlord. Real estate values soaring: three years ago, houses sold for $4,000 to $5,000; today some asking prices for shells have reached $30,000, completed houses up to $90,000.

These issues merge. Existing industrial, commercial uses concern residents, who complain about danger, noise of large trucks passing through streets. Taverns that draw nighttime crowds draw complaints from residents about noise, drunks, and parking. Diversity of population means diversity of opinions about future. All views represented in Fells Point Planning Council, set up to work with architectural and planning consultant at direction of city Department of Housing and Community Development. This group, more than SPFP, is voice of neighborhood.

Most diverse views converge due to outside threat—a segment of Interstate 83. Highway galvanized area into action. Made Fells Pointers wary of anything with "city" label. Some now want complete control over what happens in neighborhood. Furor also made city more sensitive to neighborhood desires. But guess is highway will be built—to run under historic district, under water, but some demolition of buildings, loss of jobs likely.

Commitment/ management/ tools

First phase (survey and analysis of a planning study) completed July 1975. Second phase—development of planning strategies, land use plan, and rehabilitation guidelines—to take another year. Few city programs pending completion of planning study. Then city will draw up renewal plan, probably based on minimum acquisition of properties.

But work already under way for two key blocks of Broadway (heart of Fells Point). Includes two buildings of city-owned market in middle of Broadway and a parking area. Architect has completed program for redesign of south shed of market and of key block of Broadway as plaza. Construction of plaza was to start in late 1975.

Other city efforts: fix up recreation pier at foot of Broadway; fixing library and recreation center, plus maintenance and code enforcement programs, general public works, and construction of two new schools.

Zoning is problem in Fells Point. Ordinances and maps revised when highway was thought to cross neighborhood. Area zoned for business and manufacturing, no residential. Baltimore's zoning code allows no residential use in areas zoned for manufacturing. Zoning changes await end of planning study.

Major issue is eventual disposition of 99 properties owned by city, purchased (1969–70) to accommodate original highway alignment. It includes sizable concentration of houses, visible and in important location. Half are occupied, some by previous occupants, some by new tenants renting from city. Other half vacant, crumbling. City and community want all saved if possible; community wants vacant ones occupied as soon as possible. Chance of inserting owner-occupancy clause into agreements on properties to deter speculations.

Options: (a) Fells Point as Wiliamsburg. Unlikely, not felt to be in accord with character of area; (b) Georgetown. Tavern owners and other local businessmen like this as good for business.

Also attractive to some officials in city government, who point to improved tax base and tourist money; (c) rehabilitation, no major change in character. Most residents want this route.

Probable city tools, tactics after planning complete: city housing rehabilitation loans below market rate; facade easements to help people who want to restore a property; strict rehabilitation standards for exteriors of city-owned properties that are resold; standards optional on noncity properties at resale; provide trees, street furniture, other public works.

On one key block of Broadway, some elements of community want space for neighborhood organizations rather than all shops, boutiques. Fells Point Planning Council (FPPC) set up to work with planning staff study. Gets good grasp on planning process; meets twice a month; made up of delegates from neighborhood organizations. Meetings open to public. Some Fells Pointers feel FPPC unduly influenced by city officials.

2 Housing programs in Baltimore

City's housing functions are centered in one department. This has allowed coordinated approach to redevelopment, rehabilitation, housing inspection and relocation, and public housing. Programs have included:

1. Programs created to assist public housing residents in city's neighborhoods with their social and economic problems. Management participation by residents encouraged. Programs include child development counseling, adult and adolescent family planning, homemaking services, family and personal nutrition. Planned programs include health screening of children, workshops on home and property care.

2. Recent urban renewal plans aimed at correcting problems of central-city residential neighborhoods and minimizing clearance and relocation. Renewal plans established with participation by neighborhood with emphasis on preservation and rehabilitation.

3. Design Advisory Panel established—group of architects and environmentalists who assist city's Department of Housing and Community Development.

4. Residential Environmental Assistance Loan (REAL) program established to provide city funds for loans to homeowners. Designed to complement Federal Section 312 low-interest loans. Latter available only in urban renewal or other federally-assisted areas, and program was often unfunded. City voted $1 million bond issue; when program worked, voted a second $1 million. Program is now citywide.

5. Stabilization of number of vacant houses. City's dilemma: rowhouse construction means that single-house demolition is costly and devastating to rest of block. Through Vacant House Program, more than 1,000 houses bought by city, totally rehabilitated by private contractors and put into public housing program. By saving individual houses, program helped prevent blight from spreading into entire blocks. Key benefit: housing for over 5,000 low-income individuals, most of them members of large families, which seldom can find adequate housing.

6. Housing Inspection Program organized from one chiefly of response to complaints into a positive force to prevent blight. Works closely with community groups. "Environmental patrols" reach every block in city on regular basis.

7. Some 30 neighborhood associations involved in cooperative programs under which community surveys own area and encourages neighbors to clean up and repair outside of their property. When necessary, community turns case over to housing department for enforcement through Housing Code.

8. Encouragement to middle-class families that have moved into "in-town" neighborhoods. A council of representatives of these neighborhoods meets regularly with city officials. REAL loans have been made to young couples who wish to rehabilitate houses in these neighborhoods.

9. Urban homesteading: vacant, city-owned houses available for $1, with proviso homesteaders make house habitable and move in within six months, bring structure up to Housing Code, and continue living in it for two years. City also offers financing (through REAL loan program). To date over 120 houses awarded to homesteaders, with financing approved for 35. Some 24 of the homesteaders rehabilitating in one block of houses built in 1830s, originally slated for demolition under urban renewal.

10. Blocks of houses in urban renewal areas rehabilitated, for sale to residents as co-op apartments. Focus: areas where private ownership was unwilling to make the investment, residents were unable to raise loan, and buildings were worthy of preservation. Aim: retain integrity of older neighborhoods. Program calls for 210 structures to be rehabilitated and made into 459 dwelling units.

Example: West Baltimore
Example of treatment of an area's problems: *Rosemont*—a predominantly middle-class section in West Baltimore—riddled by blight due to decision on highway acquisition, which left city owning 500 houses, most of them vacant and deteriorated. Urban Design Concept Team helped community organize itself. Overall solution: federally-assisted code enforcement, accompanied by rehabilitation loans and grants.

In addition, city-owned houses are being rehabilitated under Vacant Housing Program (see above) and sold to moderate-income families (under federal program providing for a low down payment and subsidized mortgage payments). A few houses are, after rehabilitation, being rented as public housing. Meanwhile, scattered public housing developments planned in area.

Various divisions of housing department active in housing inspection, community organization, providing homeowners with rehabilitation loans and grants, managing and maintaining city-owned houses before rehabilitation begins, administering rehabilitation contracts for city-owned houses, managing sale of houses, counseling new homeowners, planning new public housing, administering its construction, and managing it after completion.

Another section of *West Baltimore* that underwent urban renewal is now nearly complete— with a state office building complex; a rebuilt middle-class residential area, including new town houses and many rehabilitated ones; four new office buildings; a 286-unit, moderate-income tower for the elderly; a total of 732 moderate-income apartments; a 161-unit public housing tower for the elderly; plus miscellaneous units of rehabilitated and restored housing. Also three new parks, a school, and various community, medical, and shopping facilities.

Berkeley
California
Population: c.117,000

Synopsis

Across bay from San Francisco, Berkeley is composed of these elements: the university and its community, some industry, a small central business district, and variety of residential neighborhoods ranging from poor black communities in flatlands close to bay, to wealthy white hill dwellers. Post–World War II growth of university and city cramped city's ability to furnish high level of city services demanded by diversity of residents.

Housing stock in Berkeley mostly wood frame buildings dating from 1890. Condition of housing stock mostly sound but in immediate need of maintenance, rehabilitation. Landmarks board identifies nine structures as "significant."

Due to small industrial tax base and tax-exempt university land in city, property taxes for homeowner very high. Rental vacancy rate of only 1.4% (1973) inflates rents. Also, 57.3% of rental households pay over 25% of income for housing. There's a shortage of large lots for housing developments; loan capital not available for work. Property taxes highest in state.

Initiation

Berkeley emerged from its shell to political, social forefront in 1960s. Rapid change in population characteristics, demands for diverse city services exceed city's resources. Infusion of radical politics into city government has not produced reforms expected by supporters. In response, voters passed Neighborhood Preservation Ordinance (1973) mandating, among other things, a new masterplan.

Authority and commitment

Under provisions of neighborhood preservation ordinance, citizen committees creating new masterplan elements (as mandated by state law) relating to land use, circulation, housing, conservation, open space, seismic safety, noise, recreation, historic preservation, planning process.

Meanwhile, ordinance stipulates that in new construction of four or more units, 25% must be low/moderate-income units with no subsidy for owner. Demolished buildings must be replaced one for one. In addition, city's Department of Housing and Development has CD block grant funds for a combination of housing conservation tools (see below).

City's Masterplan Revision Committee is guided by policy that recognizes self-determined or identified neighborhoods as key source of input to planning process for housing conservation and public improvement programs.

City Department of Housing and Development starting to carry out recently financed housing conservation program funded by CD block grant. $1,500,000 of city's CD block grant allocated to housing program. Program is administered by city of Berkeley.

Operating tools and tactics

Components of program are:

1. Housing rehabilitation program consisting of three parts: (a) neighborhood rehabilitation inspection (to foster maintenance of housing); (b) physically disabled and elderly rehabilitation housing; (c) emergency repair (an attempt to aid owners in correcting life-threatening conditions with quick repair dollars).

2. Prepaid maintenance fund: owners will pay premium to insure against future maintenance repair costs.

3. Land banking fund: will be used as tool to acquire sites. Also may be used to acquire endangered historic properties.

4. Direct housing services: educational/information advice to low-income households on ownership, purchase, tenant's rights, rehabilitation/maintenance.

5. Relocation services: combines relocation planning; payments and services.

6. Planning and evaluation.

7. Expanded municipal loan fund: builds on existing municipal loan program.

Existing municipal loan program uses $550,000 in general funds for loans in pilot rehabilitation program areas. Loans are made on sliding interest rate scale for structures with four units or less. Absentee owners receive loans only for code violations, not general improvements. Expanded loan program will provide bankable loans for emergency repair; physically disabled and elderly housing rehabilitation programs.

City exploring sources for funding expanded loan program through sources other than general funds and CD block grant. These include:

1. Use of a secondary market.

2. Use of city's Pension Fund as secondary market.

3. Direct borrowing taking advantage of city's favorable borrowing rate (6.5% as of mid-1975).

4. City floating bonds under California's Marks-Foran Residential Rehabilitation Act.

5. State Housing & Home Finance Act. Bank of America loaned a vice president to city for 3½ months; he dealt with financial aspects of housing conservation program.

Boston
Massachusetts
Population: c. 641,000

Like London, Boston is multicentered, with cluster of neighborhood communities each with own commercial node. Thus, city chose multipronged effort, channeling conservation and rehabilitation plans through neighborhood organizations, plus own administrative offices in key neighborhoods.

Boston's growth, and resulting street pattern, created a series of discrete centers that architecturally reflect each period of development.

South-End and East Boston reflect whole of 19-century architectural taste. Post–World War II exodus of upper- and middle-income families from South End, influx of poor residents. Completion of Prudential Center (1965) placed neighborhood within walking distance of work; house prices climb steeply.

North End is special case. Mainly Italian blue-collar families, with many elderly residents. Intense ethnic pride, distrust of outsiders. Recently, white-collar and professional families attracted by charm of neighborhood, closeness to new governmental center, Faneuil Hall preservation area. Many North End structures are 1890s cold-water flats without central heating. In 1970 apartments often rented for less than $100. After rehabilitation, rents rise to $250 (1975). Housing 50% owner-occupied, rest held by absentee landlords. Housing stock is poor quality but residents do not want neighborhood to change ethnically, yet also strongly want new housing for elderly.

Roxbury and particularly Highland Park have large concentrations of blacks. In one section of Highland Park, vacant land and buildings due to abandonment form 30% of area, population declined from 10,000 (1960) to 5,000 (1970). But architecturally rich area (12 buildings on National Register). Eight of 12 are in John Eliot Square and form an historic district—other four in Highland Park.

One-fifth of Boston's housing stock is triple-deckers; much in demand in some parts of city.

Triple-deckers are three stacked floor-through apartments. Mostly wood, some of brick or masonry. Date back to 1870s but popular well into 1930s as form of urban housing.

Most triple-deckers are owner-occupied. Offered owners greater independence than as tenants, but brought with it reluctant role as landlord. Triple-deckers financial liability—little profit in them for working class, middle-income owners.

But social-psychological relationships in the triple-decker ethnic neighborhoods far outweight economics. Owners usually chose to subsidize these buildings through own time and effort, to provide decent housing services to their tenants. Phenomenon widespread, works well, but until recently overlooked by housing policy makers.

Infamous 1950s West End clearance project triggered neighborhood community members to seek voice in city's housing plans. Middle-class groups tapped for participation in new residential rehabilitation projects. Consciousness of community power emerged in 1960s. Neighborhoods form own strong organizations, many distrust City Hall and Boston Redevelopment Authority (BRA). Representation varies. West Roxbury has official elections for Local Advisory Committee established by city. But Local Advisory Committee in East Boston has an elected board; anyone who attended four of its public meetings may vote. Attitudes vary: North End, South End residents, reject open occupancy, hence denied federal housing funds.

North End opposes groups that sought to turn vast 19th-century warehouses along crumbling docks, into housing, commercial space. Elderly in North End want old age housing. Squaring-off between existing elderly and white-collar newcomers still unresolved. Real estate interests see North End ripe for development, but Italian community is politically vigorous, rejects these outside interests. City and BRA also want to preserve neighborhood's strengths while upgrading public facilities and building housing for elderly. North End residents have created 47 separate organizations dedicated to various aspects of preserving ethnic unity.

Roxbury Action Program (RAP) formed 1968 in response to virulent decay of Highland Park. Community organization, minority group staff live in area. RAP's goal: make Highland Park a model black community. Achievements: developed and manage 114 units of housing; housing management plan adopted as state model by Massachusetts Housing Finance Agency (MHFA); early 1974 undertook $9-million rehabilitation and new construction of John Eliot Square; $2,000,000 commitment from BRA to create and construct public improvements in Square. To be built elsewhere in RAP area late 1975, early 1976: 322 low- and moderate-income housing units (including 85 units for elderly).

In Cambridge, **Wellington-Harrington Program (WHP)** brought urban renewal plan around to emphasis on rehabilitation. WHP created own development corporation to rehabilitate dwellings, construct 56-unit housing complex owned by its low- and moderate-income tenants.

Management of program

Current approach is decentralization of many activities of mayor's office and of BRA.

"Little City Halls" established in key neighborhoods to deal with services, related problems. BRA divided into 15 district offices in key neighborhoods. City hopes to rehabilitate 70 to 80% of Boston's older housing stock.

Operating tools and tactics

a. **Conservation-oriented programs**
Major neighborhood conservation activities are those undertaken under city's CD block grant program. This program has led to dramatic decrease in funding levels from those of various categorical grant programs it replaced.

Other neighborhood conservation activities are being carried out under city's capital improvement program using primarily local funds.

In 1975 major focus given to housing, vacant land, neighborhood business districts, capital improvements, neighborhood services, and urban renewal:

Housing programs, which consist of four kinds of activities:

Rehabilitation: includes incentives for rehabilitation of owner-occupied housing; for example, cash rebate for repairs, protection from property tax reassessment, technical assistance.

Abandoned housing: includes thorough inspection of all abandoned houses in city to determine whether structures should be demolished or boarded and secured.

Public housing rehabilitation: includes funds for basic structural renovations of six older developments and for critical physical repairs in all developments of Boston Housing Authority.

Special housing program support: funds provided to support a high-risk revolving loan fund. Monies are reserved for proposals from neighborhood-based organizations.

Vacant Land Program. This program seeks to upgrade presently vacant land and make it available to residents. It assists homeowners who wish to buy and improve city-owned lots abutting their land.

Neighborhood Business District Program. Program is geared to reverse decline and physical obsolescence of many of city's older business districts. Elements include public improvements such as parking, lighting, pedestrian amenities, and major sidewalk and street improvements; foot patrolmen; technical assistance to businessmen in marketing, financing, physical improvement, and crime protection; a storefront rehabilitation program that includes tax rebates.

Neighborhood services. City provides funds for

human services programs—many of them funded under the Model Cities program.

Urban renewal. A sum of $89 million would be required to complete Boston's remaining urban-renewal projects. Portion of CD block grant entitlement has been allocated to the most binding commitments.

b. Preservation-oriented programs

Traditional historic preservation ranges from protection of significant monuments to planning for viable reuse of late 19th-century commercial structures. Included in range of activities using public resources are:

Boston Landmarks Commission approved by city and awaiting passage by State Legislature. Boston Landmarks Commission to be first body with citywide preservation responsibility (two historic districts now, covering Beacon Hill and Back Bay). Commission will designate, for architectural regulation, notable buildings, sites, and areas of city. It will provide for a hierarchy of designation categories so controls can be tailored to needs and relative significance of properties to be designated.

Boston National Historical Park. Through efforts of city, local residents, and congressmen, Boston National Historical Park authorized by Congress in fall of 1974. Seven sites including Faneuil Hall, Old State House, and Bunker Hill to be part of National Park System, ensuring permanent protection.

Conservation study. BRA's preservation planning staff (which also serves as staff to Boston Landmarks Commission) studying preservation opportunities downtown. Survey phase to develop a process for evaluating salient visual or urban design qualities worthy of conservation. Next phase to focus on economics of downtown conservation.

Recycling projects. BRA acquired Faneuil Hall Markets, completed exterior restoration, and leased historic Quincy Market and 40 flanking buildings. City updating several old structures for its public facilities and will dispose of surplus public buildings for new uses. For example, a fire station is now an art museum; several schools are being converted to housing. In addition, city has used its power to bring about retention and reuse of notable buildings including former offices of *The Record American*. Also, will reuse Charlestown Navy Yard—86 acres of surplus federal property that are a National Historic Landmark.

Public education. BRA producing publications and slide shows aimed at increasing local appreciation and awareness of local architecture and neighborhood environments. It is also producing a series of rehabilitation guidelines for older buildings.

Charleston

South Carolina
Population: c. 67,000

Synopsis

Charleston has been a pioneering city in many aspects of historic preservation. Established first historic district in U.S. (1931) and adopted the first ordinance to control development in an historic district. First city to use revolving fund for historic preservation (1959).

Initiation

The Old and Historic District (1931) consisted of 20-block area (about 144 acres) located on top of city's peninsula, including parts of original settlement. Area placed on National Register (1961).

Area slum when restoration movement started. Palatial houses from 1700s converted into crowded apartment and commercial buildings. First efforts spearheaded by Society for Preservation of Old Dwellings, a private, nonprofit organization founded in 1920. Later became Preservation Society (PS). Present membership 1,500. Deteriorated buildings bought, resold, often to members of PS, and restored as residences. PS continues to influence general opinion toward saving and restoration.

Historic Charleston Foundation (HCF) formed 1947. Through innovative real estate policies has had the most impact on historic neighborhoods in Charleston peninsula.

Save Charleston Foundation (SCF) formed 1973 to save approximately 3-acre block of 18th- and 19th-century warehouses to be razed for nine-story condominium. SCF saw this as developer's first intrusion into delicate streetscape, raised $1,200,000 to buy property for eventual restoration.

By 1966, original Old and Historic District included 60 blocks, 412 acres. New enlargement 1975. Also 1931 zoning ordinance strengthened to provide legal tool for HCF, PS, and interested citizens to restore areas and buildings.

Authority and commitment

Restoration activities supervised by Board of Architectural Review (seven members appointed by City Council and mayor). Board approves new construction, exterior changes, demolition of any building in historic district area. Also may for 180 days halt demolition or alteration of any building outside of historic district if it is over 100 years old. Also may require routine maintenance to forestall neglect.

HCF 30-member board represents most of leading forces and interests.

HCF focus has always been in preserving areas and groups of buildings rather than in meticulous restoration of single buildings. Committed to adapting old substantial residential buildings to modern life. Accordingly, bought and restored deteriorated buildings in target areas and sold them, often at a loss, to new private owners. Sees such losses as its contribution to city's cultural heritage.

Operating tools and tactics

HCF established revolving fund (1959) with $100,000 in donations from individuals and foundations. Policies have set pattern for many other revolving funds. Funds may be used:

• To acquire and resell properties with no strings attached, unless they are of outstanding architectural and historic merit.

• To acquire and resell properties of architectural and historic value to carefully screened purchasers with legal restrictions attached. Deeds include restrictive covenants for 75 years which grantee, heirs, or successors must agree to. Exterior alterations, physical or structural changes, change in color or surfacing forbidden without written approval from HCF. In event of resale, property must first be offered to HCF.

• To buy, restore exterior of valuable buildings unlikely to attract proper purchaser. May develop these properties into rental units (apartments, offices, stores).

• To buy, demolish properties of no value, for use as gardens or parking lots.

• To provide mortgages and home improvement loans to buy, restore, or maintain properties where owner or purchaser interested in preservation cannot obtain a mortgage or loan from local bank.

- To grant life tenancy to owners of buildings who agree to give or sell property to HCF.

Value of houses restored in early 1960s increased in value about threefold, much more than general appreciation in city. No special abatement granted by city.

In the beginning, many buildings inhabited by impoverished elderly people who could not afford to maintain them. Many times HCF found apartments for those compelled to move. In some cases owners granted life-long tenancy at little or no rent if they gave or sold building to HCF. But interest among middle- and upper-income people in inner city living within walking distance of CBD has led to displacement of most lower-income families. Statistics scarce, but city says displacement is serious problem (investigation promises better data for 1975).

Typical of HCF's operations is Ansonborough, a six-block, inner-city area, selected as target area in 1959 as it was close to CBD and because of its substantial but seriously decaying housing. Laid out in 1747. Contains more than 135 period buildings dating to 1860s.

Today Ansonborough is choice area for inner-city living. HCF sponsored first visible improvements; after that most of restoration done by private initiative.

Downtown Broad Street, a four-block downtown section laid out in 1670s, part of the Old and Historic District since 1966. Buildings date from 1717 to 1937. Today it is city's financial district. Contains several buildings of national historic importance. Principal property owners and tenants joined with HCF to preserve Broad Street. In a joint venture of private citizens, the city, HCF, and the utility companies, the four-phase program is almost complete: property owners have refurbished facades according to an HCF plan. Utilities have placed overhead wires underground. Tree-planting, sign controls, historical markers common. City allocates $250,000 of CD block grant for neighborhood rehabilitation program.

Chicago

Illinois
Population: c. 3,387,000

Synopsis

No one neighborhood stands out in conservation terms, but there are activities of interest under way in several. Five programs are summarized: Citizen Action Program (response to redlining by number of neighborhoods); RESCORP (Renewal Effort Service Corporation) in South Shore (business community involvement); Historic Pullman (active community in an old company town); the Loop (development pressure, politics, development rights).

Several features of city shape future of neighborhood conservation. Power of Democratic "machine," massive population shifts (city now virtually segregated—whites and middle class on North Side, blacks and low-income on South Side).

**1
Citizen action
program**

Citizens Action Program (CAP), umbrella for 100 community organizations, heads "greenlining" program (greenlining is a threat by groups of depositors to transfer funds from bank that "redlines" to one that doesn't). Participating communities subject to redlining. Disparity between communities in terms of ethnicity, income, goals, race. Suspicions between member groups. Some of the notable communities are:

Southeast: Hyde Park–Kenwood. Pocket within South Side black ghetto; community-based, "save our community" effort rather than preservation; some rehabilitation and new construction. Much University of Chicago housing, and influence in neighborhood of 40,000 people (70% white, 30% black). Cited as only genuinely integrated community in city.

Southwest: Beverly. Has 57,800 people in 7 square miles, 93% white. Middle-class resistance to black influx from adjacent areas.

Inner-Ring/Older Suburban. Oak Park: 62,500 people; middle-class white, late 19th-century structures (many by Wright). Evanston: 80,000 people; mixed incomes, established black population, preservation element in program. Evanston's redlining limited.

Initiation and management
Greenlining program began in Beverly. CAP carried out pledge card drive: working-class homeowners vow to withdraw savings from institutions targeted as "redliners."

CAP offers training in "greelining" to member communities. Staff examines investment by S & L institutions for geographical distribution of loans. Aim: saturated citywide greenlining drive.

"Greenlining" (South West Side–Beverly). After abortive discussions with loan institutions and receipt of bank loan figures, $55 million in withdrawal pledges obtained. One institution targeted. After media campaign, agreement for $2.8 million in mortgages in the community obtained (1975). Another institution refused; $1 million in savings transferred to two cooperative lenders.

Greenlining as a tool to stabilize integration.
Greenling used mostly in white neighborhoods that have either begun to deteriorate or fear "invasions." Says Father Ciciora, head of CAP: "Chicago does not have integration. Integration is the time lapse between the time the first black family moves in and the last white family moves out."

Legislation. National People's Action on Housing, network of community organizations with chapters in 39 states and 104 urban centers, got City Council to pass local statute: requires institutions with city of Chicago deposits to disclose their savings and investment patterns.

Focus on O'Keefe area of South Shore where RESCORP (see below) is most involved. Has 15,000 residents, 80% black, 5,000 units of housing, 85% renter-occupied. Rentals at level of moderate-to middle-income families. Vacancy rate 4–5%. Neighborhood in early stages of deterioration. Early 1900s housing and commercial buildings; one of few black lakefront communities. One-third of families in O'Keefe on public assistance. Rate is decreasing.

**Operating tools
and tactics**

**2
South shore
and RESCORP**

Management/financial tools

Chicago Area Renewal Effort Service Corporation (RESCORP) organized in 1972 by local S&L associations as vehicle to undertake rehabilitation and create neighborhood stability. RESCORP's program has three components: rehabilitation development, South Shore Comprehensive Plan, and loan guarantees.

Rehabilitation development. RESCORP as developer. Overhead paid by Chicagoland Savings and Loan (55 S & L's provide capital for operations and revenues from activities). RESCORP's charter limits investment to housing. Helps several organizations to sustain neighborhood preservation activities. Neighborhood Housing Services (NHS) gives low-interest rehabilitation loans to lower-income owners (see description of NHS program under *Dallas, Pittsburgh*).

South Shore Comprehensive Plan. Cooperation between insurance, banking, businesses, and community organizations and University of Chicago.

RESCORP, South Shore Bank, and South Shore Commission meet regularly to develop long-range preservation plan. (South Shore Commission is vocal grassroots community organization built on block groups and neighborhood groups; is an anchor and stabilizing force.)

Loan guarantee. RESCORP and Community Services and Research Corporation (CSRC). Group of lending institutions to provide $7 million for loans. City to establish fund of $500,000 in trust to protect against losses. A mortgage insurance corporation assumes further risk. Loss shared by all participants in three test areas. The insurance corporation absorbs first 15% of any losses on loans; lenders absorb next 25%, and city fund 60%. Loans are for up to 92% of appraised property value at market rates. CSRC administers the program.

Pullman has two parts—North and South. Both are national (1970) and state (1969) historic districts. Only South Pullman ("Historic Pullman")

is Chicago Landmark (1972). Population 3,000.

South Pullman: White, blue-collar workers. Industry on three sides, railroad on fourth. Made up of 60% townhouses, rest multifamily. Late 19th-century industrial town built by George Pullman (contains worker quarters, Pullman plants, institutions).

Historic Pullman Foundation (HPF) formed in 1973 to deal with long-range planning, sponsor projects, provide technical assistance to residents, operate educational activities, and buy and restore nonresidential structures. Has taken over many activities of older Pullman Civic Association. Funds obtained through general fund-raising drives, local industry, volunteer "in kind" services, national and local foundations, corporations, and individuals. All home improvements financed privately. Planning and urban design study funded by Endowment city options grant.

Prototype facade easements to be tried for restoring entire facade (10–12 dwellings.) Little displacement or out-migration of older ethnic residents. Hence no effort to attract "young professionals." Little inflation in property values despite neighborhood improvement. Why: area has not become "glamorous." The larger community (i.e., Chicago's South Side) changing rapidly, discourages typical developers of urban "old towns." Good transportation to central business district (the Loop).

Values and rents low: typical townhouse sells for $10–$12,000 (nonrenovated), $14–$15,000 (renovated).

An outline of preservation problems and issues in the Loop follows. Since the situation is complex, it is necessarily simplified.

Legal Commission on Chicago Historical and Architectural Landmarks created in 1968 by City Council. Commission submits recommendations for designation to Commissioner of Development and Planning and then to Council, which must pass on them. Only a few buildings acted on due to possibility of claims for compensation.

Development pressures in Loop. Major Chicago School high rises (late 19th century) in danger. Some do not earn enough to justify high land values and high taxes in CBD. New, larger buildings produce increased tax base, more jobs. City administration and city council (dominated by mayor) have played a passive role in conservation. Very keen on obtaining new development.

Endorsement of commissioner who heads Development and Planning Department, Urban Renewal, and Special Development (and reports directly to mayor) crucial to landmark designation in Loop.

Landmarks Preservation Council (LPC) and its service affiliate are the principal private groups working to develop new roles for landmark buildings in Loop area.

Preservation efforts in the Loop greatly aided by 1974 passage of an expanded Planned Development Zoning Ordinance. Ordinance allows increased flexibility and phasing potential of a site's development, with special concern for adaptive use and integration of landmark structures with new construction.

Incentive zoning: Development rights transfer as alternative to historic district zoning. Development rights in excess of required zoning on a landmark site could be transferred to nearby parcels. Sale of rights thus enables landmark owner to maintain building.

Two main drawbacks in its application to Chicago: first, a generous allowable zoning bulk base has yielded unused development potential on major sites. Hence, no real market for purchase of a landmark structure's development rights.

Second, several Chicago School buildings have no excess development rights that could be transferred, only hypothetical figures when combined with large-site assemblages.

An umbrella community organization in Lincoln Park area, Lincoln Park Conservation Association has spawned extensive conservation efforts in over 2,000 acres adjacent to this northside lakefront park.

**5
Lincoln Park
Conservation
Association**

Dallas
Texas
Population: c. 844,000

Dallas is a young city (130 years old); only since World War II has major growth occurred. This, coupled with healthy economy, has insulated it from problems of older cities to north and east. City has healthy tax base and·electorate committed to providing broad range of services and facilities for their city.

Several neighborhood conservation programs in older areas of town, involving both public and private effort. One is in racially-mixed East Dallas, centered around Swiss Avenue Historic District: a 13-block area of 200 houses protected by city's Historic Landmarks Preservation Ordinance.

Other historic districts planned for are: (1) West End, a brick warehouse and loft district at fringes of CBD; and (2) South Boulevard, a 6-block stretch of large old homes in "black" South Dallas.

City working with citizen groups in West Bank, Winnetka Heights, Oak Lawn, Love Field, and Little Mexico areas on variety of neighborhood conservation strategies, from low-interest loans and sensitive code enforcement to redesign of neighborhoods.

Buildings in these conservation areas built mostly between 1900 and 1920—brick or wood frame, mostly single-family (except downtown), on streets lined with mature shade trees.

Initiation

Major force for change is Goals for Dallas program—a citizen-based, comprehensive planning and action group. From 1965 inception has had continuing impact on public and private programs citywide. One area of accomplishment: major changes in structure and status of city planning function in city government (see below under "Management of Programs").

Second factor has been citizen support, both from special interest groups and neighborhood residents. Swiss Avenue Historic District originated in part due to homeowners who wished to preserve their neighborhood's character against encroaching multifamily development.

First concrete start in the city's financial community came with establishment of Neighborhood Housing Services of Dallas, Inc. (NHS) in 1973. NHS is a nonprofit corporation seeking to expand bankable lending by financial institutions to edge-of-decline areas (see also *Anacostia, Pittsburgh*).

Texas state law does not allow multibranch banks. A bank generally must cultivate its surrounding community. One bank, Lakewood Bank & Trust, located in East Dallas near Swiss Avenue, early pushed for financing bankable homeowners. It has had a big influence on Dallas financial circles in justifying lending in normally redlined neighborhoods.

Dallas is one of cities in Texas with "home rule"; allows city government to enact any ordinance not specifically prohibited by state law. This gives it freedom to respond with flexibility and reasonable speed to problems.

Authority and commitment

Under zoning power City Council passed Historic Landmarks Preservation Ordinance, which establishes an Historic Landmark Preservation Committee and gives city the power to establish special preservation criteria for historic buildings or districts. Landmark designation requires approval of three bodies: Dallas Historic Landmarks Preservation Committee, City Planning Commission, and City Council. Separate criteria and ordinances are written for each landmark or district; these criteria must be met prior to issuance of a building permit, and issuance of a demolition permit may be delayed for set time periods while alternative solution is sought.

Dallas has a manager/council form of municipal government. City manager's office has developed a program to encourage construction of new housing in inner city by private developers. City works with developer to provide an approved plan and agrees to make capital improvements, reroute utilities, etc., in accordance with plan. Also, fund is set up from which city will (at developer's option) buy back property of an approved project for a specified price (not to exceed a maximum). In this way, developers are assured of recovering at least part of investment should project run into financial difficulty. Council established $10-million fund for this purpose.

Work is underway to see that zoning policy citywide does not discourage neighborhood conservation through "overzoning". Zoning and subdivision code revision will be based on guidelines developed for conservation of various types of neighborhoods.

Management of programs

Under NHS of Dallas, Inc., lending institutions are depended upon to underwrite administrative cost of NHS program for two years and to make loans to bankable homeowners; city provides sensitive code enforcement, public works, and adequate city services; neighborhood community provides interest and leadership. Foundations provided seed funds for high risk, revolving loan fund for unbankable homeowners. A deed of trust secures all loans and repayment. Interest based upon prevailing market and borrower's ability to repay. Impact considerable, since 50 banks and S & L associations involved.

After designation of Swiss Avenue Historic District, Lakewood Bank and Trust committed $1 million in purchase/repair loans to people in adjacent neighborhoods and advertised to attract families back into area.

Lakewood Bank and city's Department of Housing and Urban Rehabilitation working on plan to establish private corporation run by consortium of eight banks and S & L associations. Corporation, independent of institutions involved, would originate and make loans to buy, rehabilitate older homes in inner city neighborhoods. If approval to use $275,000 of CD block grant funds as seed money is granted, corporation would use it to pay insurance premiums on high-

risk loans and fees to obtain money in the secondary mortgage market (FNMA and FHLMC). Goal is to generate $10 million in mortgages for inner city housing.

Historic Preservation League, Inc. (HPL), East Dallas homeowners group, carries on community action and education, public information, and media participation. HPL publicity oriented, to good effect. In first 6 months after Swiss Avenue designations spent $2,400 for advertising. During that period, $750,000 in purchase and renovation money invested in historic district; within a year, area had made dramatic turnaround.

Key element in neighborhood conservation is Urban Design Division of Dallas Department of Urban Planning. Division roles range from policy formation (input into comprehensive land use plan, preparation of environmental quality committee report), to data development (historic landmarks survey, visual form of Dallas), to tools (historic landmarks preservation ordinance, Swiss Avenue ordinance, Little Mexico project), to implementation itself (administers historic preservation program). In addition, seeks to guide, support activities of others.

Operating tools and tactics

Useful tool of research and analysis is HUD-sponsored Community Analysis Program (CAP). Purpose was to determine and anticipate major problems of city and formulate an action program. Six CAP studies deal directly with individual neighborhoods.

Another major tool is Interim Comprehensive Plan and its program of Neighborhood Plans, developed individually for each neighborhood in city. Through these plans attempts are made to coordinate citywide needs of transportation, land use, etc., with special needs and circumstances of each neighborhood.

An important tool is historic preservation ordinance and extension of zoning power for historic preservation. Historic designation carries much clout; it may include regulations on land use, lot coverage, height, floor area ratio, parking, screening, building services, signs, materials, color, design detail, and relationship among buildings.

Design guidelines have been developed for environmental protection of newer, outlying areas; next step is to draw up guidelines to conserve older neighborhoods. This will be purpose of Conservation Strategies Study, a HUD 701 Demonstration Study Grant to bridge "gap between historic preservation . . . and conservation of areas of lesser historic and cultural value." Guidelines less specific than design criteria in a preservation ordinance, but impact is over much greater area.

Synopsis

Woodward East Project (WEP) is one of several conservation projects in city. Located in 180-acre area adjacent to downtown. Near Medical Center, Wayne State University, Arts Center, has 12,000 low- and moderate-income residents, almost all black. Some 8,000 live in old (1939) Brewster-Douglas public housing. Some of the other dwellings rehabilitated since 1967 riots.

Aside from Brewster-Douglas, housing is mainly large, detached two and three stories, built 1860 to 1900 as single-family mansions, mostly brick Victorian style, set back amply (25 feet) from sidewalk.

Condition poor, but structurally sound. Many mansions split into rooming houses, efficiency units, badly maintained by absentee landlords. Law required city demolition of 20 large houses because seen as hazardous.

Near center of 180-acre renewal area, WEP picks 2½-block, 9½-acre section, designated as Woodward East Project. Will develop as planned unit. To consist of 14 to 18 renovated Victorian mansions, 104 units of new housing, two rehabilitated apartment buildings, shopping, public services, open space, new circulation system. WEP now owns 80 to 85% of land; city and private ownership balance, some city parcels will be transferred to WEP.

Initiation

Woodward East much neglected up to and since 1967 riots. City Plan Commission then put area under early building permit review to screen reuses, help residents renovate.

After riots, church groups met on how to rebuild area. From these, neighborhood leaders emerged, founded Woodward East Project. Felt that to have influence over redevelopment, must own land, buildings.

After opposition to WEP's original plans to clear 2½ blocks for low-income housing, WEP sought way to restore them. Solution: retain, rehabilitate mansions as multifamily housing for middle-income families and simultaneously build 104 contemporary town houses, in keeping with historic district, for low-income residents.

WEP adept at pinpointing wide variety of resources. Funds, technical aid from city agencies, local and national foundations, corporations, state, and federal grant agencies.

Local media cooperate; sometimes threat of real estate speculation defused as newspapers voluntarily reduce coverage.

Authority and commitment

Area designated as French Victorian Historic District in National Register and has state designation. Not a city historic district, however, as 1970 local ordinance very restrictive, requires property owners to restore historic buildings within reasonable time. WEP needed time.

Preservation control assigned to new Community and Economic Development Commission (CEDC). CEDC working with WEP on restoration plans for area, under National Endowment for the Arts City Options program, may recommend future historic designation to maintain it.

Management of program

WEP is community manager, property owner, and sponsor of rebuilding program for the 2½ blocks. Professional Skills Alliance, local nonprofit organization, provides technical (e.g., architectural, legal, planning) assistance to WEP.

Operating tools and tactics

Plan for 2½-block project designed to serve as catalyst for redeveloping rest of 180 acres (except for its public housing).

To integrate preserved Victorian mansions with compatible new housing, streets and alleys in the 2½ blocks will be closed, and old and new buildings clustered into 5 "squares." The housing program consists of:

● 104 units of new, low-income, duplex cooperative or condominium town houses financed by State Housing Development Authority.

● 14 Victorian mansions rehabilitated and restored by WEP for middle-income families for three to five families each.

● 40-unit apartment building and an old hotel rehabilitated for use by those displaced by renovation.

Plan described in detail in *AIA Journal* article (see Resources, page 260).

Original plan did not include mansions because too dilapidated. Those in good condition or privately owned will be retained. High costs and WEP's desire for mix, has led to search for middle-income tenantry for mansions.

Parts of project granted tax exemption for 1975 only, as an incentive.

Funds from local Urban Coalition, New Detroit, Inc. ($40,000 for social programs and administration), Endowment ($50,000 matching grant for feasibility studies and interior renovation plans), national foundations, and trusts.

State Housing Development Authority provided grants to acquire balance of land in project and will finance new housing (see above); first year city will spend $588,000 in CD block grant funds: $385,000 on exterior renovations for 14 mansions and $203,000 on open space in project.

WEP used part of the Endowment and NTHP grant for design "retreat" for mansions: the Endowment consultant architect did plans, specifications for one restored building. Project planned as unit, to be part of surrounding city but with own internal circulation and open space. Goal is social, economic, and physical integration of old, restored buildings with new structures.

Galveston

Texas
Population: c. 62,000

Until 1900 Galveston was Texas' only port and its largest city. Attracted many European immigrants, who built lavish Victorian houses.

The East End Historical District (established 1970) close to CBD and medical branch of University of Texas. A 40-block area, 19th-century houses, 3,000 to 4,000 residents.

Heavy decay prior to 1960s, then return of young, white, upper middle-income families. These bought and restored homes in area. Led to higher income levels and property values, and drop in minority population. Newcomers often reconvert multifamily dwellings to original single-family use. In addition, there are elderly people (long-time property owners in district) and minority families renting in homes converted to apartments.

Demand for houses in district up due to lack of other new housing in city and due to its location.

The Strand is district that contains fine concentration of 19th-century commercial buildings. Listed as an historic district on National Register. Galveston Historical Foundation (GHF), a citywide, private, non-profit organization of residents, purchases Strand properties through its revolving fund and resells them to private purchasers. In case of an historic building, purchaser contracts to restore facade within agreed upon time, and accepts deed restrictions requiring GHF approval prior to demolition or facade changes. In case of a nonhistoric building, purchaser may demolish building, but accepts deed restrictions requiring GHF approval of exterior design plans for new construction.

Initiation

Several sections in city with 19th-century structures declined, and significant buildings threatened with demolition. GHF triggered idea of historical district. Late 1960s referendum to create 100-block historic district under state laws defeated. Reason: threat of broad restrictions over large portion of city. Also, University of Texas medical branch saw threat to expansion plans.

GHF then sought more limited but politically acceptable method. After survey of significant structures by GHF, city council adds special historic district regulations to city's zoning ordinance (1970). Upon approval of a development plan by City Planning Commission, an area may be designated an historic district. The 40-block East End Historical District so designated (1970). National Register designation (1975).

City's guideline stipulates that historic designation be considered if 85% of *homeowners* in an area approve petition requesting designation.

Amendment to zoning ordinance established a Historical District Board (HDB) to administer adopted development plan for an historic district. Nonsalaried seven-member HDB (appointed by City Council) made up of: three property owners within district, one architect, one member of City Planning Commission, two members-at-large.

Operating tools and tactics

Development plan for an historic district sets forth "criteria for the delineation of the boundaries of the district as well as the criteria to be observed in the improvement, change, demolition, or reconstruction of buildings and structures within any such area." If City Planning Commission approves plan and same is filed with HDB, HDB's decisions must be in accordance with plan.

The ordinance does not cover building interiors. HDB has jurisdiction over all requests for building permits in district. Regulations also list permitted uses. HDB must act in 60 days upon requests for building permits. Its decisions may be appealed to Zoning Board of Adjustment, then to District Court. For demolition permits, HDB has power to halt, with appeal process as above.

Tax abatement or moratorium not presently possible under Texas law. Hence, taxes on restored buildings up, due to higher property values (4 to 5% per year). This has seriously slowed restoration process. Revision of state law likely to permit tax abatement for rehabilitation.

Before designation, GHF concerned with danger of banks' redlining. So, group of local banks, S&L associations, and an insurance company persuaded to pool $1 million for improvement loans in Strand. Applications to be processed by GHF. No application yet, but presence of pool reassures property owners. Many obtain loans through normal bank borrowing.

To date, 25% of homes in East End District have had major renovations. Maintenance of most dwellings improved. Incompatible new construction, alterations, and demolition prevented by ordinance. Strong support by residents.

Major funding sources: Moody Foundation, Section 701 funds for preparation of Historical District Guide. Two more 701 grants applied for to study ways to move suitable structures from other areas to vacant lots within district. (There are several of these, many in danger.) Funds from Kempner Foundation used to help save a structure: house is bought, restored by GHF, resold to interested purchaser. Costs of restoring property financed through the mortgage, but down payment *plus* mortgage fall short of costs of restoration. $3,000 to $5,000 gap per restoration made up from Kempner Foundation funds.

Two most significant of many Hartford neighborhood conservation activities are: (1) business community involvement citywide via Greater Hartford Corporation; (2) Charter Oak–South Green project.

Synopsis

City has less than 20% of SMSA's population, yet provides livelihood for nearly 50% of SMSA's workers who live outside city, without commensurate benefits to city.

City of paradoxes: rich corporate community (e.g., insurance); has 70% of all SMSA's welfare; high minority concentration (38% black, 22% Puerto Rican and Hispanic). Market for good housing is weak (5% vacancy), for substandard (only housing poor can afford) it's tight. Key to understanding Hartford are economics and power alignments: conservation versus redevelopment, inner city versus suburb.

1. Greater Hartford Corporation

Initiation/ program management

Greater Hartford Process, Inc. created to channel corporate community's resources into solution of city's social problems, without becoming arm of government (late 1950s). Shortly thereafter, Process merged with two other Hartford business groups to form Greater Hartford Corporation (GHC). In this union, Process became the executive body.

After unsuccessful attempt to create multiracial new town 40 minutes from city, Hartford Process was forced to focus on Hartford itself. This earlier failure had damaged Process' credibility with city officials and the general public. Process' involvement in city produced planning studies for many neighborhoods. Some proposals were adopted by the city. Some neighborhood studies were motivated by priorities not coined in neighborhoods, hence lacked neighborhood support.

2. Charter Oak–South Green

Synopsis/ initiation

Charter Oak–South Green neighborhood is city's greatest architectural resource: larger 1850s Italianate double houses, small workers' housing, plus older unused mill buildings. Population: about 20,000. Social transition: Italians moving out, Spanish-speaking people moving in. 95% absentee landlords.

Hartford Redevelopment Agency (HRA) contracted with Hartford Architecture Conservancy (HAC) to explore large-scale restoration effort in portions of 96-acre Charter Oak-South Green redevelopment project. HAC developed restoration concept and cost analysis which became part of redevelopment plan and guide for development of some 40 buildings in two sections of project.

HAC's educational and preservation awareness efforts include newsletters, walking tours, lecture series, exhibitions. Paid for through membership dues and grants, which are also used to explore legal convenants, facade easements, historic district zoning, as well as to do survey and inventory of architectural and historic resources of Hartford.

Operating tools and tactics

City tax policy could be used to aid rehabilitation/renovation in Charter Oak-South Green. Four programs exist:

Renewal writedown. HRA will dispose of properties at prices that are based on cost of restoration, so that at this cost approaches market value, cost of acquisition approaches zero.

Tax abatement. Local ordinance for improvement to historic preservation properties, but depends on state reimbursement, for which there are no funds.

Tax deferral. (a) Rehabilitation: assume original assessed value $10,000 and improvements valued at $2,000. First year taxes on $10,000, second year taxes on $10,000 plus 10% of $2,000, until eleventh year, when 100% taxes on improvements are paid; (b) on new construction only for properties valued at more than $10 million. Incremental increases in taxes through seventh year after completion.

Mortgage financing. Connecticut Housing Finance Agency will finance construction mortgages at below market rates with no income restrictions for tenants in cities of over 80,000 in Connecticut.

Public Development Corporation. City has established a nonprofit corporation for public improvements using labor hired with federal funds, which could be parlayed with renewal dollars for the materials only—thereby stretching renewal dollars.

HAC requested $150,000 as part of city's CD block grant plan, but only $35,000 submitted by city—for survey of historic architecture. HAC also seeks $250,000 to start revolving fund.

As for Hartford Redevelopment Agency, HRA has sought to rehabilitate and restore area via HUD renewal financing and through acquisition, rehabilitation, and condominium sales of houses on Congress Street.

HRA's commitment is based on resettlement: attracting young professionals to area. But due to city's eroding tax base, additional low-moderate-income housing in area is opposed because of higher tax burdens transferred to private housing.

CD block grant budget illustrates city's stance. Of $10.26 million allocation, $3.5 million being used to close out three urban renewal projects and to acquire, rehabilitate units that will attract middle- and upper-income families. By comparison, $1.2 million will pay for citywide rehabilitation program to provide 3% loans to low- and moderate-income families.

Hoboken

New Jersey
Population: c. 45,000

Synopsis

Hoboken is an old industrial city on west bank of the Hudson River, across from Manhattan. Current population: 50% white, 45% Puerto Rican, 5% black. Houses brick solidly built, many as rowhouses. In 1960, 65% of residential structures owner-occupied (one of highest rates for an older, industrial city in any SMSA in nation); but by 1970 dropped to 60%. Program is city-wide; no neighborhood focus.

Initiation

Over past 10 to 20 years, population shift through exodus of middle-class families and influx of unskilled workers. Deterioration, then abandonment of sound residential structures speeded by reluctance of lenders to sell conventional loans for repurchase and home repairs. To fill city's home financing vacuum and stop abandonment, Hoboken Municipal Home Improvement Project (HIP) created in 1972 under Model Cities jurisdiction. HIP initiated with $30,000 grant from Hoboken Model Cities, $200,000 from New Jersey Department of Community Affairs. City planned to use CD block grant funds for 1975–1976.

Management of program

HIP is citywide source of mortgage assistance for housing rehabilitation for current and prospective homeowners. Program is widely publicized through newspaper ads, letters, brochures to homeowners across city, meetings with homeowners in each ward.

HIP program citywide; not restricted to special target areas. No income limits for participation, but only homeowners may take part. Participation voluntary, not tied to code enforcement. Work on building has to follow HIP's priority for repair type (see below).

Operating tools and tactics

HIP program provides following tools and incentives to homeowners:

● Cost estimates for rehabilitation work.

● Helps prepare homeowner's application for conventional rehabilitation loan. Private lending institution must approve application so homeowner can participate in HIP.

● Nonrepayable interest reduction grants enough to reduce market interest rate of conventional loan to 3%. Size of grant depends on total value of intended repairs, plus the terms offered homeowner by lender.

● Provision of list of contractors in area. But choice, negotiations with contractors up to homeowner.

To receive this assistance, homeowners must:

● Occupy building to be purchased or rehabilitated at least two years after receiving HIP assistance.

● Agree not to evict tenants and to offer them a two-year lease at present rent.

● Qualify for a loan from a conventional lending institution.

● Follow HIP's priority repair schedule. This is not based on code enforcement, but requires heating and plumbing improvements before cosmetic and other work.

No special tax increases due to increase in value through effort. But property subject to any citywide rise in tax rates.

Since 1972, 243 property owners have borrowed $1.4 million for rehabilitation loans. Average loan: $6,000. Average interest reduction grant: $1,300. Thus, each dollar in grant funds generates about $4.50 in conventional improvement loans.

Agreement by landlords to retain tenants for at least 2 years has stabilized rents and reassured tenants.

To assure timely completion of work and control quality, grant to homeowner held back until job completed.

Prices have been kept down, competition encouraged as homeowners select and deal directly with contractors. Avoids public bidding procedure for contractors embodied in HUD rehabilitation loan program. Program successful, may be extended to nonowner-occupied properties. City has set aside $335,000 in first year CD block grant budget to provide grants to about 100 more homeowners.

Hudson
New York
Population: c. 9,000

City was whaling port, later distribution center for goods between New York City and upstate. Today, serves as center for governmental, institutional, manufacturing, and retail activities. Economic problems: over 65% of land tax-exempt; one of lowest per capita incomes in state.

The conservation neighborhood is Lower Warren Street, a locally and nationally (National Register, March 1970) designated historic district. It is within 55-acre North Bay Urban Renewal Area and a few blocks from CBD.

District has 400 people—low- and moderate-income Polish and Italian, with some black families. There are 39 buildings (1790 to 1900), including outstanding center-hall mansions and a rare Adam-style house. Many cases of ornate Victorian overlay of simple older buildings. At time of renewal designation, urban renewal area blighted; had 50% of city's substandard housing units.

Initiation/ commitment

Survey of impact of renewal activities on historic structures led to historic district designation in 1970 and decision to conserve historic district within context of urban renewal. District residents support rehabilitation, especially when assured urban renewal plan won't displace them.

Operating tools and tactics

After four years of planning (1969–73), cooperating city, state, and federal agencies embody innovative ideas in amended urban renewal plan. Feature: broad use of facade easements in an urban renewal project. Renewal agency takes perpetual facade easements on building exteriors and restores them. Owners in turn agree to rehabilitate interiors, preserve exteriors, make no changes to exteriors without city approval. Catch: New York State Historical Trust wanted entire 55-acre urban renewal area on National Register, thus limiting scope of intended renewal. Conflict resolved when trust accepted agency's proposed boundaries.

Louisville

Kentucky
Population: c. 361,000

Plan establishes detailed design controls over facades and public space (traditional materials, colors). Urban renewal funds used for period sidewalks, street lighting, and to rehabilitate historic park. In some instances facade easements give renewal agency right to demolish Victorian additions to buildings, with consent of owner.

City and tax assessor say postrestoration valuations will be raised only modestly, thereby moderating effect of improvements on property taxes.

Facade restoration costs are borne as follows: 12.5% city, 12.5% state, and 75% federal. Interior rehabilitation accomplished through a combination of conventional loans and urban renewal tools: some Section 312 loans and Section 115 grants for lower-income families.

Since 1959, firm of planners and architects, assisted by a historic architect, have worked within renewal agency on historic preservation project. For example, firm's architect is now assisting renewal agency in executing facade restorations by preparing plans and specifications.

Facade easements on 38 of 39 buildings already executed. The renewal agency contracts for restoration work by trade rather than by buildings. This way, same contractor works on several structures, resulting in greater economies and consistency.

Synopsis

Louisville remains city of strong neighborhoods. Part of reason: wholesale clearance, renewal of past two decades didn't take place, leaving neighborhoods with strong roots in history and their sense of identity intact.

Initiation

Cooperative spirit between neighborhoods all over city. These face same problems, mainly difficulty in obtaining money. Complain banks do not make loans large enough to cover purchase and rehabilitation of an old house; do not make loans with minimum down payments; appraise structures based on idea old neighborhoods are declining; will not approve home improvement loans for amount larger than assessed value of house. But change pending: First National Bank offers certificates of deposit, using deposits to make loans for rehabilitation of commercial structures. To date, nothing residential.

Authority and commitment

City to get $8.6 million in CD block grant and other HCD Act of 1974 funds in each year to 1978. Nearly half allocated for housing in first year. A $15-million guaranteed mortgage loan pool will be created, using $1.5 million of HCD Act funds as seed money to attract additional funds from local banks and Kentucky Housing Corporation, and provide somewhat higher risk loans at below market rates. Other CD block grant funds to go for home improvement grants; would be made to owner-occupants in amounts up to $4,500, with focus on elderly and handicapped.

Zoning is another problem facing city's neighborhoods. Thus Butchertown, zoned industrial since 1930s, now zoned for residences in some areas, result of efforts from within the neighborhood.

City's Neighborhood Development Office recognized 70 neighborhood organizations. Newspapers (Courier-Journal, Louisville Times) support neighborhood development, conservation. The Times has special section on neighborhood news. Both papers owned by Bingham family, active in historic and neighborhood preservation.

Management of programs

Neighborhood groups' efforts also coordinated by Preservation Alliance of Louisville and Jefferson County, Inc., an umbrella group for about 30 neighborhood and civic organizations. Alliance's aim is to give small groups strong collective voice in dealing with city agencies; public education, preservation expertise, and other aims.

Following are capsule profiles of three key Louisville neighborhoods: Butchertown, Old Louisville, and Main Street.

1. Butchertown

Synopsis

Settled by German immigrants in mid-1800s, Butchertown takes name from family-run slaughterhouses, meat packing business prompted by nearby Bourbon Stockyards, established 1834. Area bounded by interstate highways on three sides. 40-minute walk to downtown. Institutions: Wesley Community House, two public schools. Strong sense of community identification; many families in neighborhood since Butchertown first settled. Focus provided by Wesley Community House and neighborhood development corporation called Butchertown, Inc.

Population about 3,000, white working class. Some shifts: 22-35 age group is increasing; young professional types moving in, attracted by low housing prices.

Initiation/authority and commitment

Once a community of well-built, well-kept houses, declined seriously during this century. Industries—meat-packing and some others—made place undesirable to live. Houses were run-down, windows boarded up, streets and sidewalks in disrepair. First restoration effort came in 1950s, when a couple moved in to buy old candle manufactory (became their pottery factory) and a brick home nearby. Neighborhoodwide efforts didn't come until 1960s.

Fear of greater industrial development sparked neighborhood consciousness. Wesley House Mothers' Club called on mayor for help in stemming industrial influx in 1965; mayor turned problem over to Louisville and Jefferson County Planning Commission. Eventually, neighborhood development corporation, Butchertown, Inc., set up (1967). Corporation has power, wide membership, buys, rehabilitates, resells houses.

New businesses enter area. Complex of shops attracts smart shoppers.

Operating tools and tactics

Zoning thorn in neighborhood's side. Residential zoning only allows construction of rowhouses on sites of three acres or more. Butchertown, Inc. put together two lots on which to develop a three-unit rowhouse tailored to neighborhood needs and intended to meet requirements for FHA 235 housing (1971). But corporation still unable to start project because zoning variance not granted; sued city; federal government froze FHA 235 appropriations. Butchertown, Inc., finally sold lots, returning deposits to the three prospective buyers. City Planning Commission has since passed new rowhouse regulations that would have allowed construction.

Banks' lending practices have made mortgages elusive: refusal to grant conventional mortgages for houses over 20 years old; unreasonably low appraisals because Butchertown is "declining" neighborhood; costly short-term mortgages that often must be repaid concurrently with renovation loans; refusal to lend more than 66% of purchase price or to approve home improvement loans larger than assessed value of house.

2. Old Louisville

Synopsis

Population: 17,000, 27% elderly, plus large percentage of young people, university students. Institutions include University of Louisville, Spalding College, Woman's Club of Louisville. A neighborhood of pleasant, turn-of-century houses, a few high-rise apartment buildings. Feature is Central Park, site of recreation area of

1883 Southern Exposition. Once one of city's most fashionable districts.

Initiation/ commitment

Civic-minded businessmen set up Old Louisville Association for Restoration, Inc. to buy, restore, resell houses (1961). In 1968 Neighborhood Development Corporation (NDC) established. NDC is catalyst.

Through its efforts, NTHP funds obtained to draft ordinance calling for a preservation commission and inventory of historic structures. Such ordinances passed; city set up Historic Landmarks and Preservation Districts Commission. Old Louisville first area to be put under commission's jurisdiction (1974).

Operating tools and tactics

NDC also rehabilitating housing and reselling individual houses, helping member institutions develop housing for the elderly (840 units in four projects).

NDC also acts as zoning watchdog; has blocked two harmful projects. Has strengthened neighborhood organization—14 active block organizations are the base for neighborhoodwide decisions.

As in Butchertown, banks unwilling to extend long-term, low down payment mortgages. As a result, hard for young families to buy, restore houses.

Synopsis

3. Main Street
According to National Register and city's Landmarks Commission, the West Main Street Historic District includes collection of 19th-century, cast-iron commercial buildings cited as best outside of New York City or Portland, Oregon. Area was once commercial heart of Louisville, later suffered economic decline. Now new construction.

Initiation/ commitment

Only in past 2 years has business community along Main Street seen itself as a neighborhood. Before, it was an area of wholesaling, warehousing, light manufacturing. Part of Main Street cleared, new construction put up; but east end and western blocks ripe for adaptive use. East end includes Actors' Theater of Louisville, an 1836 landmark Greek Revival structure restored by Harry Weese. Preservation Alliance, an umbrella preservation group, moved offices to Main Street (1974); Main Street businessmen set up Main Street Association to react to area needs, talk to city with strong voice, boost property values. Got off ground in March 1975. Membership: owners pay $4 per lineal foot per year; first floor tenants $3; other tenants pay $30 lump sum per year. Votes not weighted.

Mayor's Center City Commission becomes planning element within city government, underscoring Main Street efforts.

Operating tools and tactics

New businesses flock to Main Street—all in renovated old buildings. Properties scarce, prices quintupled in 2 years. Backlog of vacancies, so no displacement problems yet.

Louisville and Jefferson County Planning Commission plans study of center city, focusing on logical uses for downtown areas (since 1930s large areas zoned for industry, but not used for that purpose).

Madison
Wisconsin
Population: c. 173,000

Synopsis

In 1974 city created $225,000 revolving loan fund for rehabilitation of housing. Housing Rehabilitation Services Program (HRSP) operated by city's Department of Housing and Community Development. Loans made at 6% interest. Program aimed primarily at two neighborhood preservation districts, as designated by Common Council, one east, one west of CBD. Districts cover older areas of city, have about 20,000 population each, and contain many owner-occupied, single-family dwellings.

Authority and commitment

HRSP created by Common Council in 1974. Housing Finance Committee sets policy for HRSP and acts on loan applications. HRSP was outgrowth of one of city's successful urban renewal projects that had included Section 312 loans. HRSP works with neighborhood organizations, or helps create them.

Other related programs:

1973 city ordinance establishes Urban Design Commission (UDC). Mayor-appointed members include architects, landscape designers, planners, and citizen representatives. Designates certain areas of city as "urban design districts." Criteria: architectural merit, street plans, vistas, approaches to major landmarks.

In urban design district, exterior building changes or plans for new construction must receive Urban Design Commission approval. UDC looks for appropriateness to total district. Appeal allowed to City Council, but none so far in UDC's 2 years of life. UDC works with builders and developers on modifying and improving plans for buildings in the urban design districts.

Landmarks Preservation Commission (LPC) deals only with individual buildings designated as landmarks. No landmark districts, but City Planning Department proposes one historic district coterminous with an urban design district. UDC and LPC would both have jurisdiction over area.

UDC set to identify critical city districts with high visibility. Plans for each district to highlight key features (must be considered during Commission's design review) and to set design goals and criteria for each area. New construction or change would have to be approved by UDC as "consistent with the design plans."

LPC prepares comprehensive plan for historic preservation. Includes structures and environmental factors. District is unit for preservation. Could be established on basis of social, historic, or architectural merit.

LPC's pending plan for historic preservation to include provisions for transfer of development rights and facade easement purchases. Sees this as incentive for keeping designated structures in private hands and in economic use. LPC's preservation planner also identifies commercial structures of merit as early step in creation of a commercial historic district.

City officials cite good cooperation from banks, commercial interests, and public on the two loan programs. City and neighborhood groups have planned parks and recreational facilities in neighborhood preservation areas.

Under revolving loan fund of $225,000, money is loaned for housing rehabilitation at 1% above city's cost.

Operating tools and tactics

Cooperatives and other nonprofit housing owners also eligible. But most loans go to owner-occupants. Priority is given to applicants in officially designated neighborhood preservation districts.

City buys "no cost" rehabilitation work for those whose incomes are too low for loan repayment. Under this program, labor is free and owner must pay for some material costs. Has helped many households.

Technical services to those above program income limits (help in securing bank loans, advice on renovation plans, work write-ups, cost estimates, and contractors) also offered.

Wisconsin law allows cities to abate real estate taxes on improvements within a neighborhood preservation area for up to 5 years. No such provision yet in Madison.

In late 1975, grant program was to be added to loan program. Grants will permit city to provide housing rehabilitation assistance to families whose incomes are too low to repay a loan. Funds for grant program to come from city's entitlement under 1974 HCD Act. Rehabilitation work to be done with outright grants, loans, or a combination, depending on applicant's income.

Middlebury

Vermont
Population: c. 7,000

Synopsis

Middlebury, like other small-scale towns in many parts of New England, is undergoing changes which disrupt community's architectural, social unity. New commercial developments, various resort projects have forced on these quiet towns new attitudes toward growth. Downtown business sections in these towns, due to new commercial ventures on outskirts, begin to disappear. But historic focus, the Common, regaining hold.

Middlebury settled in 1770s. Middlebury College, founded in 1800, has given cultural and commercial variety. New growth brings traffic, parking problems.

Initiation

New shopping mall on outskirts triggered community action to overcome downtown congestion (1972), as merchants were losing customers to more accessible mall. Chamber of Commerce creates Middlebury Betterment Committee (MBC) under prominent realtor.

MBC held contest for design to improve CBD. Led to wide publicity. Vermont Natural Resources Council retains Cambridge-based community improvement consultants. Presentation of techniques made to town administration, MBC, local banker.

Consultant completed study of downtown area (1974).

Authority/ operating tools and tactics

Vermont has state enabling legislation for design review. This law lets municipalities set up boards of interested laymen, design professionals to review new construction, renovation so they meet community aesthetic standards. Town may provide property tax relief for those who improve property according to guidelines.

Town may set facade easements to preserve historic structures. Also, may devise conditional permits on commercial uses, such as parking lots, fast-food establishments, gas stations.

MBC, major Mobil station in CBD likely to agree on desired changes to station.

Special Assessment Districts can require property owners to pay for amenity improvements over period of years, based on linear feet of public frontage. All these tools possible but remain unused in Middlebury.

Milwaukee
Wisconsin
Population: c. 717,000

Synopsis

Feature of city: strong ethnic neighborhoods. Walker's Point area is five minutes from CBD, has 150 square blocks, 8,500 people, and is south of a heavy industrial concentration. Formerly mostly Polish and German, now mainly low-income Hispanic (Mexican, Puerto Rican, South American), but still has many Polish and other Slavic, German, Greek residents. Sections of larger older homes (east), smaller houses (western half). Walker's Point—potential "preservation district"—is 20-block area in eastern half.

Walker's Point evolved as 19th-century, working-class residential and business neighborhood. One of city's three original settlements and last one still quite intact. Houses are predominantly modest detached cottage/two-flat dwellings built in mid-19th century.

Initiation

Area is solid working class. In 1920s Mexicans and other Hispanics came as migrant farm workers, remained to form strong, stable community. 40% homeownership, but absentee owners are small (2–4) buildings), and live in area. Also, most of Slavic population, institutions remain. Area deteriorating, due to age of structures and postponed maintenance, more than milking of properties.

Initial impetus for conservation efforts have come from outside area. NTHP grant to study area's potential as preservation district (1970). Grant modest, so Land Ethics, a Milwaukee preservation group, targeted a 20-block historic Walker's Point area; it and Junior League documented 200 most significant buildings.

Used grants from National Endowment for the Arts, Junior League, Wisconsin Arts Council, volunteer surveyors.

Documentation plus edcuational programs develop community identity, awareness (1972). University of Wisconsin's (Milwaukee) South Side Design Center offered neighborhood advocacy planning, self-help, architectural services.

Outcome: Historic Walker's Point, Inc. created (1973).

Authority and commitment	City offficials conservative. Consider historic preservation low-priority, private sector activity. Lack of acceptance due in part to impact on property rights. Hence little commitment to Walker's Point, except as locale for industrial growth. Working-class families in this city traditionally resist governmental assistance. Also, officials see housing and historic preservation as activities competing for public funds. Consider preservation frosting on facade, not substantive.
Management of program	Prime sponsor: Historic Walker's Point, Inc. (HWP), a nonprofit corporation. Has 30-member board (neighborhood residents, business and financial interests, Junior League, Land Ethics represented). Goal: preservation and conservation of HWP without displacing residents. Under way: technical advice to homeowners; purchase, renovation of pilot landmarks and blocks; demonstration projects; education and participation of residents; coordinated delivery of social services to residents. But HWP still only a board of directors; not representative of neighborhood. However, in process of change to neighborhood orientation.
Operating tools and tactics	**Legal controls.** No state enabling legislation for historic districts. City landmarks ordinance establishes Commission which can designate landmarks with city council approval (1967, amended 1975). But can only place historical markers. HWP being considered for local and national designation, but has requested postponement of process pending definition of boundaries and weighing of publicity and prestige versus resident stability. **Zoning.** City zoned much of area industrial, thinking St. Lawrence Seaway and Interstate 94 would trigger pressures for industrial expansion.

This did not happen. But industrial zoning kept housing values low.

Financial. Prime tool is Historic Walker's Point, Inc. Revolving Fund (1973). Only about $15,000 to date, used to buy, renovate individual houses and low-cost loans. $75,000 matching grant from NTHP is being used for restoration of Holy Trinity–Our Lady of Guadaloupe Church (National Register property). Redlining by local banks halted.

Key feature of program is desire to preserve the working class and ethnic nature of the neighborhood through land use controls, investment, and tax climate encouraging improvements without resident displacement.

City began Urban Homesteading with CD block grant. How it works: sale for $1 contingent upon compliance with codes; 5-year residency by buyer. But, city owns few properties, encourages current owners to donate properties, past taxes forgiven.

Neighborhood Improvement Development Corporation (NIDC) has secured $1 million in bank financing for home improvement loans to credit qualified owner-occupants in the Neighborhood Preservation areas. NIDC subsidizes 50% of the interest costs along with counseling and inspection service. An additional $685,000 for code enforcement financing is available at 6% interest.

Milwaukee Economic Development Corporation makes low-cost loans available for commercial rehabilitation in preservation areas as well as grants to merchants' associations involved in major redevelopment efforts.

Minneapolis

Minnesota
Population: c. 434,000

Synopsis

Neighborhood conservation activities in Minneapolis best understood via three programs: (1) decision to rehabilitate several blocks of unique residences in Seward-West urban renewal area; (2) package of housing programs used by city's Housing and Redevelopment Authority across the city, though focused on renewal areas; and (3) plans for Special Design District in Whittier-East neighborhood. Businessmen and private developers willing to work with city agencies to try innovative adaptive and mixed use developments.

1 Housing rehabilitation within urban renewal

Seward-West area federally-funded urban renewal activity started 1972. Within Seward-West, 4-square-block area (Milwaukee Avenue) is site of neighborhood conservation effort.

Milwaukee Avenue, a narrow street, built as lower-class residential development in 1883. Unique remnant "common man's" architecture in immigrant German style of that period. Contains 100 houses with 145 dwelling units—40% of them owner-occupied by lower–middle-income residents. Most houses brick with uniform roof slopes, arch windows, and open front porches.

At first all houses in Milwaukee Avenue area slated for demolition as part of Seward-West urban renewal. Neighborhood group (Seward-West Project Area Committee, SWPAC) felt condition of most of 100 houses warranted rehabilitation, and that small lots and narrow streets were asset due to "human scale."

SWPAC agreed with Housing Authority to re-survey 74 dwellings for rehabilitation feasibility. Decided that 26 too decayed; should be replaced with infill housing.

In 1973, joint planning team (Seward-West Redesign) formed to plan redevelopment of entire renewal area, including preservation plan for Milwaukee Avenue. Key criteria included need to keep rehabilitation costs down so as not to drive out current residents.

Result: plan to use $309,000 in first year CD block grant funds to restore 45 structures and make public site improvements. After rehabilitation, homes to be sold to existing families or newcomers who could afford the partially subsidized restoration.

MHRA has package of federally and locally financed programs, directed at various aspects of neighborhood conservation. (Under Minnesota law, renewal agencies are authorized to pursue several major renewal programs. Minneapolis has obtained, made use of most of them.)

- City has had spot urban renewal program since 1973. City buys, removes substandard structures to make room for new development. So far, 110 lots involved. 1975 goal is 200 units. $500,000 in first year funds earmarked under CD block grant program.

- Special home ownership program begun 1973: MHRA buys, rehabilitates, sells homes on open market. 120 units so processed in past 2 years; 150 due in 1975. City picks homes not requiring too many repairs nor too costly. First year CD block grant budget allocates $500,000 to writedown rehabilitation costs.

- Urban homesteading program (started 1974) permits MHRA to sell abandoned properties for less than fair market value to low- and moderate-income buyers. Structures must be restorable and cost of property plus cost of rehabilitation should not exceed fair market value. Applicants chosen by lot. One house repaired to date (May 1975); three more in process. Low-cost loans are coordinated with sale.

- In March 1974, city authorized by state law to establish local rehabilitation loan and grant program. Goal: augment federal programs and bring housing up to code standard. City authorized to float $10 million in general obligation bonds and offer loans to property owners at 4%, 6%, or 8% interest, depending on income. Federally-funded loans at 3% available in renewal areas; in some cases city will piggy-back loans.

2 Housing package of Minneapolis Housing and Redevelopment Authority (MHRA)

City sets contractor performance standards. MHRA sponsors a seminar for contractors. Contractors must warranty work for 1 year.

- Program is set up to make neighborhood groups more effective. Planning and Development Department staff assigned to help such groups establish priorities and prepare plans.

3
Special
design district-
Whittier-East

Whittier-East area (adjoining center loop of downtown Minneapolis) is locale for special study by residents and city's planning staff. Purpose: determine guidelines and design review process for a special design district. Area chosen because it has: Minneapolis Society of Fine Arts Park, architectural cohesion, open space, historic older residences, about-to-begin deterioration, out-migration of families, change from owner-occupants to renters. Recent years see rise of poorly built two-and-a-half-story walkups, but moratorium halts such development pending adoption of Southside Land Use Plan.

In 1971, state legislation enabled city to establish local design districts and design advisory committees, along with design review procedures to preserve city's visual appearance and environmental quality.

Currently, design study team readies final draft of Design Review Ordinance. Under it, a Design Review Committee reviews all requests for building permits for renovations, signs, and new structures. The Committee, guided by design principles and standards established by ordinance, submits recommendations to City Planning Commission. Final action is taken by City Council.

Stress on: image residents want for area, building facades, additions, yards, open spaces, graphics, lighting, fences, key building improvements.

Wooster Square upgraded in 1960s through urban renewal, oriented entirely to neighborhood conservation. In 1948, area was identified as one of city's worst slums.

The Wooster Square Renewal Project Area covers 36 blocks east of CBD and Yale University, north of harbor. Area bisected by interstate highway; leaving 24-block residential area to west, 12-block light industrial district to east. Within residential area is 10-block Wooster Square Historic District, locally and nationally designated. Of district's 100 properties, 65 are historic. Mansions built by merchants, sea captains in Federal, Greek Revival, Italian Villa styles; some later converted to three- and four-family units or other uses.

In 1950, working-class neighborhood, initially Yankee, later Italian. After conservation, some original Italian homeowners remained. Some subsidized cooperatives house a mixed lower-income population. Rehabilitated and new dwellings now house diverse population, much of it downtown business and professional oriented, as well as Yale-connected.

Before renewal, deteriorated Wooster Square subject to redlining, flop houses flourished; housing jammed cheek by jowl with factories; trucks with tricycles.

Renewal plan pioneered renovation approach to redevelopment, limited clearance in residential sectors as part of overall plan for area.

Top design, technical talent, community relations specialists staff renewal agencies. Wooster Square Neighborhood Renewal Committee (WSNRC) established as vehicle for community involvement. Close cooperation with State Highway Department, which had originally proposed road through Wooster Square green and best of residential area. Would have separated residential from downtown. Major early obstacle was limited allowed use of renewal funds for rehabilitation. But law later amended.

Synopsis

Initiation/
commitment

As city investment and commitment to neighborhood rose, redlining was itself attacked. Homeowners were able to make improvements. Approach novel in U.S., hence media coverage extensive. Redevelopment Agency's annual reports published as separate supplement in local papers; staff members kept close contact with real estate editors; brochures and site offerings widely distributed. "Before and after" pictures in papers drew homeowner attention.

Management of program

During active phase, Redevelopment Agency dominant. Field office went door-to-door telling owners how they could improve property, furnishing renderings and plans, helping with financing problems. Suggested improvements were usually at level of rehabilitating one notch below full renovation. In rare cases of owner-occupied structures with many code violations, city threatened to take property. Various properties acquired with rehabilitation as object. Agency would make sales for rehabilitation offering or hold competition for acquired properties of architectural merit. Winners were sold houses for minimum fee ($2,000) with stipulation that required level of rehabilitation be done.

City involved local banks, which reversed redlining. Key inducement: renewal plan locally adopted, residents were interested, had savings for some improvements, WSNRC had prepared owners, assured them of city's commitment.

Passage in 1970 of city's historic district ordinance (with strong impetus from New Haven Preservation Trust, a private group). Historic District Commission must approve changes to structures in 10-block historic district. But Redevelopment Agency still oversees alterations in larger Wooster Square residential area.

Operating tools and tactics

Imaginative, productive pairing of federal and state urban renewal funds with the city's one-sixth share. Allowed street system reworking, off-street residential parking, parks and schools to be developed within large coordinated action

of purchasing blighted properties and reworking use of land. Controlled land disposition. Key element to restoration was employment of renewal funds in Wooster Square to write-down houses and other property for resale. New construction and actual home improvements through private funds, some "sweat equity," owner's savings, and Section 312/115 loans and grants.

Almost no historic preservation funds available. Dislocation minimized but still substantial.

City revised housing codes, persuaded FHA to adhere to its standards for rehabilitation to secure FHA financing for owners. For owner-occupants, city staff worked up specifications based on ability to pay.

City provision of land or buildings through urban renewal enabled individual developers and nonprofit sponsors to build new housing or rehabilitate structures on scattered sites following approved renewal plan and appropriate reviews.

City's one-sixth renewal share expended through school and other public works construction. Combined with further renewal funds to support housing activities by using cleared land for parks, landscaped off-street parking, playground, schools. Central park (Wooster Square itself), already existed—it is over 100 years old. Stability of park provided focal point for renewal of surrounding area.

City's stand toward displacement: wanted blue-collar Italian and other families to remain. When clearance, displacement unavoidable, displaced families had first priority on all other dwellings. Through relocation, lower-income families, especially blacks, able to live in decent housing in neighborhoods previously closed to them. Some original residents remain in Wooster Square. Erection of subsidized coops helped stem out-migration of some displaced families.

New Orleans

Louisiana
Population: c. 594,000

Synopsis

Historic preservation in New Orleans has a long history. The Vieux Carré (or French Quarter) was designated a municipally-protected historic district in 1937. But uniqueness of Vieux Carré has obscured concern for other more commonplace areas in city. Neglect of residential neighborhoods, pressures for new development threaten to erode older sections. Now city, in recent years, has taken new look at its heritage outside of Vieux Carré. Measures included moratorium on demolition downtown, giving city time to plan both for preservation and directed growth.

Vieux Carré (260 acres) includes all land of original French capital of New World. It is center of tourism, entertainment, shopping, and a residence for many people. Adjacent to CBD, subject to strong development pressures since early in century.

Most of Vieux Carré built in 19th century. With one exception, all colonial buildings destroyed by fires in 1788, 1794. Salient examples of French architecture (1803–1835), the Greek Revival Period (1835–1850), antebellum, and Victorian architecture. Further, area is dotted with squares and parks. These confer unity, distinctiveness on entire area. Vieux Carré is listed on National Register.

Other historic areas threatened by deterioration are the Lower Garden District (entered on National Register, 1974) containing notable Greek Revival and mid-Victorian houses of the 1850s and 1860s, and St. Charles Avenue, a street of large deteriorating mansions (the St. Charles Avenue streetcar is listed on National Register). Marigny and Bywater neighborhoods have been placed on National Register. Also city has enacted legislation to create a historic district consisting of Lower Garden district and a major portion of St. Charles Avenue.

Finally, City Council has passed ordinance creating a Historic Districts Landmarks Commission (HDLC). By end of 1975, HDLC was to develop ordinance setting forth rules and regulations for governing the currently designated historic district areas. HDLC empowered to include additional areas. (It has nine members; as districts are added, it may be enlarged to a maximum of 15.)

Initiation

Many important buildings destroyed between 1905 and 1937, when Historic District Commission was established. Past 15 years, even with Commission's protection, have seen many changes to Vieux Carré. Threat of additional change persists. Internal blight and deterioration set in. Pressures for growth from adjacent CBD (especially for hotels, parking, and other tourist attractions) escalated. Severe traffic problems in and around CBD arose.

Between 1960 and 1970, number of older resident families, including blacks, dropped; young, affluent, single, white professionals moved in.

Alarmed, city applied for HUD urban renewal demonstration grant to prepare a plan and program for preservation of Vieux Carré (1968). Key was to preserve the "tout ensemble" environment, as well as designated landmarks, yet allow for construction to meet new needs. Plan recognized importance of mix of uses—residential, commercial, tourist, entertainment. Need for housing traditional population—mix of ages, incomes, ethnic groups—as well as provide new accommodations for residents, tourists was emphasized. Major stimulus to awakening preservation interest was 1968 proposal for a riverfront expressway. Citizen opposition led to review of expressway by President's Advisory Council on Historic Preservation, under its mandate to review impact of all federally-funded projects on National Register sites. Adverse report helped halt construction.

Thereafter citizens became much more conscious of architectural and historic assets outside Vieux Carré. Builders, commercial interests, civic leaders joined preservation "bandwagon."

Other preservation interests spurred by development pressures stemming from construction of Superdome (1972–5). Many 19th-century Greek Revival, Italianate, and cast-iron buildings in and near CBD torn down for skyscrapers, or turned into vacant parcels held for speculation, meanwhile used for parking lots. This burst of destruction largely responsible for current moratorium on demolition downtown.

Authority and commitment

Since 1937, the Vieux Carré protected by municipal ordinance which established Vieux Carré Historic District, plus a commission to preserve its chracter. Commission regulates all new construction, alterations, additions, demolition; also has power to prevent owner from allowing building to deteriorate through neglect.

Commission reviews all proposed actions affecting exterior of any building. The three architects on commission comprise the Architectural Committee; it authorizes permits for change or recommends alternatives.

Court decisions since 1937 have strengthened commission's authority. More recently, inclusion of Vieux Carré Commission in 1974 State Constitution gave it great prestige of endorsement by public referendum.

Key elements of 1968 plan and action program for Vieux Carré (to be followed by city and private interests) include: areawide federally-assisted code enforcement; revolving fund of at least $2 million for preserving major buildings; "selective" zoning providing for five types of districts—low- and high-density residential, low- and high-density commercial, and industrial (the last to be phased out); and a 1968–80 capital improvement program.

Reconstituted Vieux Carré Historic Preservation Commission of seven members to have broad powers to regulate district, especially as a center of tourism and convention trade.

Legislation enacted to halt demolition on part of

St. Charles Ave., the Lower Garden District, and the central business district.

City has decided to use historic district and landmarks approach rather than urban conservation zoning. However, major study of possible zoning revisions for CBD is underway. Revised zoning and a combination of historic district and/or landmarks approach are intended to protect scale and integrity of key parts of CBD.

Operating tools and tactics

Matching city capital bond money and a HUD grant are part of a $5 million restoration and open space program for the riverfront.

Other work is being constructed variously with help of a further HUD grant, a matching grant from New Orleans Public Service, and general revenue sharing funds.

Another tool is a revolving fund, authorized by City Council, for acquisition, restoration, and resale of deteriorated structures in Vieux Carré. $300,000 in public money put into fund, augmented by private contributions. City will extend revolving fund to other areas as funds permit. Funds give Commission option when faced with property owner who wishes to demolish structure or refuses to halt deterioration.

Still another tool is systematic code enforcement being tried in Vieux Carré as model for rest of city.

Tactics include partial vehicular restriction, minibuses at peak hours, and rerouting of major bus traffic out of Vieux Carré.

For residential neighborhoods outside Vieux Carré (and downtown), city has public improvement plan geared to neighborhoods in early stages of decline or undergoing renovation. In 1973, city set up demonstration project in Irish Channel, a section between river and CBD. $250,000 from general revenue sharing funds earmarked for street and drainage improvements, planting, and other beautification.

North Adams

Massachusetts
Population: c. 19,000

Irish Channel residents fear displacement due to higher rents as in other neighborhoods. Improvements delayed, however, so effect on rents not yet clear. Vieux Carré Plan underscored serious housing problems in other, older areas of city. The most historic sections also have most deteriorated housing. Differences along racial, social, economic lines arose between: (a) groups interested in historic preservation; and (b) those concerned with repairing or replacing bad housing. To resolve conflict, city commissioned New Orleans Housing and Neighborhood Preservation Study (completed 1974). Study did *not* include Vieux Carré.

Study divided city into 73 neighborhoods. Each analyzed for deteriorated housing, lack of plumbing, family income, percentage of homes owner-occupied. Study found most of city's pre-1900 neighborhoods with worthy structures in critical or severe condition. Post-1900 neighborhoods generally in acceptable condition.

Synopsis

Situated amid scenic Berkshire hills, city was flourishing mill town with prosperous leather, textile, and paper manufacturing. Industries left (1930 to 1960). Since, city marked by economic depression, physical deterioration, unemployment. Features of city are attractive location, wealth of late 19th-century commercial, industrial, residential buildings, skilled work force.

Initiation

To preserve 19th-century architectural heritage, Historic Resources Committee formed by Chamber of Commerce (1971). Program of mere historic preservation widened by formation of Hoosuck Community Resources Corporation (HCRC), private nonprofit community development corporation (1972). HCRC looks to comprehensive program for reviving local economy, via reuse of old, vacant buildings, rebuilding of local craft traditions.

Keystone is renovation of Windsor Mill, a 19th-century, three-story, 150,000-square-foot complex of buildings built around several courtyards. HCRC to adapt Mill as center for reaching, production of crafts. Wide local backing after big federal, state, and regional financial commitments.

Authority and commitment/ management of program

HCRC acts as developer, contractor. Membership open to all residents.

HCRC controls, manages Windsor Mill under 10-year purchase agreement. Sponsors exteriors, interior renovation, attracts tenants, develops educational programs for Guild School jointly with State College system. Also is sponsoring facade restoration of ten commercial buildings in downtown Eagle Street—Monument Square Historical District; facade easement program being negotiated with merchants.

To avoid isolating Windsor Mill project, extend impact downtown, HCRC picks more target areas for action. Though tax-exempt, HCRC to pay city taxes on Windsor Mill to prevent friction, endanger project.

All tools had to be developed *ad hoc*, including financing mechanisms, organization, tenant search.

Operating tools and tactics

As of March 1975, HCRC had commitments of funds from public sources totaling $300,000 including National Endowment for the Arts, the New England Regional Commission, and Massachusetts Department of Community Affairs. Plus $381,000 commitment from HUD for exterior renovation of Windsor Mill and Eagle Street; matching funds for this grant raised from city, Massachusetts Department of Public Works. Low-interest, 30-year construction loan for rebuilding Windsor Mill interior being negotiated with Ford Foundation. HCRC to obtain commitment from Farmers Home Administration to guarantee the loan.

Synopsis

City has three neighborhoods designated as historic preservation districts (two by city legislation; one, near State Capitol, is controlled by special state legislation).

The two areas regulated by city zoning are Heritage Hills, oldest neighborhood in city (1910, 130 acres); and Putnam Heights (1920s, 100 acres). Both are near downtown. Heritage Hills is middle-to-upper class, integrated, single-family, houses owner-occupied. Many houses large, luxurious. Putnam Heights is white, middle-class (professional), owner-occupied, single-family houses.

The third is Capitol–Lincoln Terrace preservation area. State Legislature established Capitol District Zoning Commission to plan growth and limit new construction in district. Preservation area itself is a section of Capitol District (10 blocks long, about 4 blocks wide, 155 houses). Integrated, middle-class, professionals, students, some blue-collar people; single-family home ownership.

Few landmark structures in any of the districts.

Initiation

Heritage Hills city designated because area, due to proximity to CBD, under pressure from commercial speculators who wished to demolish mansions for commercial buildings. Homes threatened by conversion to multifamily residences or deterioration.

Prominent residents formed Historical Preservation Inc. (1969) and identified 12 houses as significant for use as documentation for a preservation ordinance.

Mayor active in State Historic Preservation Office, helped City Council write Historic District Zoning legislation. Heritage Hills residents, many active in business and political life, worked in support. This was vital, since they were accepting limits on use of their property. Heritage Hills first district under new city 1970 legislation.

Putnam Heights residents, wary of encroaching commercial activity, noted success of Heritage Hills and, in 1972, founded Putnam Heights Preservation Area, Inc., to lobby for designation as historic district.

Residents wished to include Classen Boulevard (formerly large mansions now demolished or converted into "high class" commercial space), but Classen Boulevard property owners refused. When Boulevard excluded, district obtained designation (1972).

Capitol–Lincoln Terrace area residents concerned with deterioration of private houses, expansion of commercial interests, encroachment of University of Oklahoma Medical Center. Formed Capitol–Lincoln Terrace Historical Preservation Area, Inc. (1973). With NTHP consultant service grant, documented historic significance of area. Preservation area is approximately a 40-block residential community, within a larger Capitol district.

Special State Zoning Commission convinced that historic designation would be tool for controlling growth in the entire Capitol district. Commission used city legislation to create own ordinance for Capitol–Lincoln Terrace Historical Preservation Area (1974).

Authority and commitment

City Council passed a Historic Preservation Ordinance: created special zoning category—historic preservation zone. Nine-member Historic Preservation Commission (HPC) appointed by mayor and council. At least one commissioner must be architect and one a historian.

Ordinance limits use in district to residential, except where there is a pre-existing use. Demolitions, additions, alterations to buildings must be submitted to HPC for certificate of appropriateness. Building permit for any significant exterior change cannot be issued without such a certificate.

HPC also requires that houses be maintained. Imposes fines where allowed to deteriorate. Decision may be appealed to the District Court. Few appeals, as HPC prefers to use persuasion and peer group pressure. One court case, but authority of HPC upheld.

Capitol District Zoning Commission appointed by state governor and representatives of community.

There are no covenants or facade regulations in either ordinance (individual case decisions), but such items as off-street parking are regulated. Only Capitol–Lincoln Terrace District has design regulations.

Historic Preservation Commissions administer zoning ordinances in their respective districts. They work with homeowner groups to encourage maintenance and discourage inappropriate alterations.

Management of program

The historic district designation is major land use control mechanism.

Operating tools and tactics

One goal of designation was to enlarge community tax base, so there are no rebates or exemptions.

All restoration and rehabilitation privately funded. Since designation, banks more willing to lend money for home repairs. All three homeowner groups raise operating funds through membership dues and contributions. Use funds to hire attorneys, publish brochures, beautify streets. In Heritage Hills, Historical Preservation, Inc. Foundation bought, renovated, resold a few houses.

Little displacement. Long-time residents remain, maintain own homes.

Houses mostly in good condition. Maintenance more important than rehabilitation.

Paterson

New Jersey
Population: c. 145,000

Paterson's origins as an industrial city reach back to nation's industrialization efforts during Revolutionary War. In 1791, Alexander Hamilton, together with SUM (The Society for the Establishment of Useful Manufactures) chose area around city's Great Falls for nation's first industrial center.

Great Falls/SUM Historic District is within walking distance of Paterson's center. This 89-acre area includes a 77-foot-high waterfall of Passaic River—after Niagara the largest on east coast—group of 60 historic industrial buildings that reflect birth, growth, and change of urban industry in America, and a canal or raceway system and dams to provide power and water to adjoining industries.

Building types range from single-story shops to multistoried mills up to 400 feet long. Buildings are brick, solid, still used, but generally underoccupied. Some were vacated a few years ago due to threat of highway construction. Alterations to buildings over the years due to changes in manufacturing processes are part of the history.

City population up, with moderate- and middle-income families replaced by poorer families. Many of these cannot find jobs in shrinking industrial base. Although downtown redevelopment has been moderately successful and tax rate has stabilized, it may be hard to attract new investment and activities needed to make reuse effort work.

Historic designation has assured homeowners that neighborhoods could continue as single-family residential areas. Since buildings could not be torn down for apartment houses or offices, people were willing to maintain homes, or sell to those who would. City now considering requests for designation from other areas.

Commercial, real estate interests, wanting to develop downtown sites for apartment houses or offices, had opposed designation. Figured areas were old, ripe for change of use. Preferred redevelopment to historic preservation. But since designation, have come to terms with concept.

Values in districts have gone up, especially in Heritage Hills. Houses sold for $30,000 (1970), $65,000 (1975).

Great Falls listed as a National Natural Landmark 1969. In 1971 Great Falls/SUM listed as National Historic District. Great Falls Development Corporation (GFDC), a private nonprofit membership organization, formed same year to plan, fund, and execute restoration of the historic district.

To draw attention to the Great Falls area, GFDC has a tour guide service, publishes quarterly newsletter, and cosponsors a yearly Great

Falls Festival with the Chamber of Commerce.

When designated in 1971 historic district, included only the individual buildings. Meantime preservation interest has grown. Industrial development of Paterson would not have happened without an immigrant work force—first Europeans, later Spanish-speaking. For 200 years these lived close to the industry in the historic district. Hence, city applied for grant from National Endowment for the Arts to study inclusion in historic district of 25-block residential section next to the Great Falls area.

Spanish Community Agency, representing this section, will sponsor project. It will include preservation and rehabilitation of housing. Residents have said they want authentic restoration of houses.

Goal of Great Falls Development Corporation is to integrate the buildings and surrounding spaces into Paterson's daily life. Great Falls/ SUM District under review as nation's first historic industrial park. GFDC plans activities in these areas:

Recreation and open space. Clean up Passaic River and tie large city parks and sports facilities into future historic industrial park.

Hydraulic system. Reuse hydraulic system, including raceways, dams, and the hydroelectric plant, as functional and educational resource portraying history of energy development in nation.

Labor and industry. Upgrade working conditions in buildings in use. Find adaptive uses for housing, exhibitions, commercial space for vacant structures no longer usable for industry. Restore facades.

Housing. Provide desperately needed housing, sale and rental, through adaptive reuse of industrial buildings.

Education. Found a State Museum of Labor and Industry in district. Area has buildings where first revolver, locomotive, submarine, and air-plane engines were developed. Cotton, silk, and paper industry also flourished.

Found Industrial Arts and Building Trades School. Use as job training center for skills needed to restore and rehabilitate historic industrial park.

Transportation. Route 20 has been planned for 15 years. If built as planned, it would have destroyed two-thirds of historic district. GFDC seeks change of road alignment.

Projects underway, along with operating tools being used, include:

1. Great Falls Park: 15 acres of open space at falls developed through time and materials donated by contractors, service clubs, citizens, and city of Paterson, 1971. $250,000 project.

2. Field evaluation of Great Falls/SUM Historic District by Smithsonian Institution and NTHP, 1972.

3. City and HUD jointly redevelop additional 15 acres of parkland around Falls, including lighting, landscaping, public accommodations. $311,000 project, 1973.

4. Historic American Engineering Record survey: $40,000 project, 1973–1974.

5. Salvage Archeology Grant: Sponsored by New Jersey Department of Transportation and GFDC. During construction of storm drain, discovery of significant archeological material caused change of construction method from open cut to tunnel. $200,000 project, 1974–75.

6. National Endowment for the Arts Grant: Feasibility studied for restoration and rehabilitation of entire hydroelectric system including raceways, dam, and hydroelectric plant. $22,820 project, 1974.

7. Great Falls/SUM Historic District designated as one of five major bicentennial sites in the state, 1975.

8. New Jersey Bicentennial Commission Grant: To begin restoration of the Waterwork Building

Peekskill

New York
Population: c. 19,000

Ivanhoe, Paper Mills (c. 1840) as city's Bicentennial Coordinating Center. $3,000, 1975.

9. Economic Development Administration Grant: To clean and preserve raceway and surrounding landscape. $164,000 project, 1975.

This city, 40 miles north of New York City on the Hudson River, was bustling rail, water, and industrial center in 19th century. By 1950s had stagnated and decayed, and was beset by racial violence common to many cities in 1960s.

New city administration (1968) used massive federal urban renewal to recast city via new construction, rehabilitation, and neighborhood conservation programs.

Neighborhood conservation, relying on code enforcement, affected area of over 600 buildings with 1,000 dwelling units.

Most neighborhood conservation activity is in 200-acre Park Street area in east of city. Park Street code enforcement program covers 412 houses. Over 300 property owners (mainly owner-occupants, but some investors buying for resale) assisted with loans, grants, technical assistance. Housing (75 to 125 years old, two-to three-story frame) mostly owner-occupied, one- and two-family houses. Neighborhood is racially integrated, working class. 17% of city is black; Park Street has larger percentage of black residents than many other areas.

No structures designated as landmarks. There are no historic districts.

Initiation

New mayor committed to taking city management out of "politics" (1968). Hires a city manager and a city planner with federal fundraising skills. Officials worked with enlightened developer, concerned congressman, innovative director of poverty programs, and determined mayor and City Council. Ciy has attracted over $25 million in federal and state aid (said to be largest amount per capita in nation). City and private investment have built new low-, middle-, and high-income housing; commercial facilities, a civic center, shopping, office space, and parks. Set up broad code enforcement. Performance convinced black groups to participate. Formerly skeptical leaders become supporters.

City able to work closely with county, state, and federal agencies (New York State Office of Planning Services, State Department of Transportation, Hudson River Valley Commission, HUD administrators). Hence, benefited from agencies' expertise and from speedy project approvals.

Authority and commitment

City has consolidated Community Development Agency (CDA). Mayor and Common Council are chairman and members of Agency. Hence, elected officials directly control policy, programs, decisions.

Management of program

Code enforcement program, started in 1970, managed by CDA's Director of Rehabilitation. CDA first declared Park Street area (containing almost half of city's dilapidated housing) a neighborhood improvement area. HUD approved. CDA's inspectors then checked homes for code violations. Homeowners informed of violations, notified of HUD grants up to $3,500 or low-interest HUD loans (depending on their eligibility).

City also gives technical assistance on removing violations. Director's office is in area; he monitors program daily. City also helped establish Project Area Committee. As many residents use own funds to rehabilitate as receive federal loans and grants. At first, residents in area unable to secure improvement loans. Now, area attracts investors who repair buildings and sell at profit. Since program gained momentum, banks willing to finance home improvements.

Operating tools and tactics

City has substantial design controls over all commercial, industrial, and apartment development. City zoning ordinance requires review of all site plans by City Planner—a trained architect and city planner.

City's neighborhood conservation relies on code enforcement, low-interest loans and grants, and private investment. By mid-1975, there were 62 federal low-interest loans (over $644,000) of which 40 were to owner-occupants and 22 to owners interested as investors. There have been 56 grants (totalling $121,590) all to owner-occupants. Some 196 building owners have invested almost $689,000 of their own funds with technical assistance provided by CDA staff.

City has spent required matching funds for this program in neighborhood open space facilities and infrastructure improvements. Rehabilitation activity has taken place with residents remaining in their dwellings. Almost no displacement. CDA has community relations program to keep residents abreast of benefits and progress.

From a total of 1,089 substandard dwelling units in city (1960 census), city has demolished some and aided or carried out rehabilitation of 872 dwelling units. Remaining 217 substandard units scheduled for correction by 1976.

Philadelphia
Pennsylvania
Population: c. 1,949,000

Editors' note: Philadelphia is a city of neighborhoods. The 1974 annual report of the Philadelphia Redevelopment Authority shows activities in many of these. Of 94 active renewal projects, some, such as the early urban renewal areas that border Independence Mall, have been widely documented. This case study describes conservation efforts in less well-publicized neighborhoods such as Haddington, Fishtown, and Spring Garden. A brief look at Philadelphia's LPA Rehabilitation Program ushers in the account.

The LPA (Local Public Agency) Rehabilitation Program was launched in 1973 to buy, rehabilitate, resell 500 vacant, vandalized, and abandoned houses in 12 urban renewal areas. Patterned after earlier program that had rehabilitated 81 houses through FHA Section 235, eliminated by HUD housing subsidy moratorium. When that happened, Philadelphia Redevelopment Authority (PRA) worked with consortium of S & L institutions and local banks to develop conventional financing for low- and moderate-income families.

Program works like this: vacant houses are acquired on blocks that are still 50% owner-occupied, in neighborhoods that are declining but still viable. Houses are totally rehabilitated, resold at fair market prices for the neighborhood. Sale price usually below actual cost of acquisition and rehabilitation; difference covered by federal funds. Thus, in 1974, average rehabilitation cost was $16,754; average sale price $9,689.

For 77 houses completed or under contract, total cost is put at $1,290,119, against expected sales return of $746,070. Cost of entire program (1974 through July 1, 1975) expected to be over $4.3 million for 266 houses.

Program has been hailed as helping to save Philadelphia neighborhoods.

Rehabilitation Loan and Grant Program run by PRA for past 8 years. Eligible homeowners in approved rehabilitation urban renewal areas apply for long-term, low-interest loans (to $17,400) or grants (to $3,500). Money used to bring houses up to city and rehabilitation standards. In 1974, 371 families received loans, grants totalling $2,265,667. City employment and training program provides free or low-cost labor when appropriate, allowing grant funds to be used mostly for materials, permitting major rehabilitations with limited funds.

City-State projects. Philadelphia and state of Pennsylvania launched program of city-state projects (1971). In 1974, 17 active, accounting for total of $14,900,000. State, city share in 3:1 ratio. Money went mostly to acquire, assemble properties (mostly vacant lots or houses) by PRA for new housing construction.

Project Area Committees. Following 1969 federal guidelines for community participation in redevelopment and renewal, PRA set up first Project Area Committees. Now 17 representing residents, community groups. Eight of them funded by PRA. Committees active in planning, developing rehabilitation; offer services to neighborhood. Among strongest is Haddington Leadership Organization (see below).

1
Haddington

A 450-acre neighborhood in West Philadelphia, mainly residential, with appropriate institutions—churches, schools, recreation centers—commercial and light industrial. Housing generally in good condition. Home ownership over 50%. Population 28,000, age group 40 to 60 predominates, 93% black, median family income: $6,500.

Haddington divided into units, each with own renewal plan. Prime activity in Unit 1, with combination of rehabilitation and clearance. Rehabilitation limited to single-family houses, to be resold to increase home ownership factor. Clearance aimed at producing new housing, plus another level of clearance for public works, libraries, recreation facilities.

Successful loan/grant program (see above). 820 loans and grants for total of $2,772,413 through

1974. Program popular, as it helps people stay in neighborhood.

Haddington Leadership Organization (HLO), a community group, back of progress. HLO developed own urban renewal plan, using own consultants; selected blocks for rehabilitation. Has been part of all community organization activities, giving advice, fielding complaints, marshalling neighborhood support. Also active in services to elderly.

Haddington is also one of 12 target areas for improved city services—streets, social services, funds, etc.—selected on basis of need and potential benefit.

2
Fishtown

Fishtown is neighborhood of modest incomes—median family income below $9,000; about 11% of families below poverty level. Population (10,003 in 1970) white, 33% under 20, 17% over 65. Houses over 70% owner-occupied.

As neighborhood, Fishtown is favored because: it is close to center city, has nearby industrial base, good transportation access, a solid store of parks and other amenities, good parochial schools. It also may be the least expensive neighborhood in Philadelphia in which to buy a shell for rehabilitation.

Hence, Fishtown scene of an active, privately financed rehabilitation program for past several years. Yet no formal statement of goals; program simply one of free enterprise by local contractors who buy, rehabilitate, resell to other local residents. Lacks the pressure created by influx of new, more prosperous residents.

Some 700 units rehabilitated in past few years by local contractors. Another 700 in prospect. Large factor has been active bank, Benjamin Franklin Savings & Loan. President also trying to encourage other S & L's to follow example. Other S & L institutions have now opened branches in Fishtown. Local contractors worked without city aid until 2 years ago when industry

slumped and easy projects all done. Most are Fishtown residents; at one time 35 active in neighborhood, later only eight.

Little outside threat to Fishtown; interstate highway skirts neighborhood; rehabilitation efforts are keeping long-time residents in neighborhood.

3
Spring Garden

Spring Garden (along with Fairmount and Francisville) makes up one of Philadelphia's oldest residential sections. Developed in 1850s. Close to center city (15-minute walk) and near Fairmount Park, so area attracted wealthy Philadelphians. Area is chiefly two- and three-story row houses in variety of turn-of-century styles. Institutional, commercial uses along major arteries; scattered industrial sites.

Neighborhood falls into three communities: Fairmount (white working class of Russian, Polish, Irish descent); Francisville (largely non-white, low income but stable); and eastern part of Spring Garden (largely Spanish-speaking). Fairmount is most stable, with 50% of houses owner-occupied; Francisville is poorest, with most deteriorated housing. One small area, near Art Museum Area, enclave of private restoration and rehabilitation by prosperous professional types. Along Benjamin Franklin Parkway is wall of high-rise luxury apartments.

Neighborhood financially depressed; properties cheap, readily available. Now changing as more properties are rehabilitated.

Population is changing, due to influx of upper middle-income professionals. Rising property values that follow rehabilitation helping to drive out some long-time residents. Another factor is Franklin Town, expensive in-town development adjacent to Spring Garden.

Franklin Town is $400 million project, includes town houses as replacement housing for neighborhood residents. These are provided in "deed-for-deed" exchange of old house for new. First

Pittsburgh

Pennsylvania
Population: c. 520,000

time private developer has built new relocation housing tailored to specific needs of individual homeowners without extra cost to family.

Sponsors for Franklin Town are: the Korman Corporation; Smith Kline Corporation, a pharmaceutical firm; I-T-E-Imperial Corporation, manufacturers of electrical gear; Philadelphia Electric Co.; and Butcher & Singer, brokerage firm.

With change, issue of who is being served starts to burn: controversy over site chosen for new school; white community in Fairmount doesn't want it; but choice supported by black, Spanish-speaking areas. Similar controversy surrounds sites chosen for public housing, reuse of Eastern State Penitentiary.

City is helping to attract new, different people to area, but few programs to help deal with this pressure.

Synopsis

Pittsburgh has two neighborhoods with outstanding multiple conservation activities. Central North Side is nation's first Neighborhood Housing Services Corporation (NHS). The Manchester neighborhood has an innovative facade easement and revolving fund program.

White out-migration and overall population decline in Pittsburgh large: 14% population loss since 1960; rise in black population (now 20% of city); large ratio of elderly (19%). The housing market is soft (6.2% vacancy rate in mid-1975). 74% of residential structures built before 1939. Median value of owner-occupied units only $12,500. 11% of families below poverty level.

The two neighborhoods under study are in the Northside, contiguous, each some 2 miles north of CBD. (Northside neighborhoods are the most deteriorated, with largest population loss and highest concentration of minorities and low-income families.)

Central North Side neighborhood is residential. Population in 1970, 7,872; decline 1960–1970, 34%; black population, 46.5%; receiving public assistance, 36%.

Housing (number of units), 3,808; owner-occupied, 23%; most units 60- to 70-year-old masonry row houses.

Within Central North Side is 4-block-wide Mexican War Streets district. Site of concentrated historic preservation. Laid out in 1848 and built up in 1890s. Houses are Greek Revival, Italianate, French, and Victorian; many of them mansions. Residents of War Streets block mostly white, younger, more affluent than Central Northsiders.

Manchester to west of Central North Side. Population decline over past 20 years. In 1970, 5,500 residents, 70% black. In 1972, 43% of residents received public assistance. 2,302 housing units, 29% owner-occupied.

Residential Manchester isolated from other communities by railroad tracks and highways. Has strong neighborhood identity.

In 1966 Central North Side faced with declining population and decaying housing. Citizens oppose urban renewal and clearance, create several organizations—Citizens Against Slum Housing, Central North Side Neighborhood Council, North Side Civic Development Council). Leaders of these groups, financial institutions, and Pittsburgh History and Landmarks Foundation (PHLF) form Neighborhood Housing Services (NHS), nonprofit corporation with representatives from banking, business, architecture, preservation groups, government, local residents. When community turned down by HUD's code enforcement program, groups turn to city; city designates area a "code enforcement area" (1967). Banks agree to stop redlining. Citizens submit proposal to Scaife Foundation for a high-risk loan fund (1968). Program supported by all key organizations plus city agencies, Mayor's Office and Planning Department ACTION—Housing Inc., a nonprofit organization, well regarded by Scaife Foundation, acts as agent for any funds granted NHS. Banks assume expenses of operating loan fund. Program underway (1969).

Manchester neighborhood program heralded when PHLF, Urban Redevelopment Authority (URA), and the Department of City Planning did a preservation planning study of heart of area (1964). Large Italianate double stone houses. This was a Title I Urban Renewal Area, but PHLF sought way to restore historic properties without dislocating residents. Took several years to create legal and financial mechanisms for restoration. These evolved into Manchester facade easement program (see below).

Key local enabling legislation is Ordinance No. 128, effective April 1971. Provides for designation of historic districts upon recommendation of City Planning Commission and PHLF, following public hearings. An advisory commission must assist Planning Commission. Latter must approve building permits that would change exteriors of structures in designated districts. If permit denied, no change may be made for six months. Building inspector then rules on permit in regular way. City also has tax abatement ordinance (1971). Authorizes exemptions from tax assessment for certain improvements to deteriorated dwellings.

a. Central North Side

Prime conservation program is Neighborhood Housing Services (NHS) program of physical rehabilitation, financial assistance, and directed public services. In city's first phase, Bureau of Building Inspection and the Allegheny County Health Department inspected all structures in target area for building and health code violations. NHS then helped residents with violations find financing sources. Qualified applicants referred to group of 20 local banks which agreed to make loans for violation removal and repair. NHS has high-risk, $700,000 loan fund for loans at up to 6% for those not eligible for bank loans. Financed by $125,000 per year grants from Sarah Mellon Scaife Foundation since 1969 and grants from other foundations. $47,000 in administrative costs underwritten by local banks. The loan repayments average $100,000 per year. Delinquency rate, 10%.

NHS staff supervise, inspect properties, write specifications for repairs, review contractors' bids, arrange mortgage financing, and (since 1973) have acted as general contractors.

Preventive maintenance pilot project, funded ¢ by $125,000 from Ford Foundation, started 1975. For $96 per year, homeowners get servicing, tools, paint, labor, and access at cost to all items needed for repairs.

Between 1969 and 1974, NHS made 339 loans totaling $813,664. Loans range from $1,740 to $3,837. Since 1968, over $2 million in loans from banks. Over 80% of structures now satisfy code standards. City to commit CD block funds to a home repair revolving fund starting 1975.

NHS and local residents work with City Department of Planning on capital improvement projects. City has put in major sewage and water lines, trees, tot lots, park renovation, and new fire and police building.

Central North Side also site of historic preservation action by PHLF—in Mexican War Streets area, a designated historic district. PHLF has $500,000 revolving loan fund (started with 1966, $100,000 Scaife Foundation grant), and augmented by other foundations and bank loans.

PHLF buys houses, restores interiors and exteriors, and then rents buildings at varying prices. Seeks to keep existing rents and tenants. Federal leased housing program used to provide a share of low-income apartments. In first years of program, residents secure Section 115 and 312 grants and loans and bank loans for restoration.

PHLF has spent $325,000 directly and owns 20 to 25 buildings in area. Foundation members and local residents have spent six times that sum to buy and restore historic houses. Program has deterred residents from leaving area.

b. Manchester
Manchester is site of innovative facade easement program coordinated by PHLF and Urban Redevelopment Authority (URA). PHLF first did systematic historical and structural analysis of all buildings in area. Found 207 structures that would be eligible for federal preservation funds.

URA agrees to restore exterior of all designated buildings at no expense to owner. URA pays owner 10% of appraised value of house as a facade easement. Interiors rehabilitated by owner using 3% Section 312 loans and Section 115 grants under regular HUD financing. Owner may not change exterior after restoration without permission, under city's historic preservation ordinance. The Authority has $2 million HUD grant to set program in motion.

Other financial tools available to city for neighborhood conservation and not referred to earlier include: CD block grant funds over 3 years to be used for low-interest home repair loans. Also, a neighborhood housing program run by URA to create new housing at moderate cost. Provides $7 million to make up difference between cost to developer of producing dwelling on selected site in designated neighborhood, and realistic market price house can command.

Other operating tools and tactics

Portland
Maine
Population: c. 65,000

Conserving historically and architecturally rich downtown peninsula area of Portland has been struggle against forces of decay, and physical and economic change.

Settled in 1632, peninsula area laid waste several times. Peninsula's East and West End areas rich in soundly built Federal, Greek Revival, Victorian houses, and commercial structures, as is Old Port Exchange Waterfront Area, with its old commercial buildings and wharves.

Large shopping mall 5 miles from city siphoned off shoppers from CBD. Concurrently, city officials launched a major downtown upgrading, called Maine Way Project. Some 19th-century cmmmercial buildings demolished for civic center and two parking structures.

Old housing stock, much of it deteriorating. Below average income. Efforts by city councilors and grassroots neighborhood groups to marshal federal assistance to rehabilitate older neighborhoods, supplemented by new subsidized housing construction at selected sites. These efforts, in concert with downtown revitalization, and use of urban beautification funds, sought to recapture in-town peninsula's historic legacy as good place to live.

Initiation/ commitment

The 1888, Richardson-style Union Station demolished (1961), so citizens form Greater Portland Landmarks, Inc. (GPL). Several 19th-century buildings placed on National Register in 1960s, but several demolished by owners for private developments. GPL bought, resold some buildings with restrictive deeds.

From 1970 on, Spring Street and Waterfront added to National Register as historic districts. These mostly restoration efforts. MICAH founded in 1969 by local clergy to preserve existing housing stock of peninsula and stabilize neighborhoods. Same year MICAH taken over by Model Cities Program.

After MICAH came in with Model Cities, local banks loosened loans in East, West End. Through Model Cities–MICAH, 700 homeowners aided with maximum subsidy of $1,000. On occasion federal grants were used. MICAH also aided owners of multiple dwellings (up to three units). Proviso: no rent boosts in rehabilitated buildings.

City granted to MICAH a total of $2.2 million in funds as of May 1975. Eight-member board includes three area residents.

Operating tools and tactics

Under Federal Neighborhood Development Program city has used $2.3 million in past 4 years for conservation of stable but precarious neighborhoods. Vehicles: Section 312 loans and Section 115 grants.

CD block grant program received $5.3 million to be spent in 1976, with heavy emphasis on residential conservation. Goals include: communitywide conservation program based on neighborhoods; 100% housing code compliance; $500,000 rehabilitation loan fund; extensive street and sidewalk repairs.

Consultants readying set of regulatory controls establishing city historic districts, but design control probably not suitable for downtown area, already blanketed by "Maine Way" restrictions.

Innovative conservation proposal for Portland
Portland Plan, if approved, would create public purpose Mortgage Guarantee Corporation (MGC) via grant from city, using CD block funds. Acting jointly with HUD's existing mortgage insurance program (as expanded by Emergency Home Purchase Assistance Act of 1974), MGC would enable local banks to make low-cost loans for housing. Low-income and elderly housing provided through federal leased housing program, allows Maine State Housing Authority to assume these loans from local banks. Eligible under the 1974 Act are buildings on National Register or buildings in a National Register Historic District.

Another plan

Maine Historic Preservation Commission and GPL have prepared Maine Urban Conservation Fund (MUCF), which would use vacant downtown commercial, industrial structures for low-, moderate-income and elderly housing. Would offer private redevelopers long-term financing when unavailable from local banks.

GPL also using labor hired with federal funds to restore exterior of houses with restrictive covenants for resale. Value of labor effectively becomes a subsidy, allowing building that would otherwise be economically unfeasible, to be restored.

Synopsis

Providence made first conservation efforts in College Hill district around Brown University (1950s, 1960s). Upper-class effort, directed against university's drastic expansion in center of district. City initially opposed conservation. Providence Preservation Society (PPS) formed 1956. Working with Providence Redevelopment Agency, which originally planned to clear area, PPS gave necessary citizen support for federally funded pilot study to explore ways to save College Hill. Houses, multifamily dilapidated tenements, not up to code. No cooperation from absentee landlords; impossible to rehabilitate and keep former tenants. Influenced by PPS education program, local people began buying houses for their own use.

No funds from city or PPS. Restoration program entirely dependent on private investment. Houses now occupied by new owners. Project, one of the early successful area preservation programs in country, instrumental in changing city's attitude toward area rehabilitation of historic structures.

In Elmwood neighborhood, local groups fought for stabilization, upgrading throughout late 1960s, early 1970s. New city administration elected whose political support was in neighborhoods (1974). Reversed earlier policy, began intense program for conservation.

Initiation

College Hill residents galvanized into action by city plans to bulldoze its fine but dilapidated Colonial and Federal town houses for expansion of Brown University (1956). Benefit Street houses had been divided up into small living units for low-income families; whole district in decline. PPS launched campaign to publicize urgency. Theme: "Buy, restore." Mrs. Chase buys, restores houses in concentrated area. Result: people of lesser means able to get bank loans to do likewise.

College Hill listed on National Register (1960). Gave impetus to potential buyers. Prices for restored buildings rise sharply. City holds off upward reassessment of property tax during tenancy of first purchaser.

Elmwood area at edge of downtown Providence. Showplace for new wealth (1890s). In 1930s Elmwood Avenue became commercial strip; Victorian mansions converted. In 1960s influx of blacks from South Providence triggered exodus of whites. Diminished owner occupancy; larger houses divided into rooming houses, nursing homes. Absentee landlords neglect maintenance; high abandonment rate develops. Elderly owners of Elmwood's numerous single-family houses and triple-deckers (three-story, floor-through apartment buildings) cannot afford maintenance, speeding up neighborhood decline. Ethnic unity also down; crime rate up.

Blockbusting: housing costing $65,000 on city's East Side goes for $25,000 in Elmwood. Redlining sets in.

People Acting Through Community Efforts (PACE) became active in Elmwood in late 1960s. Local people stressed pragmatic solutions to specific problems—street lighting, police protection, building code enforcement, repairs, maintenance, zoning to control excessive occupancy, neglect by absentee landlords, redlining.

PACE originally supported by Roman Catholic Church. PACE efforts at stabilization begin to bear fruit. City's administration responding to community demands. White exodus is stemmed. Public services improve. Redlining subsides.

Authority and commitment / operating tools and tactics

City completed extensive survey of housing. Expects $9.1 million in HUD funding, of which 70% will go for neighborhood rehabilitation, in form of loans, grants, subsidies, to low- and moderate-income homeowners, including non-occupant owners. Funds to be administered by city agencies, with 80-member advisory committee from neighborhoods. CD block grant plan grew out of desires of neighborhood groups.

Seven historic districts designated in Providence; 43 individual structures have been placed on the National Register. The other neighborhoods under survey. Designation makes homeowners eligible for grants-in-aid from National Park Service.

Owners to be treated individually; will be offered whatever combination of subsidy approaches required to keep housing costs to owners and tenants under 25% of income. Community groups in neighborhoods to be involved in setting priorities, in some cases also in evaluation of loan applications.

Citywide reassessment of taxes may help lower Elmwood's high taxes.

Large-scale displacement of families unlikely due to strong neighborhood community groups which would vigorously fight dislocation.

Richmond

Virginia
Population: c. 250,000

Synopsis

Two programs reflect Richmond's concern for neighborhood: the restoration activities of private Historic Richmond Foundation in Church Hill; and a rehabilitation loan program operated by the urban renewal agency.

Church Hill area (originally settled 1611) is 20-block area in center of city, with one edge 10 blocks from the CBD. Its 300 residential buildings range from early to late 19th century in variety of single-family types: small free-standing, double-unit structures, and some grander Greek Revival mansions. Prior to conservation, was slum with high proportion of absentee ownership.

Initiation

In 1956, group of well-to-do Richmond citizens became concerned over deterioration of old Church Hill area. Opted for private restoration effort, with minimum of government involvement. Secured State Charter as nonprofit Historic Richmond Foundation (HRF).

Authority and commitment

Conservation activities advanced, safeguarded by local historic district designation (St. John's Church Historic District) granted by City Council (1975). With designation, City Council established Commission of Architectural Review, which passes on all construction, demolition, and exterior alterations in historic district.

City involved minimally but has assisted conservation activities through public works (street and sidewalk improvements), installing gas lights, enforcing housing and building codes to hasten restoration activities, and turning over buildings it has acquired (e.g., by tax foreclosures) to HRF.

To avoid controversy and retain public confidence, HRF selects restoration projects carefully.

Operating tools and tactics

HRF buys, restores, resells architecturally or historically important houses. Using private contributions as well as monies from a revolving fund, HRF has found restoration to be a viable real estate business; has rarely lost money on resale.

Lately, HRF able to purchase, resell houses with a minimum of restoration, leaving such work to purchasers. Includes restrictive covenant in deeds: retains right of first refusal at original sales price for a period of 5 years for all restored houses it sells. Financing comes from two main sources: revolving fund and a private "security deposit" maintained by one board member. By 1975 revolving fund has grown to $88,200; assets listed as property and equipment in Financial Report totaled $614,597.

The second resource is a large sum one board member has deposited in local bank. Bank uses money as security for purchase and renovation loans (both construction and permanent financing) to homeowners. After five years, bank releases security money on an individual property to make it available for another loan.

Market in Church Hill initially weak, now rapidly strengthening. Currently, HRF buys only structures that cannot be sold or are hard to restore. Sometimes will invest its money in common improvements (e.g., fencing and site improvements), leaving building improvements to buyer.

After HRF took initial investments risks, created viable market, owners now able to get financing directly from banks.

City has granted no tax incentives for restoration, as property taxes in Richmond are relatively low. Yet assessed valuations as a result of conservation in district have tripled since 1956, only doubling in rest of city.

Many low- and moderate-income residents of Church Hill displaced. HRF relocated these, paying all moving expenses. Families displaced by individual owners not guaranteed relocation aid. Recent review of displacement has led HRF to explore federal rent subsidies for restored

Sacramento

California
Population: c. 254,000

structures: would continue to sell important buildings to middle- or upper-income people; lesser dwellings would be restored, rented at subsidized rents to low-income tenants.

In addition to Foundation's effort, a locally funded public conservation program started by Richmond Redevelopment and Housing Authority after federal government suspended Section 312 loan program. Authority obtained loan commitment of up to $600,000 for rehabilitation loans from four Richmond banks, at 5% for a 15-year term, in return for Authority revenue notes. Added $200,000 of its own (nonfederal funds) in interest-bearing bank account (interest used to cover defaults). Authority charges homeowners 6% interest, securing loans by first or second deeds of trust; deposits loan repayment in escrow account to make payments on its notes to the banks.

Since agreement completed in 1974, over 15 loans made.

Founded in 1839, Sacramento became jumping off point for prospectors after gold was discovered in the Mother Lode, 35 miles to the east. In past 30 years Sacramento has grown outward into residential suburbs. The inner "Old City" generally grew and changed in the direction of commercial, office, and high-density residential uses. Remaining historically and/or architecturally significant structures in "Old City" being conserved through two programs.

The first of these, "Historic Old Sacramento," a National Register Historic Landmark along banks of Sacramento River adjacent to CBD, is a leisure-time business, tourist, and recreational area. This area has great concentration of historic buildings dating back to the California gold rush (1849–1870). There are 120 buildings on 28-acre site. State Department of Parks and Recreation owns one third, rest being sold to private developers through Sacramento Housing and Redevelopment Agency (SHRA).

Sound conservation effort carried forward for the larger "Old City" area, where many single-family houses remaining date back to gold rush period. Rehabilitation activities in "Old City" focus on preservation program prepared by Historical Structures Advisory Committee (HSAC), and adopted by Sacramento City Council. Program calls for historical preservation ordinance, preservation board, a comprehensive inventory of historically and architecturally significant structures, a demolition review procedure, and a public information program.

Old Sacramento project begun 1963 by SHRA. Impetus came from within agency as planners sought to save yet another severely blighted and neglected part of original city.

Redevelopment Agency did $100,000 HUD-financed planning study. Construction began 1966 and is nearing completion. Early concerns by local interest groups (such as Sacramento Old City Association) and city officials brought into focus need for conserving historic structures and areas. This concern formalized by city appointment of an Historical Structures Advisory Committee (HSAC), charged by City Council to develop preservation program for "Old City" area.

Authority and commitment/ program management

City Council enacted a preservation ordinance, appointed preservation board and preservation director, authorized survey leading to official register of significant buildings.

Under ordinance, demolition permits for buildings on register can be delayed up to one year while alternatives for preservation are sought. Also calls for a Preservation Area Plan to contain: a statement of goals for architectural review; a representation of existing land uses; historic and architectural data on area; standards and criteria relating to height, bulk, architectural details, materials, and landscaping.

Also at work in "Old City" area is Central City Study Committee (CCSC) charged with updating existing 1961 masterplan for this area. CCSC is developing masterplan guidelines and recommendations for "Old City" area as a whole and neighborhood subunits.

In Old Sacramento, the historic/commercial area of the waterfront, authority rests in hands of SHRA and the State Department of Parks and Recreation (DPR). Of 120 buildings in this area, DPR is investing $9 million in the restoration/reconstruction of nearly 40. Within these buildings will be five museums telling story of transportation and communication in the early West. DPR financing, managing all construction on buildings under its authority. SHRA, on other hand, sells property in Old Sacramento to private developers, who will end up financing one-half ($15 million) of total project cost. Balance from issuance of $8 million in local bonds and from HUD two-for-one matching of locally committed monies.

Operating tools and tactics

In Old Sacramento (claims more historic sites per acre than any other city in nation), design

control by SHRA made up of deed restrictions and facade easements. Developers restoring existing buildings required to use only historically authentic material on all exposed facades. Color of facades, outside illumination, signs, landscaping of private courtyards clearly specified. Large investment by developers expected to be offset by estimated 2.5 million visitors spending $20 million per year.

Despite these actions by city, financial institutions reluctant to commit much loan money in Old City neighborhoods.

Area redlined by conventional money lenders and no alternative mechanisms (revolving loan funds, low-interest federal loans, high-risk loan pools, etc.) operating in area.

Sacramento hopes to allocate portion of first-year CD block grant for planning, organizing, and establishing a Housing Rehabilitation Assistance Program. Other first-year CD funds allocated to preservation program, including comprehensive listing of significant structures and preservation areas.

St. Charles

Missouri
Population: c. 32,000

Synopsis

Conservation neighborhood is the First State Capitol Urban Renewal Project downtown. Within renewal area is 8½-block section designated by city as the Historic Site District (1966). District put on National Register (1970), includes 125 structures, of which 60 noteworthy, 10 "of major importance."

Buildings mostly stone, brick, built in early 1800s. Most have always had commercial uses on first floor, residences above.

Initiation

In early 1960s, several individuals concerned with deterioration of state's first Capitol and other early 19th-century buildings, founded St. Charles County Historical Society, Incorporated (SCCHS). Working with the Missouri Historical Society, aroused interest in legislature for restoring the Capitol, then in private ownership. State and city cooperated in assembling block of buildings composing original Capitol. State bought two of them, city the balance of site. Restoration of Capitol with state funds completed (1972).

This effort awoke residents to meaning of historic buildings in other neighborhoods.

Authority and commitment

A 1966 city ordinance created Historical Site District, and five-person Board of Architectural Review (BAR). BAR rules on all exterior alterations, renovations, or removals in district; certificate of appropriateness required for a building permit. BAR has final authority; no appeal to City Council. Redevelopment Authority's renewal activities must be approved by BAR, as with private activities.

Management of program

In 1972 urban renewal plan focused on rehabilitation not clearance. Initially, some resident-owners in district disliked restrictions on physical changes to their own property, resented going before BAR for changes approval. Others, attracted by concept of historic preservation, more cooperative. 30 of 125 buildings in district

privately restored. Public commitment and controls seen as beneficial to area's long-term stability.

Designation helped upgrade area, newcomers to buy, restore deteriorating buildings in District. Almost all kept as mixed use dwellings (residential/commercial) after restoration.

Except for city/state sponsored restoration of Capitol buildings, financing has been through private investment and HUD renewal funds, Section 115 and 312 grants and loans.

City used $145,000 in revenue bonds to pay for its portion of State Capitol site. SCCHS aided city by buying bonds and selling some to others. Bonds being repaid from revenues from city parking facilities in area. Little displacement.

Operating tools and tactics

St. Joseph

Missouri
Population: c. 73,000

Synopsis

St. Joseph lost most of a downtown historic district in face of aggressive urban renewal program, a highway, and contrary political and business interests.

Market Square Historic District (now revised to Missouri Valley Trust Company Historic District) included downtown half-block of mid-19th-century buildings plus adjacent 1½ blocks with late 19th-century structures. Area entirely commercial. District comprised 27 buildings entered on National Register 1972. Since then 24 buildings demolished due to urban renewal. Three designated historic structures preserved in the CBD. (Conservation focus also on 1873 Buchanan County Courthouse and block of late 19th-century warehouses. These preserved to date).

Initiation

St. Joseph Historical Society (SJHS) organized 1949. Current activities triggered by city's urban renewal program, which began to demolish many old city buildings. SJHS and city contributed a third of the cost of a HUD survey to determine buildings of architectural and historic significance in 1972.

With $400 grant from NTHP, SJHS did feasibility study on preserving 19th- to early 20-century city center. Also received $16,545 City Options grant from National Endowment for the Arts, for staff to coordinate work of several preservation groups (e.g., Pony Express Historical Association and Heritage 1776, Inc.).

Movement to preserve Market Square Historic District opposed by city officials and downtown merchants. These feared jeopardy to interstate highway connection that would serve St. Joseph's CBD. Also, Land Clearance for Redevelopment Authority (urban renewal agency) claimed many buildings were beyond economic restoration.

Authority and commitment

City's conventional urban renewal program, using federal and city funds, directed at downtown commercial area; within it lay Market Square Historic District. SJHS delayed demolition of some buildings in Historic District through court order requiring Environmental Impact Statement for urban renewal program. But contract for urban renewal plan signed with HUD several months before placement of Market Square on National Register. Hence, lacking protection of designation, these buildings demolished. Historic district ordinance not enacted until 1974. Created district encompassing many Victorian mansions.

Management of program

One developer has bought with own funds two buildings in Market Square District and restored them as retail and office space. Seven other buildings in CBD also retained and preserved. SJHS wants to pass bond issue to restore 1873 Buchanan County Courthouse; opposes competing bond issue for a new courthouse. SJHS now encouraging owners to restore block of late 19th-century warehouses downtown; hope to convert to modern uses.

St. Paul

Minnesota
Population: c. 310,000

Synopsis

Historic Hill contains many of the oldest houses in St. Paul. Over 400 structures identified by Minnesota State Historical Society as historically significant. Area had 8,000 residents (1970), 3,160 dwellings, one-third owner-occupied; median family income $10,700 (1969).

District is large (5 square miles); has some of the most costly houses and some of worst housing in city. Of several neighborhoods, two (Ramsey Hill and Summit Hill) are the oldest (settled 1870–95); sites of larger single-family houses; residents most concerned about historic restoration.

The other neighborhoods in Hill are part of Model Cities area, the locale of most of renewal clearance in the district—poor rental neighborhoods—about 15% black and the most deteriorated.

Initiation

Old Town Restorations, Inc. (OTR) formed in 1967 by local residents: nonprofit neighborhood corporation to buy, restore, resell old homes in danger of demolition due to code enforcement and urban renewal. By 1972, middle-class families return from suburbs—many are descendants of early residents. They, plus poor and minorities still living there, all realized the advantages of saving Historic Hill's moderate-priced, spacious houses suitable for rehabilitation.

Historic District Act (enabling statute for local preservation commissions) passed in 1971. Hill designated as state historic district (1973). Concurrently, state legislature directed mayor and City Council to establish a Historic Hill Commission with review power over district.

OTR begins comprehensive planning to preserve, develop district (1974). Stress on citizen involvement, as district is large, has many groups, often with conflicting goals.

Authority and commitment

Responding to state's mandate to City Council, OTR and local residents prepare local ordinance. Provides for a Historic Hill District Board and Preservation Commission to regulate construction, alteration, and demolition within district.

A year passed, but ordinance still not enacted. City Planning Commission wants heritage commission for entire city, not limited to Hill District. Other areas in city (such as Irvine Park Historic District, created in 1974) also need regulation and conservation. Within Historic Hill, preservation activities hindered by: (a) interest of speculators in high-rise apartments; (b) State Highway Deptartment's concern with roadways; (c) some residents' concern as to degree of homeowner control that ordinance will provide.

Management of program

Historic Hill District action program run by OTR, along with Housing and Redevelopment Authority of St. Paul, City Planning Department, mayor's office, and four neighborhood associations. Funded by over $120,000 in grants from State Arts Council, National Endowment for the Arts, Hill Foundation, plus volunteers.

Activities of residents, including data gathering, coordinated by planning and other professionals. To be completed in 1976.

Key element of plan: define options for land use and community facilities; balanced transportation system; viable shopping facilities and commercial services.

One difficulty: goals of black and poor residents do not always coincide with those of more prosperous white residents. Black community (severed by Interstate 94) promised new housing, but reconversion of multi-unit rental to single-unit, owner-occupied structures through restoration further reduced low-income dwelling units. Participation achieved through neighborhood meetings, at which policy and operations discussed. OTR supplies the resources: materials for premeeting discussion, organization of task committees, and distribution of minutes.

**Operating tools
and tactics**

St. Paul has several housing improvements programs that could be used in Historic Hill. One is a rehabilitation loan and grant program to bring houses up to code standards.

Funds come in part from $3 million city bond issue, used as leverage to obtain other loan funds from banks and state Housing Finance Agency. Using the city's borrowing power, loans are made to homeowners at 4% or 8%, depending on their income. Only 5% of funds in program used for grants. Loan program to focus half of funds on only five or six areas, with many old, owner-occupied homes with moderate-income families. Hope is that concentration of municipal loan funds will stimulate residents to invest in home improvements. According to 1973 state law, property taxes frozen for homeowners over 65.

There is also a modest program of home construction grants in black community.

To avoid conflict among diverse ethnic and income groups, OTR supporting creation of coop apartments in restored structures. Various types of units and ownership arrangements, at different prices, to be made available.

Synopsis

Conservation neighborhoods all built after 1849 Gold Rush and before earthquake fire of 1906. Neighborhoods grew in crescent around original commercial center of city; now form boundaries of CBD. Known as Pacific Heights, Alamo Square, Western Addition, Mint Hill, Buena Vista, Duboce Triangle, Haight-Ashbury, Eureka Valley, Noe Valley, Inner Mission, Bernal Heights, Potrero Hills, and others. These areas, filled mostly with Victorian era (1860–1900) houses and small commercial buildings, take up 25% of city's area. Most buildings wood frame residential, single-family but with many two- to four-unit buildings and occasional large apartment houses with up to 50 units. Total: 89,000 living units, 238,079 people live within area (1970 census). Over past decade, population declined but recently outmigration stabilized, reversed.

Many units "improved" by asbestos shingle and stucco, aluminum windows, removal of interior and exterior embellishments. Except for Western Addition, none of these neighborhoods heavily hit by redevelopment.

Initiation

1. Urban design plan prepared by Department of City Planning (1972) set goals, guidelines for physical evolution of San Francisco. Includes strong directions for revitalizing, reinforcing city's sense of neighborhood identity. Urban Design Plan went bigtime—three-screen narrated slide show seen in schools, auditoriums, churches, living rooms. Became catalyst for public awareness and urban design tool.

2. Citizen groups. During the same period many citizen-organized groups began forming. Each came together for a different reason, or a different issue, and today, several remain with reasonably broad based programs and memberships. These groups are: Foundation for San Francisco's Architectural Heritage (citywide urban conservation organization); The Victorian Alliance (a 250-member group of Victorian homeowners organized around grassroots program of information and politics); and over 20 neighbor-

hood group. Several umbrella neighborhood groups act as areawide cleainghouses and representatives.

Authority and commitment

State law mandates strong planning process. Each of state's cities and counties must have general development plan, broken down into required elements and local option *permissible elements.* Latter include: community design, housing and demolition planning, redevelopment, historic preservation.

Other applicable state authority is Marks-Foran Residential Rehabilitation Act of 1973. Allows any size city to issue revenue bonds for residential rehabilitation. City must first adopt a comprehensive code enforcement program and establish guidelines for financing of such rehabilitation. City must also adopt public improvement plan for areas designated for loan program. Law helped create city's locally financed code enforcement program (see below).

At city level, Department of City Planning (civil servants), which is directed by Planning Commission (mayor's appointees), does planning and zoning administration. Other administration is through mayor's office and Department of Public Works.

Management / operating tools and tactics

Regional programs (private). Savings Associations Mortgage Co. (SAMCO) very active in Bay region. Alliance of 27 S & L's. Is source of loan money to nonbankable people. Has made a few loans to Model Cities Development Corporation in Inner Mission neighborhood.

Code enforcement programs used as lever to correct both code and noncode deficiencies. FACE (Federally Assisted Code Enforcement) used HUD Section 115 rehabilitation grants up to $3,500, and Section 312, 3% loans for rehabilitation up to $17,500. Plan for public improvements accompanies homeowner's efforts. In four pilot FACE neighborhoods, 91% of buildings had some sort of code violation. From 1967

through 1970, 93.7% of violations (2,797 buildings) corrected, 622 loans made, totaling $4,581,200. Made 230 grants totaling $463,800.

Rehabilitation Assistance Program (RAP) designed to replace discontinued FACE program. Voters approve RAP (1973). Qualifies under state Marks-Foran Act (see above).

Designation of residential rehabilitation areas is initiated by Director of Planning, approved by Board of Supervisors, city's top legislative body. By and large, programs will be conducted only after major groups in area have joined in support of program. To date, two areas designated as RAP areas.

Under RAP the city will issue revenue bonds. Bonds will provide for payment of interest only at end of first year. City will then make equal annual payments of interest and principal; entire reserve fund becomes due at end of terms of bonds.

City to establish reserve fund out of bond proceeds equal to 15% of face amount. Despite limitations on what city can earn through investment of bond proceeds and still have interest on bonds be tax exempt, any surplus funds generated may be used for hardship loan and relocation assistance funds. Property owners will be charged interest rate the city pays on the bonds plus an amount to cover administration and anticipated losses due to defaults.

Bank of America has agreed to submit a bid at public sale for up to $20 million in 20-year revenue bonds, with an interest rate for the first 10 years not to exceed current market rate for "Aa" rated, 10-year general obligation securities. Interest rate for the last 10 years will be market rate at end of first 10 years. As security, city to pledge deeds of trust on property to be rehabilitated, monies received in property owner loan repayments, and the reserve fund.

Each responsible owner of property located within a residential rehabilitation area will be eligible for financing under RAP program. Loans covering minimum code work may be granted up to $17,500 per unit; maximum repayment period is 20 years or 75% of economic life of building (whichever is less).

If enough funds are available, hardship loans may be granted to low-income applicants up to $3,500 per building for owner-occupants of one- to four-unit buildings. Interest-free loan is lien against property; no repayment required until sale or transfer, or at end of 20 years.

Program delayed, however, because city awaits IRS ruling that city's bonds will be exempt from federal income taxes.

HUD has released $598,606 in CD block grant funds for administration, relocation benefits, hardship loan interest subsidy, acquisition for rehabilitation/resale, and temporary rent payments in the Inner Richmond RAP area.

City expects to issue $8 million in RAP bonds during first year of operation, and $3 million in each of 5 succeeding years.

Zoning study. City under interim zoning ordinance during residential rezoning study, which Department of City Planning is doing in cooperation with neighborhood groups. Expected result will be rezoning of most residential neighborhoods; 70% of city now zoned above existing use.

Landmark preservation. City Planning Code provides for "preservation of historical architectural and aesthetic landmarks," through City Planning Commission as advised by Landmarks Preservation Advisory Board. Designation (individual buildings or districts) temporarily freezes development rights on structure(s), but yields no tangible tax benefits. By 1975, only district was Jackson Square.

Bicentennial. Celebration theme is competition aimed at improving streets, parks, shopping areas, and homes. Contest categories include neighborhood oriented improvements. Award: total of $600,000 in public improvements, programs for neighborhoods, cash awards to aid public service objectives of community groups.

Foundation for San Francisco's Architectural Heritage features three programs: 1. facade easements—owner conveys development rights of property to Heritage; 2. Urban Conservation Fund, revolving fund to buy, resell endangered structures; 3. some 15 threatened Victorian houses in Western Addition district moved to create small "historic district" in cooperation with San Francisco Redevelopment Agency and Landmarks Preservation Advisory Board. New owners found to restore the houses. Mixed response: much staff time given to move, plus long-term tie-up of capital ($30,000) in resale of buildings.

Santa Fe
New Mexico
Population: c. 41,000

Synopsis

City founded by Spaniards on remains of Indian pueblo (1609). Because of mixture of American-Indian, Spanish-American, and Anglo-American culture, it is one of most picturesque cities in U.S. Plaza created by Spanish has been commercial core of city since 1610. Features of city are narrow, often unpaved streets, sidewalks protected by arcades, and low, adobe-style houses. Tourism now city's second largest source of income.

Initiation

Private, nonprofit Old Santa Fe Association, Inc. (OSFA) founded 1926. OSFA encouraged City Council to pass historic zoning ordinance to preserve existing architecture and control style and size of new buildings (1957). All building activities in the historic district supervised by an Historical Style Committee.

Smaller historic district expanded to include one-third of city (1972). Expanded area includes downtown, historic and new buildings in other parts of city, and undeveloped land. Land uses regulated by Zoning Ordinance, upon which are superimposed the "H" Historical District Regulations as design control (see below).

Much of Historical District plus other sections placed on National Register (1973).

Authority and commitment

The Historical Style Committee is a standing committee of City Planning Commission. Seven members serve staggered terms; appointed by mayor with approval of City Council. Community representation.

In 1957 Santa Fe's zoning ordinance amended to include historic district regulations for "H" Zone—a Historical Style Zone. "H" Zone comprises about one-fifth of city, including downtown. Purposes of "H" Zone include "harmonious, orderly, and efficient growth and development of the municipality."

Operating tools and tactics

Ordinance recognizes two styles: "Old Santa Fe" and "Recent Santa Fe."

"Old Santa Fe" style (adobe brick construction), goes back to Spanish settlement (early 1600's), one- to two-story oblong buildings have flat roofs and are surrounded on at least three sides by firewall. Solid wall space is always greater in any facade than window and door space combined. Wall colors are natural adobe (light to dark earth colors).

Old buildings in "H" Zone must be preserved in "Old Santa Fe" style. Owners wishing to alter nonconforming buildings must change them to old style.

New buildings in "H" Zone must adhere to follow the "Recent Santa Fe" style: masonry blocks, bricks, or other materials with which adobe effect can be simulated are permitted but exterior walls must not be less than 8 inches thick and "geometrically straight" facade lines are avoided.

Historical Zoning Ordinance (1957) upheld by state supreme court in 1964 when tire company forced to divide plate glass windows into tiny panes to conform to historical style. Ordinance said to have kept some businesses out of downtown (e.g., those whose building design is part of their form of selling, such as franchise operation). For others, historic-style architecture has increased business.

Most recent construction has been institutional and commercial. Private citizens see little incentive in building in a historic style. Property values within district have gone up sharply; there is no tax policy to encourage homeowners to restore houses.

Expansion of local historic district to western parts of the city (which are already on National Register) opposed by poorer residents (most of them homeowners) who fear influx of richer people who could afford to restore and build according to the Historical Style Regulations.

Despite strict regulations for "H" Zone, gradual erosion of townscape has not been prevented.

Savannah

Georgia
Population: c. 118,000

Some recent building follows superficial details from historic vocabulary, but thought alien to Santa Fe due to scale and mass differences. Also, diversity of city's history slighted: many brick and stone buildings from late territorial and early statehood periods lost or transformed into adobe-like "Santa Fe style." Also, "many aspects of Santa Fe's unique townscape are not recognized. These include the acequias, historic trails, colonial street patterns, and block forms." (Quoted from grant application to National Endownment for the Arts.)

Under the Endowment grant, city planning department to make inventory of all historic structural elements typical of city. Will produce three-dimensional model to help guide decisions for all new construction and redevelopment.

Synopsis

Savannah's program one of oldest efforts in nation. Conservation neighborhood is entire original old city of Savannah—2½ square miles, largely built around 24 landscaped city squares. Historic district portion of old city has 1,100 buildings rated of notable quality. Most between 100 and 150 years old; earlier structures destroyed by fires in late 18th, early 19th century.

Area formerly blighted, most homes deteriorated. Today, 850 of the 1,100 units rehabilitated (all or part); now mostly middle-class, upper middle-class residences. Current costs $15,000 to $40,000 for a shell, $40,000 to over $100,000 (restoration). Low-income Victorian area south of old city recently added to historic district.

Initiation

Three city squares destroyed for a highway (1950s). In 1954, old city market torn down for parking. Davenport House (1820, listed in HABS) threatened. Seven women raised money privately, bought Davenport House, founded Historic Savannah Foundation, Inc. (HSF) in 1954. Had 800 members by 1975. HSF founded visitors' council in Chamber of Commerce to emphasize tourism. Aroused interest of city business and professional leaders. Other allies: mayor, urban renewal officals, Junior League, Visitors Council, Chamber of Commerce.

In 1966, City Housing Authority, using HUD grant, prepared Historic Preservation Plan for Central Area General Neighborhood Renewal Area, the 200-acre historic area of old city. Area contains 253 of the 1,100 important buildings. Plan set design criteria for renewal in historic area and safeguards for preserving old buildings.

Authority and commitment

HSF involved in buying and selling of historic real estate. In 1960s city attorney set two-week delay between application for demolition and its issuance; gave HSF little time to seek buyer for threatened dwelling. In 1966, the 2½-square-mile old city declared National Landmark.

Restoration largely privately financed from HSF's revolving fund. Some activity by City Housing Authority's Department of Urban Renewal: city loans made to individual building owners, Housing Authority upgrades utilities and public space in six squares. Banks finally willing to lend in Central Area after city showed commitment. But city did not enact a historic ordinance until restoration was already socially, economically, and politically established (1972).

Some builders, developers, architects resent restrictions on new construction.

Revolving fund activity and big push on restoration between 1959 and 1969. HSF raised $1,000,000 in cash in that period and $4,000,000 in loans from banks and interested individuals. Often syndicated buying of properties by its members and was able to save 850 houses, which involved $40 million of restoration construction and $18 million in real estate sales.

Management of program

In acquiring properties, HSF cooperates with banks and real estate agencies; pays full real estate commissions.

Some 150 houses acquired from or through HSF are protected by restrictive covenant: prior HSF approval required for all exterior renovations; no demolition for 75 years; restoration must start within 6 months of purchase and be finished 18 months after starting date. HSF is catalyst—restores architecturally, historically significant houses to attract individual homeowners to neighborhood and continue efforts. Also buys marginal properties next to restored dwellings; removes same to gain open space. Of 850 rehabilitated houses, 150 bought and resold (or held for resale) by HSF to buyer willing to restore. The other restored buildings institutionally financed.

Housing Authority's complementary program for historic renewal in 200-acre historic district has three parts: prevent loss of building continuity around squares and connecting streets; retain historic structures; remove incompatible structures and signs.

During important 1959–1969 period, HSF was willing to buy threatened properties. Chief control tool was restrictive covenant attached to any property sold by HSF revolving fund. In 1972 city adopted Historic District Zoning Ordinance.

Operating tools and tactics

Covers 200-acre historic district. One year later, seven-member Historic Review Board appointed by mayor and aldermen. Board must approve exterior changes of structures.

Under Historic Preservation Plan of 1973, Housing Authority has set and used criteria for renewal activities in 200-acre historic district. Criteria cover: height and proportions of buildings, front elevation, openings, space of buildings, materials, textures, colors, details, roof shapes, landscaping.

City has no authority to create special tax exemptions. Hence, homeowners who invested in restoration have had taxes increased, even though restorations benefit city via tourism, etc.

HUD Section 312 loans and Section 115 grants used in Central Renewal Area. City funds used to upgrade utilities, do major landscaping in six of city's squares.

Until recently city had no housing policy other than restoration. Now has added to historic section a Victorian area of moderate-and low-income blacks.

In 1950s when preservation movement started, no displacement, as buildings abandoned. Now problem for existing tenants in Victorian area. Desire to have residents remain to achieve racial mix important to Savannah.

HSF raises $1,000,000 in fund drives, over $700,000 for William Jay's Scarborough house (1819) to be new headquarters for HSF, and to spark west side revitalization. Savannah Landmark Rehabilitation Project (HUD-sponsored) attacking low-income housing problem.

1970 Save-The-Bay Committee formed to prevent high-rise construction on riverfront. Had 40-foot height limitation. Save-The-Bay won battle through Georgia Supreme Court.

Troy
New York
Population: c. 63,000

Population exodus cuts across all income groups. Many housing units lost through urban renewal, highway construction. Little relocation housing available. Low vacancy rate but many abandoned buildings—100 alone once owned by city; $3½ million potential in property values. Following marginally successful 2-year city program to sell buildings at public auction, city still owns about 60. Many only fit for demolition.

Character of city's troubled neighborhoods as described in A Housing Action Plan for Troy, (1975), typical of many other cities:

"Several neighborhoods in Troy are badly deteriorated. They have developed poor reputations with their residents, institutions, and the city as a whole. They ring the CBD, surrounding the entrances to it and most of the entrances to the city. Their poor condition contributes to a negative perception of the city on the part of some residents and visitors. . . .

"These neighborhoods contain a high percentage of substandard housing—from 20 to above 40 percent of the units contain housing code violations. Often all the mechanical systems, including the heating system, are inadequate. Few buildings are insulated. The incidence of fires is high. And the problem is not soluble on a building by building basis, because of the lack of private financing. The inability to borrow money to make home repairs or to obtain standard term mortgages to purchase housing has led to disinvestment and abandonment. This lack of financing results from the low value of the buildings (and contributes to its decline) and the high proportion of residents who don't meet standard banking credit criteria. The problem can only be approached on a neighborhood scale.

". . . While many residents would choose to live there because of family and social ties, few have any choice. Economics and the residual effects of racial discrimination have trapped them.

"While at present something of a liability, these areas should be viewed as a substantial resource. They contain a large recyclable housing stock; some of which has historic and architectural value. Most of the housing can be brought up to standards at much lower cost than clearance and new construction. There is an existing social fabric in these neighborhoods that takes years to develop in new developments, but is the heart of our city. A significant percentage of the city's population and work force resides in these neighborhoods. They are still our greatest asset."

Of several uncoordinated programs, most active is Troy Rehabilitation and Improvement, Inc. (TRIP).

City has several recognized (but not designated) historic districts—Washington Park (including planned development of 46 buildings around private park from 1840s). Historic district ordinance awaits city Council approval. No major objections anticipated.

Initiation/ commitment

Out of a group of volunteers who had rehabilitated abandoned houses in Troy for low- and moderate-income families grew TRIP (1968), a private, nonprofit, tax-exempt membership corporation.

TRIP began by buying city-owned abandoned buildings (for $1.00) in inner, deteriorated neighborhoods, rehabilitating them. Has since switched to cluster rehabilitation; easier to obtain financing and only way for sustained impact on neighborhood.

All mortgages from Troy banks. FHA guaranteed since 1971.

Management of program

TRIP's 21-member board represents tenants, homeowners, businessmen, bankers, govenment officials, and church people. Elected annually by members.

Rehabilitated buildings unsold and still owned by TRIP are leased to Troy's Housing Authority, which rents units to families under Section 23 public housing leasing. Waiting list.

To date, $314,000 in assessed valuation has been returned to tax rolls through TRIP effort, translated into $16,700 in current annual taxes.

Urgent TRIP project is 6th Avenue superblock: redeveloping four-block area with rehabilitated housing, new infill dwellings, playgrounds, shopping and social services. Area one of most blighted in city. Core of superblock has 30 houses, 400 people (after rehabilitation), and old abandoned school. With neighborhood people, TRIP prepared comprehensive plan: includes street closings, vest pocket parks, playgrounds, landscaping, demolition of unsalvageable structures for off-street parking. Also rehabilitation and conversion of old school into neighborhood center (opened 1975) via part of $300,000 HUD Neighborhood Facilities Grant.

Via $40,000 grant from State Office of Planning Services, TRIP and an architectural firm developed infill housing system for use in older sections, including 6th Avenue. Erection of demonstration infill pending. Resistance of banks to processing FHA applications subsides as rehabilitation is at significant scale; TRIP does packaging for FHA applications, reducing load on banks.

TRIP's activity on block encouraged owners of adjacent buildings to repair their houses. They use same contractors as TRIP; encourages reasonable prices, quality work. $210,050 of first-year CD block grant funds allocated to a Neighborhood Improvement Program for a 30-block area. This program will extend TRIP's experience into public realm.

Operating tools and tactics

Wilmington

Delaware
Population: c. 80,000

Wilmington one of first medium-sized cities with a majority black population. After high degree of outmigration, population is stabilizing as areas are upgraded and some younger families return to city.

City has two kinds of neighborhoods. First are close to city center; have not suffered major deterioration; stable population and newer housing. All improvement efforts privately financed by owners. Example is Delaware Avenue area. Racially mixed; blacks live in modest late 19th-century housing, younger families return to Avenue to restore its large Victorian homes and row houses. Little redlining. Area has many hospitals and nursing homes.

Second category of neighborhoods is more deteriorated, inner city, with high ratio of black, Puerto Rican, and poor white families. Suffered from redlining, abandonment, considered for urban renewal. Extensive upgrading. Example: Eastside (15 years ago city's worst slum) now stable, black working-class area; high proportion of homeownership. Even so, absentee landlordism, abandonment still plague area.

**Authority/
management of
program**

Tax exemption, urban homesteading are key city-sponsored, managed programs.

Five-member Homestead Board selects homesteaders, provides technical services. Properties selected reviewed by City Planning staff (for appropriateness of zoning and future land uses) and by Licenses and Inspections (survey of structural condition and rehabilitation feasibility). Individual Homestead Board members assigned homesteaders to whom they provide direct assistance throughout 3-year homestead period. Periodic inspections by Licenses and Inspections.

City officials set policy for tax, homesteading programs. Little citizen participation. Strong mayor; large Democratic majority in City Council. Both programs approved with little opposition.

In another program, business community founded Greater Wilmington Development Corporation (GWDC) in 1960 in part to trigger activities through spin-off groups. One such group is Community Housing, Inc. (CHI), involved in 4-year rehabilitation-homeownership program in sounder neighborhoods.

Tax exempting. Two types of partial tax exemption encourage investment. Another partial tax exemption program for the elderly furthers homeownership. Partial exemption mechanism for existing structures: 50% of the increased value, based on cost (labor and materials) of residential or commercial improvement, deducted from pre-improvement assessment for first five years after improvements. After five years, value of improvements incorporated into assessment and full taxes are paid on both existing and improvement value. Any owner can qualify. Partial exemption for new construction mechanism is different: upon completion, no taxes for first year of operation; second year, taxes are 10% of assessment; third year, 20%; full taxes begin in 11th year. Anyone and any type of structure eligible.

Homeowners' exemption limited to elderly, disabled homeowners earning less than $3,000 per year. First $7,500 of assessment exempt from taxes. If home assessed for more than $7,500, owner pays regular tax rate on excess.

Urban homesteading. City wanted to return some of 96 abandoned houses it owned to private hands. Some 750 buildings are vacant in city. Properties are advertised; families evaluated in terms of overall suitability (financial resources, size) for a particular parcel.

Properties are awarded by lottery if there is more than one applicant. Homesteaders given conditional deed: repairs to be completed in 18 months, family to stay for three years. But in early stages (1973), due to conditional title, families couldn't obtain financing, had to get personal loans at 18% interest. Now city and Sa-

**Operating tools
and tactics**

Wilmington

North Carolina
Population: c. 46,000

chem Fund partially guarantee mortgages from local eight-bank consortium, and city gives lender a first lien on property. Financing is at 9% for 10 to 15 years. Partial tax exemptions used; past taxes forgiven.

Of 23 homesteading properties offered and awarded, six repaired through personal resources, other used bank consortium. Statistics: 17 black, five white, one Spanish homesteaders.

Properties scattered, little overall impact on conservation. Upgrading costs $7,000–$10,000.

Synopsis

Within a 200-block downtown section (which is on National Register), a 35-block neighborhood designated by city and state as historic district. Area bordered on north by CBD, on west by Cape Fear River. These two amenities added to its growing popularity as residential area.

About 3,600 people live in 35 blocks. Many houses date to late 18th and early 19th centuries. 65% of houses single family; others divided into apartments or rooming houses. Structures vary from sound to decayed. 90% of residents are white. District is socioeconomically diverse: many young couples, elderly, middle to high-income persons restoring homes.

Initiative

Between 1954 and 1974 over 200 buildings in 200-block section demolished through urban renewal, active city code enforcement. (Many demolitions were of homes abandoned by elderly who could not afford to bring them up to code standard.) In early 1960s city community leaders realized city's older, inner areas were becoming less livable, that property values were falling. Key individuals (architects, civic leaders, elected officials) noted restoration in Savannah, Georgia, and Charleston, South Carolina. Decided on similar remedies.

A 1962 city ordinance established a Board of Architectural Review (name later changed, by state legislation, to Historic District Commission, HDC). In 1966, private Historic Wilmington Foundation (HWF) was started on volunteer basis. These two groups spawned a third—Residents of Old Wilmington, a neighborhood association of historic district residents.

Authority and commitment

HDC appointed by City Council; operates as adjunct to City Planning Department. Nine persons serve four-year terms. Majority of board must have strong interest in history, architecture, planning real estate.

HDC has strong architectural review powers, works with the other two groups, business, and

Management of program

real estate firms to retain neighborhood character, attract new homeowners. Banks are cooperating.

HWF has bought, rehabilitated, resold 11 houses. Due to limited funds, HWF also encourages individuals to purchase directly and restore homes in district. Another 50 buildings thus sold to potential restorers. HWF counsels new owners on costs, mortgage sources, suggests contractors, appropriate restoration styles, details, colors.

HDC approves any exterior changes in 35-block district. May delay demolition for 90 days to allow for negotiation. Close ties with HWF, which may buy building for resale to potential restorer.

When HWF sells building, puts restrictions in deed: building may not be torn down for 90 years, HWF has first refusal to buy back. It must approve exterior changes, as well as Historic District Commission.

Some homeowners object to HDC's certificate of appropriateness concerning exterior changes, appealed to City Council, but to no avail. No court test as yet.

Real estate taxes assessed by county. In early stages, assessments on restored properties, based on value of house in a restored neighborhood, often led to more than twofold increase. Under pressure from HWF, county now raises assessments only by actual value of improvements. City Task Force examining a program of tax relief for historic preservation.

HWF has revolving fund of $70,000 obtained from several banks. Uses same to buy homes for resale. Buyers must get own loans, but HWF assists in obtaining second mortgage. Several Foundation members on boards of local banks and savings and loan associations encourage loans to individuals.

Financial institutions now decide case by case, rather than on condition of neighborhood.

Before restoration, city cleared buildings that did not comply with code. Now, will delay until buyer buys, rehabilitates dwelling. Restoration started with abandoned buildings, hence little displacement. Displacement expected to rise as abandoned buildings are used up, so HWF exploring use of CD block grant funds.

Expansion of 35-block area to entire 200-block district sought.

Chapter VI

Three Cities under the Microscope

Cincinnati
Seattle
New York

Cincinnati

Ohio
Population: c. 453,000

**Cincinnati:
Power to the
neighborhoods**

"Forty-Four Neighborhoods, One Great City." That is the rallying theme of Cincinnati's controlling Democratic-Charter Committee coalition. It is apt, for Cincinnati is a city with remarkably strong neighborhoods, a characteristic attributed to several sources.

Foremost are the city's uncommon topography and social history. The city's original settlers came to a small basin along the Ohio riverfront surrounded by sloping hills and plateaus. Later, as technology and affluence enabled some to escape above the basin's industrial pollution, the plateaus provided the sites of "suburban" settlements, while deep ravines between the plateaus separated communities. To Cincinnati came waves of immigrants of different ethnic stock and races: pioneers, railroad barons, laborers, industrial magnates, and farmers. Some used the city as a way station; many came to stay—in settlements defined by character, place, and name. Never a melting pot, Cincinnati's history is scarred by battles between the already settled "ins" and the newer "outs."

Today, through neighborhood organization and planning, Cincinnatians are looking for good ways for people of different racial, ethnic, and economic backgrounds to extend control over their ways of life and to mediate their differences.

The focus on neighborhoods also happens to respond to Cincinnati's form of government. One of the nation's largest cities to have a city-manager, Cincinnati also has a citywide elected city council that selects one of its members as mayor. Thus "neighborhood power" is a countervailing force to the lack of ward-elected councilmen and a reaction to the feeling of many Cincinnatians that, until the last city manager, their interests were neglected by a downtown-oriented administration.

The neighborhood emphasis has given communities a chance to think about their goals and priorities and how these relate to budget levels. Out of this exercise, perhaps more formalized in Cin-

cinnati than elsewhere, has come a clearer idea of what people value in their neighborhoods, what they see as threats, what they want and need from each other and government.

The stress on conservation jibes with the city's noted conservatism—it still proudly remembers its solvency during the Depression days. Now that new steps inherent in any conservation strategy are in sight, Cincinnati is moving slowly. An influential constituency is calling for stronger commitment and more innovative tools to protect the city's unique natural environment—the hillsides, especially—and its lovely structures of the past. Downtown interests, however, argue that conservation would further dull construction activity in the central business district. They are also critical that too much city money is going out to the neighborhoods instead of into downtown development.

This paper discusses conservation in general in Cincinnati, but focuses too on several neighborhoods where specialness-of-place and architectural character have served, with varying success, as levers for neighborhood upgrading. These are profiled later in this paper.

Synopsis

Population 27% black, 73% white. Median income, somewhat below national average, ranges widely among neighborhoods. Each has different perceived and real problems, varying degrees of economic, social, community health. Throughout, there is rising concern with condition of existing housing stock, with complex system of local values, priorities, leadership, and with citywide policies and resources.

Among the 44 neighborhoods are Westwood (retains homogeneous character of affluent white Catholic residents of German descent); Clifton (nine landmarks, baronial residences of 19th-century industrial magnates, as well as apartments, split levels, and large open tracts of private estates and no longer viable religious institutions); Madisonville, North Avondale, and Bond Hill ("transitional" neighborhoods, with rapid racial turnover, seeking to deal with cycle of blight and abandonment before it gets worse); Mount Adams (multifamily working-class dwellings over 70 years old); and three old communities, Mt. Auburn, West End, and Over-the-Rhine (reached bottom, have tried to stabilize and turn around).

How movement began

Preservation is only lately emerging as more than the concern of an elite minority. This broadening of constituency stems from a fusion of interest among those who care about "historic preservation" and those trying to save neighborhoods.

The first citywide preservation group, protection ordinance, and historic districts were created in mid-60s, as a result of urban renewal and highway construction in the West End, the city's oldest residential area. The districts—the elegant 19th-century Dayton Street homes of former millionaires and the Lytle Park District—were saved by the nonprofit Miami Purchase Association, formed by a group of three prominent and wealthy ladies concerned over razing of the city's past. These two are still the only districts "listed" by the city.

A tougher landmarks ordinance was passed by the city in 1973 after a major national corporation leveled the Wesley Chapel on a cold Friday night to clear the site for a new corporate headquarters. Demolition of listed buildings, which are designated by the city planning commission, can be delayed up to six months. Protection can be extended to interiors. Although the language of the ordinance is broad, designation has been limited. The city, though civic-minded, has thought of landmarks in traditional terms—of a music hall or a Taft House—rather than of their broader potential for neighborhood rebirth. The Union Terminal, which is less than 50 years old, was saved amid considerable controversy.

The most recent clash between those who believe in a narrower role for preservation and those who seek to preserve more of the city's old character took place in Fountain Square, at the heart of Cincinnati's CBD. At issue is the south side of the square, a block of neglected old buildings including the 47-year-old Albee theater (on the National Register), and the recently closed Sheraton-Gibson Hotel. A developer's proposal to replace the block with a high-rise was withdrawn after public conflict, but an attempt in 1974 to protect the old buildings via the listed properties ordinance did not win city planning commission support.

Awareness is rising through the work of people in groups such as the League of Women Voters, the American Institute of Architects, the American Bar Association, the University of Cincinnati, the Cincinnati Institute, the Miami Purchase Association and Environmental Preservation, as well as individuals working at the neighborhood level.

Triggers

Urban renewal and highway construction were, until very recently, embraced by most Cincinnati residents. The effort produced some of the nation's handsomest and most successful results in revitalizing downtown. It also indiscriminately levelled, as one "pile of junk," much of the city's earliest housing, destroyed what semblance of community existed in the West End, and relocated low-income black residents in adjacent communities with little thought as to the mutual impact. Many whites fled.

As neighborhoods tried to cope with change, they organized. Some say the middle class learned from the poor, others that the affluent were the first to band together to cope with racial change. While there were many bitter exchanges, these were people who were committed to staying in the city. For some the reasons were economic. You could get more house for less in the city. Taxes are much lower. For some, bound by discrimination or the rigors of age, there was no choice. For others, it was taste and aesthetics, nurtured by the interesting array of old housing in the city. The business interests did not abandon downtown, and its vitality and cultural attractions remain an important magnet. The winding river, its flat floodprone shores surrounded by green hillsides, provides a distinctly European charm, sharply visible from the surrounding neighborhoods atop the hills. The broad avenues and handsome old buildings and trees lend a country air to neighborhoods minutes away from downtown.

Many Cincinnatians may not yet have found stability, but their efforts seem to be strengthening the city as a place to live. Population turnover continues high (36%), but in 1974, for the first time in 13 years, Cincinnati had a net gain. Newspaper articles report a noticeable gain in middle-class children in neighborhoods that have undergone renewal.

Resources and leadership
The city has a wide array of "movers and shakers"—an establishment of civic and often arts-oriented people of wealth and influence whose leadership has tended to reflect a conservative "company town" orientation. The big corporations—Procter and Gamble, Monsanto, Kroger, Federated Department Stores—have always wielded considerable power.

But these resources, though large, have not generally been directed to conservation and environmental issues. The clergy has been influential both citywide and in such neighborhoods as Over-the-Rhine and College Hill, where the Episcopalian community is working with commercial interests to preserve neighborhood businesses.

Management of program

The city's only two historic districts are small, status-quo oriented areas in which no building, demolition or exterior modification can take place without a permit from a seven-member architectural board of review. The two districts are islands in a sea of urban decay.

In Cincinnati, conservation of physical structures is taking place as part of the neighborhood strategy. Citizens and officials have evolved ways to channel neighborhood goals and priorities into the city's decision making.

Rehabilitation programs in the three neighborhoods profiled below vary sharply. Mt. Adams is a private effort, with no special government help. The other two neighborhoods have a more complex history of public/private involvement. Both Mt. Auburn and Over-the-Rhine are Model Cities neighborhoods, and the community organizations have spun off neighborhood development corporations.

Mt. Adams

The neighborhoods

Mt. Adams was the first Cincinnati neighborhood to demonstrate what could be done with the older, blighted housing stock on the hills of Cincinnati's in-city "suburbs." What Mt. Adams is, and is not, has strongly influenced the rest of the city.

Sited on Cincinnati's steepest hill, with winding streets and trees opening up to magnificent views of river and downtown, Mt. Adams in the main has multifamily, working-class frame homes over 70 years old.

One-fifth are single family. The neighborhood with its pottery works and taverns has always had a citywide bohemian appeal. Until the early 1960s, it was a stable neighborhood of low-income, white Cincinnatians of Dutch, Irish, and Italian stock. Blight and slum conditions mounted, however, as Appalachian whites new to Cincinnati, and blacks from adjacent urban renewal projects, moved in. Absentee ownership rose.

Private developers who began renewal in the 1960s identified its "new town" amenities. Important cultural and recreation assets include: wooded 185-acre Eden Park, Art Museum, Natural History Museum, Playhouse in the Park, planetarium, remains of an old incline that pulled city residents up from downtown.

Mt. Adams is an urban island, reinforced by physical separation due to surrounding ravines and new highways that lead in minutes to downtown shopping, jobs, city life.

Key data are shown in table below.

(Sources for this, Mt. Auburn, and Over-the-Rhine neighborhoods: Housing Development Office and Dept. of Buildings and Inspection, City of Cincinnati, 1974; Federal Housing Administration, HUD; Cincinnati Metropolitan Housing Authority.)

Mt. Auburn

Until World War II, Mt. Auburn was one of the most influential and affluent "suburban" enclaves in the city. Like Mt. Adams, it is sited high on hills, with striking city views, winding streets, country atmosphere, and easy access to downtown. Auburn Avenue was bordered by large mansions built in mid-1850s by Taft and other city leaders.

Housing is largely single or multifamily detached, semidetached, and row houses. Diverse neighborhood institutions and businesses include Baptist churches, TV station, county juvenile detention center, large hospitals, insurance companies, social service institutions, and professional offices. OEO and model cities funds were catalysts for extensive neighborhood organization, such as the Memorial Community Center, Mt. Auburn Community Council, Mount Auburn Good Housing Corporation, and block clubs.

In the late 1950s and 1960s, changes led to a cycle of blight, abandonment, and social disintegration. Physicians tore down some of the fine big houses and replaced them with nondescript professional buildings. Many low-income blacks, dislocated by urban renewal in the city's West End, were relocated here. Tensions arose among old and new residents; whites fled, often holding buildings for speculation or income. Mt. Auburn, largely white until 1967, changed to predominantly black by 1970.

Key data are shown in table at right.

Over-the-Rhine

Over-the Rhine is a basin community adjacent

Mt. Adams (222 acres)			
	1950	**1960**	**1970**
Population	7,437	6,535	3,491
Race			
White	87%	84%	95%
Black	13%	16%	5%
Median Income		$4,152	$9,740
Citywide		($4,603)	($8,894)
Median Price of Housing		$8,150	$15,150
Citywide		($15,000)	($18,800)
Number of Dwelling Units	2,242	1,930	1,622
% Ownership	25%	24%	18%
% Rental	73%	68%	67%
% Vacancy	2%	8%	14%

(Calculated from averages of census tract data within neighborhoods.)

to the city's CBD. As its name implies, Over-the-Rhine was once a solidly German, working-class neighborhood, with a section of canal (now covered over), and many German "kirches" that reminded residents of the homeland. Over-the-Rhine has been torn apart by many forces: in a trek that often led to welfare, unskilled Appalachian whites came seeking jobs in the early 1950s; blacks, dislocated by urban renewal and highway building, moved here.

Over-the-Rhine is now a series of fragmented subneighborhoods, each with its own cast; business people who don't live here, social service personnel, clergy, low-income blacks, Appalachians, elderly Germans. There are many street gangs, and crime and welfare rates are high.

Physically, the most distinctive building stock is around Findlay Market, the last open-air market in the city: "A 19th century urban residential neighborhood composed of related and unrelated row, semi-detached row, and single-detached dwellings . . . By and large the area is homogeneous in building uses, types, styles, forms and materials" is how a 1972 study aimed at creating an historic urban district, defines it.

(Only the Market and facing streets were listed on the National Register.) Mixed residential, commercial, industrial uses permeate the neighborhood. The three-, four-, and five-story 80-year-old houses have stores at the street level, but a high vacancy rate. There are many small units, but few large ones to accommodate the poor families relocated here. Important citywide uses include, in addition to the open-air market, the Music Hall and Washington Park. Also there are many social service institutions spurred by Model Cities and OEO funding programs.

Key data are shown on following page.

Mt. Adams
Overall, the aim at Mt. Adams has been selective upgrading, which developers say sells better in Cincinnati than restoration. About 50 to 75% of the houses have been worked on—some only on the outside, or inside, others totally redone. On all streets, there is a new caring attitude. Risk capital has been followed by broader investments. Banks are more willing to finance renovation, and individuals are renovating for their own use.

Mt. Auburn (391 acres)

	1950	1960	1970
Population	13,853	13,823	11,213
Race			
White	97%	90%	25%
Black	3%	10%	75%
Median Income	$2,507	$3,872 ($4,603 citywide)	$5,628 ($8,894 citywide)
Median Price of Housing		$10,667 ($15,000 citywide)	$11,342 ($18,800 citywide)
Number of Dwelling Units	4,893	4,901	4,343
% Ownership	26%	23%	20%
% Rental	71%	68%	64%
% Vacancy	3%	9%	16%

(Calculated from averages of census tract data within neighborhoods.)

The Appalachians and black low-income tene- ment dwellers have largely been displaced, some by an expressway, many because their tene- ments were purchased by developers from "slumlords" who were not investing in the prop- erty. About half Mt. Adams' residents are "old stock," 40% singles, young couples, or people re- turning from the suburbs after their children have left, and 10% low-income blacks and whites.

Renovated houses now sell for $25,000 to over $50,000, depending on view, size, quality, and extent of rehabilitation. These are mostly owned by developers or speculators, and are rented, two or three units per dwelling, at about $200 for one bedroom, $250 to $300 for two bedrooms.

Two major new buildings have been built, a con- troversial high-rise and condominium. Property values have quadrupled since 1960. For years, appraisers did not reassess properties, but are now required by state law to do so regularly. Yet city taxes are not a barrier to rehabilitation, as higher rentals and property values outpace higher taxes.

While Cincinnatians in other neighborhoods have tried to emulate Mt. Adams' approach to change, they see it as a one-of-a-kind neighbor- hood.

Mt. Auburn
Mt. Auburn has tried to attain a racially and economically integrated community of families and homeowners. Means include reduced den- sity, recreation areas, large units for families, parking. Says Carl Westmoreland, former head of Mt. Auburn Community Council:

"The neighborhood's historic past has had vary- ing degrees of significance. We didn't originally make it a great big issue in the community be- cause it . . . has traditionally been something the white upper class has been involved in, and our idea was to provide good sound housing. The way we brought the historical thing in was in marketing . . . We would say, the finest people in Cincinnati have lived here.

"Once we began to make physical change, we knew that middle income and upper income people were going to come back on their own, and they would have their own values and own

Over-the-Rhine (442 acres)			
	1950	**1960**	**1970**
Population	34,237	30,275	16,363
Race			
White	97%	87%	58%
Black	3%	13%	42%
Median Income	$2,068	$2,941 ($4,603 citywide)	$4,893 ($8,894 citywide)
Median Price of Housing			$8,352 ($18,800 citywide)
Number of Dwelling Units	12,772	11,721	8,875
% Ownership	7%	5%	4%
% Rental	89%	85%	75%
% Vacancy	4%	10%	21%

(Calculated from averages of census tract data within neighborhoods.)

sense of history. But ordinarily poor white and poor black people couldn't care less about the historical significance of something. They're more inclined . . . to be attracted to new things."

The objective of Mt. Auburn's Good Housing Corporation (GHC) was to buy up houses and rehabilitate them. With $7,000 seed money from a wealthy ex-Cincinnatian and other local grants, GHC began to take options on key pieces of property. Aided by savings and loans institutions, GHC obtained housing for next to nothing—including a 125-year-old mansion it rehabilitated for $180,000 (contributed by corporations and individuals) as a headquarters and neighborhood services center. GHC has created 104 subsidized rental living units (including units for larger families), and owns 60 to 70 key parcels of vacant land and two renovated office buildings.

Although much of Mt. Auburn remains blighted, key view streets have undergone substantial change. Property values have risen and houses until recently virtually given away are selling for $5,000 to $15,000. Doctors, young couples, architects, students are investing sizable amounts in rehabilitation. There has been no turnover in fixed-up houses. Financing, for purchase or rehabilitation, is still hard to come by. In the past only blockbuster realtors operated; now, some are committed to the area's revival.

The blacks, both low income and middle class, are not much a part of this effort. The poor did not want the houses when they were being given away; if they attain middle-class incomes they move to the suburbs. "They have bought the *Life* magazine version of success," says Westmoreland. "When I see middle class blacks stay here, I will know the neighborhood has made it."

Mt. Auburn has a high crime rate, and the community criticizes the police for the wrong kind of protection: actions against loitering and parking violations, but not enough vigilance against drug pushers. The community has instituted a TELL program to rid Mt. Auburn of professional pushers by informing the police. The community has also fought rezonings for bars and additional professional offices on Auburn Avenue. Its request to have Auburn Avenue declared a historic district is currently before the city planning commission.

Over-the-Rhine
Over-the-Rhine was the first neighborhood target of the city's urban development department, because the health department wanted to tear down the deteriorated, vermin-ridden market. Instead, planners restored it, and combined old and new buildings in a "town center" for recreation and social services. Both efforts were viewed as public investments to give local residents a "new perspective on the value of their present physical environment." One-third of the $1 million market restoration fund came from the federal Neighborhood Development Program; two-thirds from city funds. The town center was two-thirds federal (mostly from a pre-Model Cities pilot program) and one-third city capital improvements money.

But these levers do not seem strong enough to turn around a neighborhood so fragmented and despairing. The residents distrust the citywide institutions in the area: money to restore Findlay Market, for example (which is owned and operated by nonresident merchants who take the profits out of the community), was not seen as something for them. The town center had more participation by residents. The architects set up their offices in town and responded to the community's preference for new buildings by tearing down more of the old than they intended.

City officials blame the 1973 federal housing subsidy moratorium for the break in momentum in Over-the-Rhine. (Example: in 1971, $3.9 million of housing repair permits were issued; in 1974, $471,000.)

Response in other communities
Conservation is happening throughout. In some neighborhoods the emphasis is on self-protec-

tion—maintaining an existing quality of life that is often characterized as elitist. In Clifton, large, open space acreage surrounding no longer viable estates is watched carefully, and developer requests for apartment rezonings are fought.

The efforts of Clifton's civic group cover a broad field—it fought the widening of a highway, attracted city support for a park on the grounds of an obsolete Roman Catholic country school, and developed walking tours of its lovely streets. In Westwood, the Victorian Town Hall and nearby buildings have been put into an historic district, and extensive renovation is underway.

These efforts, still suspect, now have their counterparts in those city communities that seek successful integrated lifestyles, such as those described earlier in this study.

Response of financial institutions
Cincinnati banks have been widely accused of disinvesting in urban neighborhoods and contributing to the cycle of decline and abandonment. As banks withdraw from conventional loans in a neighborhood, would-be buyers are discouraged, and the proportion of FHA-insured loans increases. Poor home maintenance, default, and abandonment often follow.

According to a local study of banking policies between 1960 and 1974, banking reluctance to lend in urban neighborhoods varies according to racial composition. The study, funded by United Appeal and religious groups, concludes that in neighborhoods of people similar in income and personal criteria, and housing of comparable physical condition, Cincinnati banks are first likely to lend to whites in white neighborhoods, second to blacks in black neighborhoods. They are *least* likely to lend in "transitional" communities.

A resident who bought into one such neighborhood describes the "invisible war": "When I came to Bond Hill, I had no idea that real estate people were steering whites away from my neighborhood, that banks were declining loans, that only FHA loans were being granted, that welfare agencies were steering clients to my street. I only saw the end result, the abandoned house."

The first national class action suit against redlining practices has been filed by a resident of North Avondale in Cincinnati.

Some members of the city's financial community are attacking these problems. One of these is the president of Cincinnati's Home Federal Savings and Loan Association, who took over the assets of a bankrupt bank with defaulted mortgages of 400 abandoned homes and 2,000 dwelling units. He set up a subsidiary to rehabilitate the houses for either sales or rental. For renovation loans, he insists on owner-occupancy. He suggests that: (1) mortgagees should have more control over rehabilitation programs; (2) contractors should be subject to rigorous audits; and (3) rehabilitated homes should carry a strong warranty from the industry to the buyers.

Response of schools
One of the hardest questions to resolve in neighborhood conservation strategy is that of schools. Cincinnati neighborhoods have been torn apart by conflicting demands on the schools, with proponents of both integration and "neighborhood schools" dissatisfied. White families continue to move out, followed increasingly by blacks who can afford it. Busing in the city has been resisted, districts gerrymandered, and even the placement of black teachers and administrators throughout the system challenged. Many schools have far higher percentages of blacks than the neighborhoods because of high white parochial school enrollment and a higher black birthrate.

Under a liberal school board president and a conservative school board, "magnet" schools are being established in key neighborhoods. Along with citywide open enrollment, this is seen as a road to integration on the basis of shared skills and education needs. However, citizens turned down a bond issue, and funds are scarce.

Operating tools and tactics

State constitution

At least two state constitutional provisions apply: one gives strong home rule to municipalities; the other provides that "the credit of the state shall not in any manner be given or loaned to any individual, or in aid of, any individual, association or corporation whatever."

The first raises questions about the extent to which municipalities can delegate power to implement community protection or development guidelines (see discussion under environmental quality zoning, below).

The second relates the the use of CD block grants for rehabilitation loans to individuals and neighborhood corporations. Some say these federal funds must be considered state funds, subject to state constitutional limitations. Others argue that the public purpose of rehabilitation should override any restriction. The law is in a state of flux and precedents are not clear. Meanwhile, Cincinnati plans to set aside two revolving rehabilitation funds from its CD block grant: $1.2 million for nonprofit neighborhood corporations, and $1.4 million for individuals.

Land use and development controls

At the municipal level, a 1948 municipal plan is still officially the basic citywide planning document. The aim is to replace it with individual neighborhood plans.

Many of the neighborhoods have seized upon zoning as a tool to control change, and in recent years the approval of strongly organized neighborhoods is considered essential before the city planning commission will approve variances.

In 1974, the city council adopted a single-family, planned unit development regulation. This form of zoning, sometimes known as "overlay zoning," permits the construction of clusters of detached or attached single-family homes at overall densities no greater than the "underlayed" district. This is important in a neighborhood like Clifton, with its tracts of open estate land. Clifton's town meeting overwhelmingly opposed a developer who would have clustered development, but at a higher density than permitted by existing zoning.

The protection of Cincinnati's hillsides are a growing concern. Much acreage remains green, but technological "improvements" have created new physical and visual problems. Highway construction around Mt. Adams, the new headquarters of the Women's Club in Clifton, and demolition in Mt. Auburn are but a few of the new sources of slides and erosion. The Cincinnati Institute has engaged geologists to map a unique topography of the hillsides for use as a guide to permissible activities. While longer range controls are considered, a cut-and-fill ordinance was passed in 1974 requiring a permit for excavations and landfills involving 100 or more cubic yards of earth.

Environmental quality zoning

In recent years, citizens have explored the concept of environmental quality zoning to supplement two-dimensional zoning. The Cincinnati Institute, assisted by the National Endowment for the Arts, has underwritten a study of constitutional approaches to such protection. As differing pressures arose in the city, the concept evolved into a citywide system of protective zones established for a variety of public purposes: protecting hillsides, historic buildings, open space, areas of high public investment, the riverfront.

Developers in a protection zone would request a permit from the city council showing consistency with a series of guidelines and criteria—a kind of impact statement. Some fear this will lead to more delay due to bureaucratic fear of possible court challenge, but the Institute's consultant believes it meets essential constitutional requirements.

Interim control guidelines, due to expire in late 1975, have been passed for Fountain Square and the surrounding central business district. Two are pending for Findlay Market District and East Price Hill neighborhood. The guidelines range broadly over design controls, physical relation of building materials and color, sign controls, and land and building uses. They have been used also to protect sensitive areas from construction that is not approved by the neighborhood or city council. Demolition is not covered.

The system envisioned for the permanent environment quality zones is quite different from that in historic districts. The latter is viewed as status quo oriented, whereas quality zoning is a flexible way to guide change. But in some key ways the historic districts are more protective. There is also the question of enforcement: an injunction by the architectural review board would have to be issued through the city attorney (something that has never been done before), whereas the zoning regulation process is more routine.

Taxes
State enabling legislation permits abatements for new downtown development and renovation, but the city has not acted on this. The city has low taxes compared to the suburbs, and this may be a prime attraction for residents. (A house in Westwood neighborhood with a market value of $30,000 would pay taxes of $504; a comparable house in the suburb of Delhi would cost $45,000 and be taxed at $913.) Reassessment after rehabilitation is not a burden in most neighborhoods, reflecting the assessors' attitude that the houses are old and that the neighborhood's upswing or stability is not assured. Mt. Adams' reappraisal took place five to seven years after values started climbing. In Mt. Auburn, there have been no reassessments. However, a 1973 state law requires annual reassessment, and the assessor is sent a copy of each building permit to help him arrive at the new assessment.

There are no tax abatements for listed properties.

Building codes and enforcement
Cincinnati has its own code, which must be at least as strong as state requirements. The issue of enforcement is complex. Code enforcement can accelerate decline in neighborhoods with high absentee ownership, high social pathology, or where loan programs are not available.

Many neighborhoods have criticized the building department for lax enforcement. "But the only thing that fixes up houses is money," a city official has said. Federal assistance for code enforcement was used in six neighborhoods. When federal money ran out, the city picked up some inspection costs, and in Over-the-Rhine these were coordinated with loans by several savings and loan associations. But funds were scarce, causing rancor in allotment.

Abandonment
The last stage in disinvestment is the abandoned building. There are about 1,400 of these. Nearby residents often call on the city to demolish them as hazards. The city is spending much on demolition ($400,000 in 1974 for about 250 houses, and the same in 1975). Demolition is increasingly controversial in the neighborhoods; residents say many good buildings are being lost. The vacant lot is a magnet for litter and gang activity, and many feel is not likely to be built on again.

As demolition continues, emphasis mounts on stopping the downward spiral in a community before the end result of failure—the abandoned house—becomes widespread. The Madisonville experiment by the Urban Reinvestment Task Force is part of a nationwide experiment in this approach (see below; see also *Pittsburgh* case study, Chapter V).

Federal assistance
Cincinnati has worked with a full range of federal categorical programs. Changing rules have stymied many local officials. Cincinnati was designated a Project Rehab City and has participated heavily in FHA-insured rehabilitation

programs, primarily 221(d)3, 235 home ownership, and 236 rental housing.

In all, 6,000 units were rehabilitated. The publicly funded rehabilitation programs ended under a cloud of public and private mismanagement. Over half the mortgages are in default. Over-the-Rhine, where most of the 221(d)3 funding was, reported widespread bonanzas by developer speculators, aided by inadequate FHA standards and supervision.

Many units were not designated to accommodate the lifestyles of people who would live there. Units were too small for families; cheap materials failed to withstand normal wear; workmanship was shoddy; sandblasting ruined the soft Cincinnati sandstone. Lesson: "We learned that if we want quality housing related to our needs, we have to participate more directly in planning and carrying through programs," according to the city manager's aide.

The Urban Reinvestment Task Force
The Madisonville neighborhood is taking part in the nationwide Urban Reinvestment Task Force pilot program. A neighborhood corporation has been set up in Madisonville, an area which is buffeted by rapid racial change, economic decline in its commercial section, blight, and some abandonment. Mostly single-family homes, there is 68% home ownership.

Under this program, every house will be inspected. Through cooperation of local financial institutions, conventional loans are assured; a contribution by the Edna McDonnell Clark Foundation of New York will extend high-risk loans through a grant of $100,000, matched locally by banks, local businesses, clergy, and foundations. Interest ranges from 0 to 6%. A community board will review and screen loan applicants and manage repayments. Twenty-nine savings and loan institutions are contributing operating funds for the neighborhood corporation.

The housing information system and other mechanisms
1. A housing information system set up in 1974 aims to provide computerized census tract data that will in turn help to quantify and evaluate statistics about housing and demographic changes in the neighborhoods. The system brings together data gathered by R.L. Polk & Company (an organization specializing in survey techniques to plot changes in shifts in population and housing), city planning commission data, crime reports, welfare data, housing permits, and other sources. Initial cost: $400,000 (city funds).

2. Neighborhood improvement services: with $1.2 million each in 1974 and 1975 (supplemented by $300,000 in block grant funds), this coordinated city program of street improvements, dead tree removal, sign review, etc., aims at high-impact, short-term visibility in neighborhoods with good, but deteriorating residential housing stock.

3. In 1974, the City Council adopted a comprehensive housing policy for neighborhoods. Types of neighborhoods are defined and standards set for review of neighborhood plans.

A look ahead

Cincinnati's neighborhood planning and budgeting effort is innovative and offers a sound lever for neighborhood conservation. But as neighborhood plans are readied, complex questions arise: Who represents the neighborhood? How will plans be coordinated and carried out? What happens to citywide social and economic goals—open housing, integration, downtown, and riverfront development? Are the affluent being given a legal vehicle to "turn inward"? Will poor neighborhoods get a fair shake?

Do 44 neighborhoods indeed make one great city? Advocates of neighborhood planning argue that destructive razing has been slowed, and many neighborhoods, with dispatch and little rancor, came up with sensible plans and priorities in the new community block grant process.

To forestall a feeling of illusion, the role of city leadership needs to be clarified. Through the block grant process, the city is on line to test its ability to manage difficult programs. Officials, who previously could complain about federal regulations and changing rules, now must test new relationships between city hall and the neighborhoods.

These relationships must be built around programs and resources, or infighting will result. Cincinnati's federal allotment of $18.9 million in CD block grants (about the same as in the past) is due to fall to $10 million in a few years. Perhaps it will find more resources within its boundaries. A citywide bond issue could raise funds for neighborhood plans. The activities of Cincinnati's financial institutions, linked with the city's development patterns in the past, could be reoriented.

Private capital is desperately needed to make bold new investments downtown, especially on the riverfront. Perhaps the state will find new ways to help the city (it appropriated $1.5 million for the riverfront when federal funds ran out).

Like many other cities, Cincinnati has so many immediate problems that long-range planning may fall by the wayside.

Seattle

Washington
Population: c. 531,000

**Seattle:
City hall
makes
a commitment**

It is less than a decade since some people in Seattle began to rethink the nature of urban blight. These early challenges to prevailing views were at first largely centered around the city's historic heart, Pioneer Square, a once lusty, vital section that became a bleak turf for winos, flophouses, and cheap stores. Earmarked by city business interests for parking lots, Pioneer Square took on new life through the vision of several architects bewitched by the arches, turrets, bays, and low scale of its Romanesque and Gothic Revival buildings; through a publisher's wife lured by stories of old miners and bordellos; and through merchants inspired by the magnetism of San Francisco's Ghirardelli Square.

In a city so shaken by economic despair that way-out solutions were not ruled out, ideas about preserving, adapting and reusing buildings, and even fostering less-than-respectable lifestyles, took political and institutional roots. They did so with the support of a newly elected nonestablishment mayor, some freewheeling emigrés from eastern cities, and an arts-oriented civic group of young Seattle citizens known as Allied Arts of Seattle.

Today, amidst professional, political, and popular acclaim, the ideas and tools used in the Pioneer Square effort have radiated to other sections of the city. The needs differ there, but the people are increasingly concerned with regulating the pattern of change to protect existing buildings, uses, and lifestyles as new needs arise. This different emphasis has led Seattle both into traditional landmark preservation (thought of as irrelevant in the past in a city founded in 1852), and out into neighborhoods where citizens are looking anew at their old homes and views.

Yet urban conservation in Seattle, embraced at high levels of government as well as at grass roots, continues to face serious tests, many inspired ironically by its very success. The business community, now an ally of Pioneer Square's economic revival, is nervous about the wide-ranging sweep of its example. Always, preserva-

tion is easier to endorse on someone else's turf. The mayor, who faced a recall threat in mid-1975, was less outspoken on contentious issues. Conservationists are hopeful that his leadership will now be strengthened as a result of his two-to-one victory over his opponents.

The new federal allocation system for community development block grants also has created a new wrinkle. Although they welcome the new flexibility in allocating funds, Seattle officials, who operated the categorical grants game superbly, now face sharply reduced funding despite heightened demands and higher costs.

Officials are also concerned that in the fray of citizen participation it may now be harder to sustain the essence of Seattle's approach—long-term public commitment in priority areas as a magnet for private support.

**Pioneer
Square**

Of Seattle's two historic districts, Pioneer Square is the more conventional and, in retrospect, less controversial. The district has an architectural unity that dates back to two separate surges of construction at the turn of the century. The current sense of public involvement is neither to preserve in the sense of Williamsburg nor to create the affluent chicness of a Ghirardelli Square. Rather, the aim is to restore an urban vitality in sympathy with the area's past and present, to attract private investment, and to create an interesting urban enclave—which means missions and alcoholics are welcome—for both residents and tourists. Pioneer Square is protected by National Register listing, city ordinance, and a mayor-appointed preservation board empowered to review and approve all proposed exterior changes to buildings, including demolition.

City officials have advanced the area's renewal with policies ranging from special street lights and fountains to selective code enforcement, arm-twisting, and a knack for attracting federal grants.

Private money is now investing heavily in restoring the handsome buildings, and business interests agree, at least in this previously derelict area, that "preservation pays." Some of the other goals—retaining the Skid Row population, building housing (neither low–nor higher-income levels are viable without subsidy), and avoiding dominance of an artsy-craftsy, boutique atmosphere—are less assured, however. Taxes are rising and a controversial "minimum–maintenance" program is now being enforced to spur code-compliance and curb speculative holding of property; a Pioneer Square Special Review District Board has power to enforce or modify a Building Department order. If the owner doesn't comply, the city may make repairs and collect costs from the owner.

Pike Place Market

The challenge in Pike Place Market, some blocks north of Pioneer Square, is quite different. Here, the attempt is less to make something happen than to protect activities already there. The colorful city market, dating from 1907 and run largely for and by low-income people as a subsidized farmer-to-consumer center, has also over the years attracted the loyalty of many middle-class people for its bargains, gourmet delicacies, and the adventure of shopping there.

It took a wave of citizen support, and skillful organization of that affection, to stop a strongly backed high-rise urban renewal plan and save the market by setting aside a 7-acre historic district within the 22-acre urban renewal area. The National Register listing protects uses as well as buildings in the district, as do a city ordinance and guidelines of the citizens' commission that reviews and approves new activities and architectural changes.

Despite the citizen vote, however, change must be part of the market's life. Officials are coming to grips with the realities: dilapidated structures and code requirements, rising property values, the need for low-income housing, decline of local agriculture, tensions between farmers and counterculture "hippie" crafts merchants, and

the economics of running the market so that public subsidy is not endless.

The issues in the area beyond the market itself are even more complex. The urban renewal plan for the entire area has been revised to emphasize rehabilitation and preservation. With public money scarce and costs escalating, private money has been leery of significant investment in the area. Since if most of the buildings are to be saved it must be done under public ownership, a public development authority has been set up to acquire properties and oversee the effort. Early in 1975, the project's managers urgently requested $8 million of Seattle's total three-year CD block grant allocation of $31.5 million; they received $3 million.

Some of the pieces are beginning to come together, however. Publicly funded (both federal and city) renewal efforts already underway in the historic district include the restoration of a corner market, sanitary upgrading of the main market, and the construction of a pedestrian incline from the water's edge up to the market. In the summer of 1975, two Seattle banks made the first mortgage commitments in Pike Place Market since revitalization began.

Ripple effect

The impact on Seattle has been widespread. In the broad sense, the perspectives, tools and tactics learned in the two historic districts have permeated the city's policies, which now stress rehabilitation and restoration of deteriorating areas, upgrading neighborhood services, and attracting private investment in key "action neighborhoods."

Seattle has many plans—for the waterfront, for pedestrian walkways, for bikeways and parks, for trolleys, for rehabilitation loans—all of which reflect a concern for exploiting existing resources and for restraint before using the bulldozer.

The following account takes up eight conservation issues that emerge from the Seattle experience.

1. Nature of Seattle's concern with conservation

Until recently, residents of Seattle—like those in many other cities of the American West—did not place much value in their older buildings. Seattle's awakening interest in its "old" buildings in the late 1960s thus did not evolve from any previous involvement in naming individual landmarks or setting up historic museums, or from an elite establishment of "daughters" who clustered around the symbols of their ancestors. Nor did it come initially from established environmental groups. Although the lives of Seattle's citizens are very much shaped by their enjoyment of the city's physical amenities, the fact that much of their wealth comes from the exploitation of natural resources has splintered organized support.

In a broader sense, however, the new attitude has come out of a genuine commitment and affection for the city—the hills, the relationship to water, the lifestyle of its residents, the commercial vitality, as well as the harmony and scale of the buildings.

Seattle's new policies are traceable to a cadre of individuals, beginning with the mayor, who sought to capture the city's ambience and shape public policies to protect it as development needs were met. Seattle is new, less bureaucratized than older cities and able to respond faster to awareness among its citizens and officials.

Without a single landmark, Seattle's first efforts in historic preservation evolved into full-scale sophisticated attempts to marshal public tools and private involvement in entire neighborhoods. While both Pioneer Square and Pike Place Market Districts were saved in the name of "history"—invoking the police power to justify special ordinances, development guidelines, sign controls, review boards, etc.—neither one was a preservation effort in the strict sense. Both identified what was worth protecting (including people), and considered how change would be accommodated. As the emphasis shifts from historic buildings to people, lifestyles, and harmonious streetscapes, the criteria, public purpose, and guidelines for change become harder to define and defend. But many of the tools and tactics are transferable, and Seattle, amid controversy, is exploring the ways.

First, the city council has passed a tough landmarks ordinance, with power to designate both individual buildings and districts and to lay down strict controls. This set down a uniform citywide policy to govern designation. Yet the first district considered under the ordinance (First Avenue) was not approved, and the only significant landmark designated was torn down. The ordinance is now under attack and will probably be weakened.

Special review districts have been established, both as an additional protection in an historic district and as a land use control in districts where the tie to history is more tenuous. In the Pioneer Square special review district—which covers an area larger than the Pioneer Square historic district—land uses (especially parking and other automobile-oriented uses such as garages and drive-ins) are controlled by an elected board. The aim is mainly to reduce adverse impact from the King County Stadium now being constructed. The nearby International District is also a special review district. The chief purpose was to protect the neighborhood's Asian lifestyle as well as its low-scale quality, but now its historic buildings too are being surveyed.

Property owners in the Ballard neighborhood have shown interest in designation as an historic district. They feel this will revitalize their neighborhood's turn-of-the-century commercial district and enhance the community's Scandinavian character. The Queen Anne neighborhood, which has lovely old houses sited on hills overlooking the water, may take the special review district approach because this neighborhood seems too diverse, in uses and styles, for the historic district designation.

2. What do people want to protect or create?

A main goal is often protection, from physical change or people change, in neighborhoods of distinct physical, social, or historic character. The Queen Anne neighborhood objects to high-rise structures blocking the view to the water. Mt. Baker was declining until selected as a "priority neighborhood" for city attention. In some areas the aim is to stop high-income residents from moving out, or to protect diverse lifestyles or even one lifestyle, such as the Asian in the International District. This may mean special protection of low-income uses, including thrift shops and cheap hotels. It may mean controlling the impacts of large-scale development, such as the stadium.

In many instances the instinct for protection is linked to a vision of the future. In Pioneer Square, merchants and city council were won over by Ghirardelli Square. Others eschewed this image, hoping instead to build a diversified urban enclave more respectful of its history. The Ballard community, while disavowing commercialism, sees economic advantages in being designated.

3. Role of individuals and government in spurring conservation

Many in Seattle link the conservation approach to a handful of significantly placed, innovative people: architect Ralph Anderson who organized a successful development team that proved out the potential of Pioneer Square; Mayor Wesley G. Uhlman, who found it a good political issue and made it the hallmark of his administration; Arthur Skolnik, City Conservator and formerly manager of the Pioneer Square District, whose creative, nonbureaucratic style meshed cross-agency policies, leveraged grants, and "sold" adaptive reuse; Bruce Chapman, former City Council member and advocate of conservation-oriented policies; Victor Steinbrueck, architect and author of books of affectionate prose and drawings about Seattle's cityscapes and a veteran of community battles against public and private demolition.

Despite the decisive 1972 citizen vote to save Pike Place Market, and Seattle citizens' civic-mindedness, the first ingredient of Seattle's success seems not to be citizen support, but rather the use of municipal policies to assure business of continuing public commitment. That means public investment in lighting, cobblestones, and parks; hustling and coordinating grants; delivering police, sanitation, and other city services; regulating code compliance, etc. Official city policy as to locating its offices gives first priority to adapted buildings, thus both setting an example and offering a financial guarantee.

4. Economic benefits

Pioneer Square, say supporters, has spurred a sense of history and identity, reinforced civic pride, and retained human perspective in the city. Officials concede these benefits but stress Pioneer Square as an economic success story. Here, they say, "a run-down, unsightly, and sometimes unsafe area was transformed into a vibrant center with a minimum of relocation expense, without the lengthy planning process required for urban renewal, without land write-downs and, most importantly, without having to raze the architectural showpieces that make up the District." An investment of $807,870 of municipal funds has been combined with $200,000 in private donations and over $1 million in federal funds. There have been no major demolitions since 1968. And the public's investment is easily paid back in tourist spending in the area, according to a city study.

The area now houses offices of lawyers, advertising agencies, and city departments. It has new urban open spaces and street benches, accessible and pleasant vistas. There are good taverns, shops and restaurants, and restored structures linked to Seattle's past. The volume of permits for renovations is on the rise, and there is increasingly heavy private commitment, new jobs, higher sales tax revenue, and business taxes. The rise in property taxes (property values are up as much as 1,000% in key restored areas) is a mixed blessing as it displaces tenants with limited resources.

5. Attitudes of financial interests

The downtown development association and financial interests, who once opposed Pioneer Square, now list it as one of the city's attractions. Yet their attitudes do not carry over to similar undertakings in other sections of the city. Each new effort is a new battle, and some say the fight is becoming harder, not easier.

For example, University Properties, which controls 10 key downtown acres owned by the University of Washington, says that historic preservation has strangled growth in Seattle, and that Pioneer Square would have survived without help. Adaptive office building use (as in Pioneer Square) has a limited market, according to a former University Properties president. To fight suburban sprawl, keep the city strong, save energy, and preserve vitality of city streets, property owners must invest and rebuild, he adds, and meet the demand for new, air-conditioned, efficient office space.

On the other hand, the chairman of Seattle Trust and Savings (the bank that has provided the most substantial backing to adaptive restorations in Pioneer Square) believes adapted office buildings can be a safer investment risk than high-rise towers. But the financial community on the whole is said to be divided and angered over what it sees as a "conservationist-environmentalist-historic preservationist conspiracy."

Seattle bankers have yet to make shared-risk arrangements.

6. The legal issues

Seattle's policies—which have depended on private investment and therefore had to be conciliatory to business—have not attacked basic legal doctrine. Limitations on the property owner (the taking issue) are still matters for sharp debate, for example, and more so in terms of individual landmarks (where an individual property owner, like the University of Washington, is involved) than in terms of historic districts, where property owners tend to gain from shared restrictions.

The city has experimented widely, however, with new legal tools, such as special zoning, review boards, design criteria, and development guidelines. In an area where there are no precedents, criteria may be subject to charges of capriciousness and imprecision (one legal suit over signs in Pioneer Square was lost by proponents of controls).

The Washington State constitution prohibits the city from guaranteeing loans and providing loans to individuals or corporations. This restriction—which it shares with other Western states—hampers the city's ability to carry out innovative fiscal policies with federal CD block grant funds. Yet an opposite interpretation views these as public purpose funds, with the city merely serving as a channeling agency. There has been no such difficulty with federal categorical programs, such as Section 312 loans, which have been extended in a limited way through August 1976.

7. Problems of innovative policies

Economic incentives. As of mid-1975, tax incentives have not been a part of Seattle's programs. Real estate assessments are made by the county; the assessor responds solely to current valuation criteria. Thus valuations are rising. Increased yield of the property tax is cited as a benefit to municipal revenue, but also can be an unwanted pressure (i.e., costs of public acquisition in Pike Place Market are rising, as are rents in Pioneer Square). A city task force report supports a range of economic incentives related to landmarks preservation. These include tax relief for landmarks (such changes must be sought at state level), along with assessments that reflect current use in historic districts, rather than the development potential of "highest and best use."

Innovative tax increment financing, which would have targeted the increased revenues accruing from district improvement to finance additional improvements in the neighborhood, was turned down at the polls. One city official fears that a weakening of landmarks preservation law would ease the pressure on the business community, and thus weaken their interest in tax incentives. Without their support, these policies will not be passed, he argues, since financial interests would prefer freedom to tax benefits tied to restrictions.

Revolving fund. In 1973, Seattle allocated $600,000 of its general revenue sharing funds to a historic preservation authority with a wide range of powers. This innovative institutional arrangement has been stymied, both for the legal reasons noted earlier, as well as for tactical reasons. The city's policy is not to compete with business and so the authority seems limited to projects in which the economics are shaky. The fund's managers have been uncertain about whether to "use up" the fund on several such properties or to find a way to make the fund "revolve." The authority is not tax exempt, and has therefore not received donations.

Marshalling city policies. This is Seattle's great strength, its impact largely traceable to city conservator Skolnik, whose effectiveness, in turn, reflects the mayor's personal support for urban conservation.

8. CD block grant priorities

If CD block grant priorities are any indication, citywide enthusiasm for "historic preservation" is mixed. As in other cities, allocation of CD funds for preservation or conservation competes for funds with sewers, street improvements, daycare and neighborhood centers, services to the aging, etc. Citizens did not have to face this dilemma when they voted to save Pike Place Market years ago. On the other hand, the city's CD plan does stress rehabilitation and conservation as a broad theme throughout, and the mayor has earmarked three "action neighborhoods" for concentrated services—a sign that the city is still committed.

New York

New York
Population: c7,895,000

**New York:
Case study in
innovation**

New York City's efforts at conserving neighborhoods are notable both for their forward-looking planning and their relative lack of integration or unity.

The city is responsible for the most advanced concepts in landmark and historic district preservation, zoning, community service decentralization, and housing preservation. It has tended, however, to approach these four as separate areas, with little by way of coordination. This separation may be traced back to the different forces (political and social) which gave rise to each effort.

Neighborhood conservation in New York City was in fact not planned as a uniform program. Rather, five separate movements developed and blossomed into programs. Each program was backed by a different constituency which impelled its formation. And each program followed excesses that have left irreversible damage. These movements were:

1. The cultural effort to preserve landmarks and historic districts which gained its most effective momentum after some of the city's more notable landmark buildings and areas were already lost or substantially marred.

2. The economic development efforts to preserve the financial vitality of primarily Manhattan commercial areas, such as the retail district.

3. The shift in the real estate industry's concern away from new construction to reclamation of abandoned housing or preservation of deteriorating structures. This follows a decade of overbuilding of commercial buildings, unrentable office space, and the fiscal reality that new unsubsidized residential construction is now unmarketable.

4. The movement led by urban planners to cut density and block the already established trend to overbuild city areas.

5. The dual effort of community and ideological leaders to return political power to communities along with efforts to preserve community identity. This came as a reaction to the centralization of city government, and to the recognition of what had been lost on the community level in the urban renewal sweep of the last decade.

Some very basic trends and ideas have also developed in the past decade that underlie each of these separate movements and serve to tie them together. Most fundamentally it has been the fierce reaction to the urban renewal programs of the past that defined progress by massive new building complexes. New construction was the only acceptable game, and to play one had to accept the bulldozing of entire neighborhoods..

The results have been recognized as mixed blessings, but out of the experience came the lesson that neighborhoods do not get built from scratch. They evolve over time, and once developed can only survive with a mixture of the old and the new, the planned and the unplanned. The urban renewal goal now is no longer simply new construction, but instead mixed development. Interests which once clashed now agree that this is the appropriate direction.

It has also been recognized that while the city was giving the lion's share of attention to new construction, entire blocks of structurally sound housing were left to deteriorate. The city is now pockmarked by whole neighborhoods that have been abandoned because the voices calling for imaginative conservation tools were ignored. Ironically now that those voices are being listened to, money and resources are scarce—and for some areas there is too little, too late.

These five separate movements and underlying trends resulted in:

• The Landmarks Preservation Commission program of landmark and historic district preservation.

• The City Planning Commission's creation of special zoning districts to promote such economic development efforts as protection of the theater district and the strengthening of the retail strip along Fifth Avenue.

- The former Housing Development Administration's program known as Neighborhood Preservation, involving loans for renovation of deteriorating property.

- The City Planning Commission program to offer increased density as trade-off for enhanced amenities in new construction projects.

- The Office of Neighborhood Government's program to decentralize city services delivery; and a state law providing for locally elected school boards to govern all but high school education.

These programs developed separately, with pressure from varied interest group—preservationists, planners, real estate investors, community groups, political groups, etc., which led eventually to citywide responses.

Of late, however, the different groups have taken to working closer together under various influences such as the federal Housing and Community Development Act of 1974, the earlier National Environmental Policy Act, and other assistance and regulatory programs.

This report examines each of the program areas separately and attempts to draw common links and problem areas. The material is arranged in three sections. The first section deals with the housing renovation program and with the services decentralization effort; the second with the landmarks and historic district preservation program; and the third with two efforts of the City Planning Commission—zoning control over density and social amenities, and economic development incentives through zoning.

In all of the city's varied preservation programs one common factor appears throughout. The major preservation effort in each neighborhood and within each program has been accomplished by the people living in those neighborhoods, who too often found that the biggest hurdle was overcoming the city bureaucracy. Invariably, local residents were ahead of the city agencies in recognizing the need, initiating preservation efforts, and pushing for appropriate programs. In some cases there are private groups, such as Brooklyn's Brownstone Revival Committee, that started earlier, worked harder, had a greater impact, and accomplished more with private efforts than any public agency. City agencies in the past few years have just begun to catch up.

New York's Neighborhood Preservation Program (NPP) originated in 1971 with an intensive two-year analysis of local conditions in the city's neighborhoods that included landlords and residents as well as the physical condition of housing and other structures. Its focus is in fact not preservation in the narrower, historic sense, but rather a broadly based program to conserve the city's neighborhoods as healthy, viable communities.

In principle New York's NPP is one of the pioneer efforts in the nation, but as with many of New York's innovative programs it has been criticized for being too little, too late.

Beset by waves of neighborhood decline and abandonment, the city launched a directed effort—beginning in the late 1960s—to salvage neighborhoods which seemed on the decline or on the verge of advanced deterioration.

During this 1965–68 period New York joined the rest of the nation in experiencing major riots. This surge of community protest against what was seen as neglect by City Hall was a factor in expanding pressure for local control of city services within local communities. Polarization and growing alienation became a subject of political debate and led in due course to efforts to decentralize.

The deterioration of housing, coupled with abandonment, continued. Rather than the scattered decay which had previously touched urban centers in New York, deterioration now began to include entire communities. Large parts of neighborhoods such as the South Bronx,

Neighborhood preservation program (NPP)

Brownsville and Bushwick (both in Brooklyn), tottered and were abandoned. The issue was no longer deterioration—which meant poorer living conditions—but neighborhood death.

In 1968–70 New York City built 49,000 units of housing of all types. During the same period it lost over 70,000 units of housing through abandonment. Planners increasingly realized that new housing, which may cost up to $60,000 a unit to build, could never be produced at a sufficiently rapid pace to keep up with the process of abandonment.

The process of decay had its refugees. They clogged city neighborhoods that were still viable and made it increasingly difficult to preserve the areas into which they moved. As these families fled from Brownsville to Brooklyn's Crown Heights, or made similar moves within the Bronx and Manhattan, new areas seemed in danger.

To cope with this exodus and stem the pattern of abandoned areas, and following a detailed analysis in the years 1971–72, the Neighborhood Preservation Program (NPP) was launched. This followed years of community pressure, bureaucratic resistance, and the loss of valuable time. Five city neighborhoods were declared special preservation districts. It was hoped they could be preserved by focusing major resources. These areas were Crown Heights and Bushwick in Brooklyn, Clinton and Washington Heights in Manhattan, and East Tremont in the Bronx. This report will focus on two of these areas (Crown Heights and Washington Heights) due to the interesting contrast in conditions between the two.

Crown Heights is located on the border of Brooklyn's most deteriorated area. To its north and east lies Brownsville, a substantially decayed and partially abandoned area. To its south lie Flatbush, East Flatbush, and Canarsie, the heartland of Brooklyn's stable residential housing stock. It is a beautiful neighborhood dominated by "barbell" blocks of one- to four-family houses (with corner buildings of 20–100 units).

Washington Heights lies at the northern tip of Manhattan. With Harlem stretching up to 155th Street, Washington Heights lent stability to the northern half of Manhattan. Its lovely Jumel Terrace houses, the Columbia–Presbyterian Medical Center, the beautiful Fort Tryon and Inwood Hill parks, and the medieval Cloisters Museum, all made the area a vital one to save. Washington Heights' northern area is largely Irish, its middle sector Jewish, and its southern sector black and Hispanic.

The preservation program proceeded at two levels: (a) a housing renovation effort to bolster the housing stock of the communities; and (b) a municipal service decentralization effort to upgrade the quality of service delivery in each area.

The theory behind this effort was that relieving deteriorating areas was essentially a housing problem. If housing could be renovated before it no longer paid its way for the owner, a neighborhood could be salvaged. This philosophy was supplemented by the view that by improving the quality of life through stepped-up service delivery, it would be possible to keep stable families and businesses from leaving the communities, and to reduce crime and vandalism.

While these theories left gaps which were to emerge later, they recognized a subtle reality. To onlookers, neighborhood deterioration appeared to represent the invasion of "good areas" by people from "bad areas"; but to newly arrived residents this very process represented important upward mobility. The low-income black entering a Jewish neighborhood may signal the start of its deterioration as seen from City Hall; to the black family the move is a dramatic event marking the end of a long-drawn-out desire to leave the ghetto.

The New York approach also took into account the various stages of deterioration. Far from the simple black-replaces-white or poor-replaces-rich formulations, the framers of the program recognized three stages to neighborhood demographic change. In the first the traditional—usually white—population declines in income and wealth while increasing in age. As children leave the neighborhood, a middle-class wage-earning white population evolves increasingly to an elderly, retired one.

In a second phase deaths among the white population open the area to an influx of middle class nonwhites. Sometimes with higher incomes than their elderly white predecessors, they are often fleeing deterioration in nearby areas. This ethnic change is likely to be quite rapid (Crown Heights was 80% white in 1960 and 80% nonwhite in 1970). Finally, in the third phase poor nonwhites drive out middle-class nonwhites and deterioration sets in.

The program also recognized the variable impact of neighborhood change. In Washington Heights ethnic and economic change has been slower in part because of physical barriers such as the George Washington Bridge, the above-average width of Broadway (which splits the neighborhood in two), the huge Columbia—Presbyterian Medical Center complex, and the hill whose summit is 155th Street. Population and deterioration are apt to be quite different on one side of these lines than on the other.

In Crown Heights deterioration centered upon certain types of buildings—in this case the corner multiple dwelling. While corner structures were often in bad condition, the smaller, owner-occupied buildings in midblock were likely to be quite sound.

By recognizing these relatively subtle variations the city's policy concentrated on several goals:

• To prevent the exodus of middle-class non-white households.

• To eliminate decayed structures amid otherwise sound housing.

• To preserve natural boundaries from decay

and reinforce them via renovation of buildings along such boundaries.

The NPP effort centered around two programs: (1) a municipal loan program (which offered loans at tax-exempt interest rates to owners seeking to renovate their property; rent restructuring and tax abatement after renovation; and rent subsidy where funds were available) provided a sophisticated tool to foster renovation; and (2) the Office of Neighborhood Government (ONG) program which sought to decentralize city services through formation of local service "cabinets" of district directors of each major service such as police, fire, and sanitation. These local offices were set up in eight of the city's 62 community planning districts, and were headed by a district manager appointed by ONG. By giving the local service chiefs somewhat greater authority than before, and by means of more intensive contacts with community representatives, it was hoped that local services would be sharply improved.

The municipal loan program was based on state enabling legislation and a city capital budget appropriation. It has been financed by bond sales which were repaid by rental income from renovated properties. The ONG program was rooted in a mayoral executive order and was directed by the Office of Neighborhood Government within the mayoral cabinet.

Private resources to support these conservation efforts have been lukewarm. Disinvestment by savings banks and savings and loans associations is a major cause of deterioration. Both had been disinvesting in declining New York City neighborhoods for some time.

Some efforts by banks to reinvest were made. One that was supposed to be a major breakthrough is the Community Preservation Corporation, a private nonprofit housing finance corporation created in 1974 by 11 New York City commercial bank members of the New York Clearinghouse Association and 23 city savings banks. The plan was to work with local government to conserve the housing stock in Washington Heights and Crown Heights by providing construction and long-term mortgage loans for one- to four-family dwellings. Conventional mortgage insurance from FHA, REMIC (see below), and the Veterans Administration would be available.

The Corporation's commitment comes in three parts: (1) $400,000 from member banks for operation of the program; (2) $8 million to form a revolving fund for construction financing; and (3) up to $32 million for permanent financing through sale of collateral notes whereby each institution participates in each mortgage and thereby spreads the risks among all members.

Income is expected to come from interest on construction loans and related fees. But by the end of 1975 not one loan had been given in any one of the preservation neighborhoods, and only the first loan was in preparation. However, the $400,000 in operations had been spent.

The municipal rehabilitation loan program
Within the designated areas the municipal rehabilitation loan program operates through identification of strategic buildings (even though it may lend any place in the city). These are structures whose deterioration is advanced and which if abandoned or allowed to decay further would disrupt materially the pattern of stability in the surrounding area. Typically, community attitudes, the extent of deterioration, proximity to such community institutions as churches and schools, and building size, are key factors in these decisions.

When a building is ready for renovation and both owner and the city seek it, a loan from the city is negotiated. The decision to lend includes an evaluation of the property's ability to support the extent of renovation proposed within the incomes of the current tenants. Often renovation decisions must be scaled down to avoid overtaxing the rent payment ability of local tenants. Typically, in mid-1975 a prerenovation building rented for approximately $15–35 per room per

month, and after renovation rents would increase to about $40–50 per room.

Rents are restructured to take account of increased costs, and renovation is usually done with tenants in occupancy. The aim is to avoid the risk of permanent relocation by moving tenants out while work is in process.

Once renovated the property improvement is in effect tax abated under Section J-51 of the city's Administrative Code, which provides for abatement in instances of substantial renovation.

Renovation typically involves mortgage refinancing and about $7500 per unit in brick and mortar costs. These usually involve replacement of heating, plumbing, wiring systems, and repair of bathrooms and kitchens.

Although the municipal loan program is only one tool in the preservation mixture it is considered the key one, and so far its actual application has been limited. And the fiscal crisis has forced a virtual freeze in new loans. In Clinton, for example, two buildings—one with eight units, the other with 53—have received municipal loans totaling $957,836. In Washington Heights three buildings—with 30, 33 and 55 units—have received loans totaling $881,417. And in Crown Heights five buildings—with five, 40, 39, 65 and 86 units—have received loans totaling $2,435,540. That makes 414 units in the three areas combined.

Recently, some stress has been placed upon transfer of ownership to cooperative formats. While such a change is needed, it is often difficult to carry through. Over one-third of Crown Heights owners are either quite elderly or live outside the area, having generally acquired their buildings through inheritance. In a public opinion poll, over half said they would gladly sell their buildings if they could.

Given such owner disinterest, the cooperative conversion option is attractive. But NPP planning surveys indicate that fewer than 20% of

Crown Heights tenants would consider cooperative ownership at any price. Such tenants are unused to home ownership, have little faith in the area, and are in too low a tax bracket for the deduction afforded by cooperative conversion to matter very much.

The Office of Neighborhood Government programs (ONG)

The ONG program is the outgrowth of intense popular agitation to decentralize city government. Coming on the heels of a state legislative act providing for locally elected school boards to govern elementary and intermediate education, the purpose of the effort was to foster administrative decentralization and citizen involvement.

Embracing departments of sanitation, police, parks, health, highways, drug addiction, and social services, the ONG program rested on a mayoral executive order directing that local service administrators, previously stripped of any power, be delegated some additional authority.

These local service directors met monthly in the community under the chairmanship of a district manager appointed by the mayor through ONG. These district managers had virtually no command authority, and their influence rested on their ability to develop dialogues between service departments—and between them and local leaders. A key factor, however, was that the district managers did have the authority of the mayor's office behind them. At (and between) these meetings some service delivery patterns were altered for greater response and coordination.

Thus police assignments were changed to cope with local street gang problems. Housing renovation policy was coordinated with vacant lot cleanings by the Sanitation Department. Police enforcement of parking laws was coupled with greater street sweeping frequency.

Both the ONG and NPP programs sought community input. In each area advisory boards were organized, often different for each program and often reflective of local or central city political conflicts.

Interest groups in each area vary in their reactions to the problem of conservation. In some neighborhoods they are largely oriented toward communitywide issues and in tune with general NPP policy at city level. In other more ethnically diverse areas there is a strong desire to keep up barriers against in-migration of other ethnic or racial groups. Such neighborhoods are more heavily divided along ethnic or racial lines; they focus on issues such as school integration, and pressure groups in the community have less time to be active in issues of housing renovation or generalized service delivery.

Has it worked?

Any assessment of the city's Neighborhood Preservation Program must deal both with the efforts at renovation and service delivery and with the gaps in conservation needs not met by the city's programs.

The key constraint on the municipal loan program has been a shortage of loan applicants. Wary of renewing investment in transitional areas, owners hesitate incurring the risks involved in renovation. A related constraint has been the city's inability to build stable management techniques into any renovation proposal: the city is often faced with a choice between making a loan to an owner whose ability to manage real property effectively it doubts, or watching a pivotal building continue to deteriorate.

As for ONG, it was limited from the start by the lack of any real authority delegated to the district managers. On the other hand, neighborhood perceptions of service delivery levels improved as did coordination among services. (Columbia University has made a detailed assessment of the ONG program.)

The ONG suffered more than most programs with the changeover in City Hall leadership in 1974. Despite its early difficulties the offices had been staffed with professionals who were beginning to develop solid working relationships with local groups, and this was bringing results. Many of those professionals were replaced with personnel selected more on politics than skill, and considerable momentum was lost.

Programs such as this went into a state of transition because of the cutback in services during the fiscal crisis and pending enactment of city charter amendments approved in November 1975.

Given the record of the NPP and ONG programs, several factors must be considered:

The economics of real property. Far more important than structural decay of housing stock is loss of opportunity for the real estate industry to make profits in conservation neighborhoods. Owners may view their properties as long-term investments to be protected against temporary setbacks due to the promise of long-term profits, or as short-term targets for "milking" and disinvestment. On such bases rest essential decisions concerning repair, investment, and management.

NPP has done nothing to alter these basic circumstances.

Some observers contend that the city's rent control law is a prime disincentive to proper maintenance. They argue that rentals are simply inadequate to allow ample profit and more than minimal maintenance. Others challenge this, noting that large numbers of units were decontrolled between 1971 and 1974—and rentals have risen to market levels. They assert that any cash flow shortfall is not due to legislative constraints but rather to the underlying lack of rent-paying potential in transitional areas.

Apart from the rent control debate, several bills considered in the New York State Legislature in its 1975 session were aimed at reviving bank investment in inner-city neighborhoods.

These bills rest on the assumption that a resale or refinancing market can rekindle owner interest in long-term maintenance of housing in such

districts. Lack of such incentive merely relegates the realm of property profitability to that of cash flow—a measurement by which property is sure to lose in such areas.

One bill would create a New York State Bank to make mortgage loans on the same basis as a savings or commercial bank and receive deposits in competition with such institutions. A second would require that 60% of all savings bank financial commitments be in long-term instate mortgages, a move designed to curb the export of capital from such institutions to out of state mortgage markets.

A third measure would permit a savings bank to register as a Neighborhood Preservation Bank and to agree to lend 40% of its mortgages in conservation areas. In return the bank would be permitted to engage in a wide variety of banking practices limited to commercial banks under current state law (personal loans, greater branching, lower reserve requirements) and to pay New York State income-tax-exempt interest to its depositors.

None of the proposed legislation passed in 1975; and prospects for reintroduction and eventual passage are not considered bright.

These measures were designed to complement the Rehabilitation Mortgage Insurance Corporation (REMIC) program, established in New York in 1973 to insure loans in NPP areas. REMIC is an independent municipal public benefit corporation. It is authorized to insure 20% of refinancing on acquisition loans and 90% of renovation mortgages, providing that the total amount of insurance does not exceed 50% of total loan value. By the end of 1975 not one building had yet been insured by REMIC, although it has an operation budget of over $200,000.

Management and ownership. While concentrating on renovation NPP has by and large ignored the need to assure proper management of buildings in such areas—renovated or not. Many feel long-term good management is far more crucial than the physical state of the building structure.

Unable to assure adequate maintenance, city lenders demur at lending money to certain types of owners—often precisely those whose properties need it most. At a loss to find an alternative owner, banks are reluctant to foreclose—and the city to condemn—such properties.

Landmarks and historic district preservation

In the early 1960s a concern for architecturally and historically salient buildings began to gather momentum in New York City. Spurred on by this and by the loss of Pennsylvania Station and other architectural gems, the New York City Landmarks Preservation Commission (made up of 10 nonpaid commissioners and a paid chairman who are appointed by the mayor for three year overlapping terms) was created in 1965 by Local Law #46. Its charge was to "designate and preserve those buildings and districts of historical, architectural and cultural importance and of special value." The law was amended in 1973 to include designation and preservation of publicly used interiors as well as scenic landmarks.

The chief purpose of the Commission at first was to designate the architectural gems. Since its start in 1965 it has moved to protect over 450 individual landmark buildings (a landmark must be 30 years old) and 27 districts. These districts contain over 11,000 more city structures. While some are only one or two block sections, others consist of such areas as a 40 block section of Brooklyn Heights, a 24 square block area in Cobble Hill, a large section of Greenwich Village, and other such communities. By the beginning of 1976 there were also six scenic landmarks, including all of Central Park. The intent was to use this new municipal mechanism not only to preserve the best of the city's historic heritage, but also to maintain the social and economic health of a large number of neighborhoods.

Designation of areas is a complex matter, the culmination of a long process of research and consultation including a public hearing. The Designation Report, which must be filed with the Board of Estimate (the city's eight-member executive and legislative body), is a legal document that includes the pertinent historical or architectural background on which the decision to designate is based. Designation by the Landmarks Preservation Commission must be approved within 90 days by the Board of Estimate after ratification by the City Planning Commission.

The Commission's designation is an effort to protect the important features of the landmark or historic district. Essentially a method of controlling alteration of such features, all changes in a designated structure (or to a structure within a designated area) must receive Commission approval in this manner:

● Changes to the interior which do not affect the designated features receive a "Certificate of No Effect" (to the protected architectural features) and are permitted.

● Changes which do not modify the essential character of the building's protected features and which are of a maintenance nature not requiring Buildings Department permits receive a "Permit for Minor Work" and may proceed.

● Major changes which affect the protected features require public hearings during which the Commission decides whether to issue a "Certificate of Appropriateness."

Two key trends have emerged in the Commission's policy and the reactions to it:

1. Greater designation of *neighborhoods* as opposed to *individual buildings*.

2. Mounting difficulty in reconciling the Commission's mandate to protect designated features with the statutory requirements that such designation not prevent a reasonable economic return to the owners.

Designation almost always affects more than the individual landmark or historic district; its unofficial influence extends to the surrounding community. Designation is an assurance that a building or small area will survive change in a city that is virtually replaced from decade to decade. This assurance has made designation a much-sought-after protection for many communities pressured by development and deterioration.

Thus the preservation constituency has expanded beyond the intellectual elite who enjoy landmarks for their aesthetic merits to everyday citizens who depend on landmarks for their community identity.

Alterations and economic return

The Commission has come out quite actively in favor of "living" landmarks and permits alterations that will introduce such modern necessities as air-conditioners. It works with owners to ensure that any attempt to make alterations and additions is sympathetic to the landmark. Usually the alterations alone do not determine whether or not a building is viable economically, however, and a landmark building in good repair often gains in assessed valuation.

Often, however, only through alteration of the designated features can a structure survive economically. In such cases the obvious alternative is to make such alteration in a manner consistent with economic *and* architectural needs. But such alterations to a facade are often much more costly than would be the case were the latter consideration disregarded.

The Commission is granted the power to devise a plan for partial or complete tax abatement whenever it has been determined that a reasonable (6%) rate is not being realized on the property. This tax relief is limited to situations where an owner is threatening to demolish a landmark. It may not be granted to an owner simply because his property has been designated. So far this tax relief power has not been used.

While the landmarks preservation law regulates alterations to landmarks or to buildings located in historic districts, the basic economic realities which force owners to want such alterations in the first place remain. To aid them economically, a zoning amendment was passed to cope with the economic problems by permitting a landmark's development rights to be sold and transferred. This has tended to work well only in high density central commercial areas under development pressure.

The tool used in the city's NPP—municipal loans to cover the costs of renovation—has not been used in landmarks in any systematic fashion. The landmarks program, seen originally as an aesthetic effort, was not thought to have need of a development loan "arm."

On occasion the Commission has been asked to tread outside the bounds of its legislative mandate in defining unique areas worthy of protection. Yet legally, designation must hinge on the objective citywide value of the architectural/historical/cultural characteristics of the building or neighborhood, not on the desire of residents or city planners wishing to preserve a community.

Of late preservation has begun to attract individuals and groups whose first interest often is improving the quality of life rather than preservation of architecture and history.

Comprehensive plan

The Commission has said it plans to tap this widening interest and in 1974 evolved a comprehensive plan which seeks to:

1. Reinforce its management resources to protect city areas with architectural, historical, and cultural character or environmental unity;

2. Make historic preservation part of a balanced program of community development;

3. Insure that future development is compatible with the existing character of an area.

To conform to this plan the Commission designed or embarked on a series of specific programs, of which the following are highlights:

1. The agency was restructured so as to supplement its professional research and preservationist staff, with expertise in such areas as community relations, law, and planning. The chairman moved from parttime to fulltime. Volunteers were integrated into the staff as fulltime, nonpaid members. Furthermore the Commission, whose activities had been seen as largely in the private and volunteer domain, now was a coequal agency within city government with all other departments.

2. With a grant from the National Endowment for the Arts and from the New York Community Trust the Commission decided to explain its enlarged conservation role by means of a variety of media. This was to be followed in the future by organizing community groups to help initiate, lobby for, and monitor districts.

3. The Commission is in the process of getting all city landmarks listed on the National Register of Historic Places.

4. Liaison with other agencies (a weakness in its early years) was being expanded, especially with the City Planning Commission and the departments of the former Housing Development Administration, to link new construction with historic preservation.

Since 1974 the Commission has been writing reviews on the impact of federally aided programs on landmarks, in line with Section 106 of the Historic Preservation Act of 1966, the President's Executive Order 11593 of 1971 (extending Section 106 to include both listed and eligible landmarks), and now the HCD Act of 1974. The City has allocated $200,000 of these CD block grant funds for this purpose. The City Planning Commission has given Landmarks some of HUD's Section 701 comprehensive planning funds to assess what kind of impact the City Planning Commission's long-range plans will have upon landmarks and districts.

5. Landmarks and districts have enjoyed an in-

crease in value often outstripping the pace of increase in structures nearby. A study will try to determine precisely the dynamics which increase the value of an area, what happens to the indigenous population, and what programs are needed to cope with the consequences of designation.

6. The landmarks law is being rewritten to meet the challenge of court decisions concerning relief to nonprofit eleemosynary groups. Meanwhile the city successfully appealed a New York State Supreme Court decision removing the landmark designation of Grand Central Terminal, and it has brought court action against a known violator of the Certificate of Appropriateness for alteration of a landmark.

Although the Commission is moving ahead in several areas, it continues to be criticized for avoiding some designations that might incur stiff opposition from important political and real estate interests. For example, well-known skyscrapers such as the Empire State, Chrysler, and Woolworth buildings, and Rockefeller Center have never even been considered for designation. At the same time, the city has been criticized for leaving many of its own public landmark buildings undesignated and unused while strengthening the landmark law's application to private property. Both the city and the real estate community have come under strong fire for their lack of creative responses to the challenge of reusing noteworthy buildings that are unused but structurally sound.

Zoning and planning policy

Traditionally, New York City zoning policy has concentrated on limiting development to certain densities and scales compatible with the area's ability to provide services. By the mid-1960s, however, the City Planning Commission (the city's zoning agency) advanced into a program of incentive zoning.

At first the program sought imaginatively to barter the right to build at higher than permitted density in exchange for installation of various design amenities in the complex. Developments throughout the city were awarded density for the construction of pedestrian malls, arcades, open spaces, park sitting areas, subway stations built into the building, and other improvements. No longer was zoning an absolute decision to permit or deny development. Rather it was a forum within which to negotiate—promoting development, but in such a manner as to heed as much as possible the public interest. The guidelines were: flexibility and the case-by-case approach.

In due course, as incentives became more sophisticated, special districts were created in which a policy of incentive zoning was formulated as part of an overall plan for community growth and protection. Such districts have proliferated throughout the city. Each is a response to a different kind of pressure. The following examples illustrate some of the variety and scope of the program:

Special Theater District. The erosion of Manhattan's midtown theater area has been a source of concern for some time. The number of theaters dwindled during the early 1960s and threatened to drop further—casualties of rising land values and pressures for commercial and office building development on their sites. Most theaters were housed in small uneconomic structures and could not support an adequate return.

In 1967 the City Planning Commission adopted a plan for a special theater district, running from 40th to 57th Street and from 6th to 8th Avenue, in which developers were offered a bonus of up to 20% (up to a floor area ratio of 21.6) if a legitimate theater were included within the building. The offer was not a carte blanche to each developer, but rather the basis for individual applications. These were to be examined based on the relative merits of design, density, and theatrical space on each site.

Lincoln Square District. The construction of Lincoln Center for the Performing Arts in the mid-1960s on Manhattan's West Side sparked a rapid development of housing in the surrounding area. However, this residential influx pointed up the lack of such amenities as pedes-

trian malls and other public places, covered plazas, retail space, and convenient subway access.

In 1969 the City Planning Commission extended the concept of incentive zoning to leverage the development pressures in this area and promote the construction of such improvements.

Once again, using a 20% floor space bonus formula, the Commission was able to promote a variety of design amenities.

Fifth Avenue Retail District. The development of retail centers outside the core of New York City became a threat to New York's traditional retail areas along Fifth Avenue. Moreover, unable to compete with the rentals which air-

Special Clinton Preservation District. Growth of the midtown office area and business district was a threat to the residential Clinton community throughout much of the 1950s and 1960s. Located between 42nd and 59th Street from 8th to 11th Avenue, this threat came into sharper focus by the decision, later rescinded, to build a convention center on the northwestern perimeter of Clinton.

The Clinton community is uniquely integrated, providing low-cost housing to black, Hispanic, and elderly white population. As development opportunities rose, so did fear that land speculation would doom much of this housing stock and destroy one of Manhattan's last ethnic neighborhoods.

The Housing Development Administration's Neighborhood Preservation Program (NPP) was designed to include the Clinton community as one of its five districts; however, the need remained to protect it not only from deterioration, but from development as well.

The Commission dealt with these concerns by creating the Special Clinton Preservation District. The district paralleled conventional zoning techniques in that it constrained development or demolition within the district's core while encouraging development of the perimeter. Along with this, the Commission developed a program to control the deterioration of the core of the Clinton community by awarding increased density (on an incentive basis) to developers on specially designated avenues of Clinton if they agreed to renovate property or finance other improvements within the core area.

Atlantic Avenue District. Another example of an imaginative use of zoning powers to help conserve neighborhoods is the special district declared along Court Street and Atlantic Avenue in Brooklyn. These blocks faced development pressures which threatened to destroy the harmonious red brick storefront character of the blocks.

The City Planning Commission, in its special Atlantic Avenue designation, stepped into the breach and forbade development along certain parts of these blocks, if they failed to conform to the height, setbacks, design, and coloration of the other structures along the blockfront.

Conclusions
In terms of impact the special zoning districts have produced some tangible results, The first mixed use (residential/office/retail store) structure was completed in mid-1975 in the Fifth Avenue Retail District. Several new theaters have been erected as part of new development in the Times Square Special Theater District. On the other hand, there is no consistent monitoring procedure, and in a strongly residential district such as Clinton a closer look is needed at demolition procedures.

Nevertheless, by thus exercising zoning powers to protect the character of an area, the Commission has defined its zoning mandate very broadly so as to attempt to protect communities in neighborhoods in all parts of the city.

The City in Folksong

by Roy Berkeley

When I was asked to prepare a program of folk-songs for the 1975 Neighborhood Conservation Conference in New York, I was confronted with the fact that very few appropriate songs exist. Our Anglo-American culture is rich in songs of nostalgia for the countryside or the small town, reflecting the population shift of the last hundred years or so. But I was asked for songs that express a feeling of urban identity and community and I soon realized that the real message was in their scarcity.

From the parlor songs of the post–Civil War period, through the vast bulk of the country music of the World War II era, through modern Nashville products like *Detroit City*, the message is clear: it's back in the hills that happiness, identity, and fulfillment are to be found; the cities are places of alienation, loneliness, and *anomie*. I understand that Puerto Rican music is also rich in songs about having to leave the old home place to earn a living in the cold cities of the north, songs replete with nostalgia for the home folks, the dearly familiar hills and valleys, and a more humane way of life. Never mind that it ain't necessarily so; it's the way a lot of people have felt for a lot of years.

In fact, rural life, especially in the past, was often characterized by isolation, back-breaking toil, and a poverty that went beyond just economic considerations—which is why those millions of people left the countryside of North America, the Caribbean, and Europe to come to the industrial cities. Perhaps the old song should have asked "How You Gonna Keep 'Em Down on the Farm After They've Seen the Farm?"

Another old song says ". . . I think with regret of the dear home I left . . . Oh why was I tempted to roam?" and was very popular among the Appalachian folk in cities like Louisville, Chicago, and Akron—people who knew very well why they'd been tempted to roam and who were now firmly lodged in the cities.

An interesting exception to the pattern is a small number of *urban* nostalgia songs associated with Glasgow, Scotland, in recent years. Scotland's folk and parlor music has been characterized almost entirely by paeans to the old, rural, quaint, traditional way of life, in response to the urbanization and proletarianization of most of her people. But in recent years, urban renewal schemes have threatened (and occasionally destroyed) both the physical and cultural structures of community in that city—a familiar story.

Singers and songwriters associated with the folk song revival movement in Scotland are producing a literature of very articulate and attractive songs which affirm the existence and worth of urban community and attack the architectural and bureaucratic scale of the redevelopment of Glasgow. What I find unusual and impressive about these songs is that they seem to have found quick and ready acceptance outside the university-educated folk-club audience. These songs, written by and for people who earn their living manipulating *symbols*, have been accepted and are being sung by people who earn their living manipulating *objects*. It does happen but it usually takes a long time.

The best of these songs are those of Adam McNaughton. He writes in the local working class dialect and needs occasional annotation for us outsiders. For example, his *Height Starvation Song* speaks of "pieces," which we call "sandwiches." Well, after all, the eponymous Earl *was* one of the hated Sassenach—and the slang word makes possible a lovely pun. A "wean" is a wee-un or little one—a kid. I personally think that every architect, builder, and housing official in this country should take this song to heart.

Height Starvation Song

I'm a skyscraper wean, I live on the 19th floor
But I'm not going out to play anymore
Cos since we moved to Castlemilk, I'm wastin'
  away
Cos I'm getting one less meal every day.

Oh ye cannae throw pieces oot a twenty storey
  flat
700 hungry weans will testify to that
If it's butter cheese or jelly, if the bread be plain
  or pan
The odds against it reaching earth are 99 to one.

We've wrote away to Oxfam to try and get some
  aid
And all the weans in Castlemilk have formed a
  piece brigade
We're goin' tae march tae George Square
  demanding civil rights
Like nae mair hooses over piece-throwin' height.

The same goes for McNaughton's *The Buildings:*

The Buildings

I am a city gent and I live in a tenement
In the heart of one of Glasgow's biggest slums
But they're going to improve and I've been told
  to move
By those mansion-living corporation bums.

They're tearin' doon the buildings next tae oors
And they're sendin' us to greenbelts trees an' floors
But we dinnae want tae go and we daily tell them
  so
But they're tearin' doon the buildings next tae
  oors.

They say we'll realize our dream in some lovely
  housing scheme
For the air out there is always clean and sweet,
But we're happy where we are, think we're better
  off by far
With a pub on every corner of the street.

In another McNaughton song, *Where Is the
Glasgow?,* two of the six verses are of special
relevance.

Where Is the Glasgow?

Oh where is the Glasgow where I used to stay
Wi' white wally closes done up wi' pipe clay
Where ye knew a' yer neebours frae first floor tae
  third
And to keep yer door locked was considered ab-
  surd.
Do ye know the folks livin' up stairs frae you?

Oh where is the wee shop where I used tae buy
A quarter o' tatties an' a fourpenny pie
A bag o' broken biscuits and three sody scones
An' the women aye asked "How's yer man get-
  tin' oan"
Can yer big supermarkets gie service like that?

One comes away from these songs wondering
whether the American folk song revival will ever
produce analogous songs. I doubt it, and it's
something to think about.

Roy Berkeley is a folklorist, singer, guitarist, historian, writer, and photographer. In recent years
he has taught a course at The New School for
Social Research which ties together most of
these pursuits.

Resources

The resource chapter is divided into two sections. The first section lists organizations which readers may contact when in search of additional facts on progress in the 45 cities that appear as case studies. This section is arranged by city, and in a few cases also lists specialized documents (such as innovative zoning ordinances or neighborhood analyses) that apply to that one city.

The second section consists of books and articles that are useful resources for those who wish to explore a topic in greater depth. These books and articles are arranged roughly along the lines of the five issue categories of Chapter III. There is also a special category on the role of the states in neighborhood conservation.

Organizations

General

Advisory Council on Historic Preservation
1522 K St., N.W.
Washington, D.C. 20005

The Conservation Foundation
1717 Massachusetts Ave., N.W.
Washington, D.C. 20036

Division of Community Development and Management Research
Department of Housing and Urban Development
Washington, D.C. 20410

National Endowment for the Arts
Architecture and Environmental Arts Program
Washington, D.C. 20506

National Trust for Historic Preservation
740-748 Jackson Place, N.W.
Washington, D.C. 20006

Office of Planning Management and Assistance
Department of Housing and Urban Development
Washington, D.C. 20410

The President's Council on Environmental Quality
722 Jackson Place, N.W.
Washington, D.C. 20006

Albany

Albany Urban Renewal Agency
City Hall
Albany, N.Y. 12207

Bureau of Cultural Affairs
City of Albany
545 Broadway
Albany, N.Y. 12207

Historic Albany Foundation, Inc.
194 Elm St.
Albany, N.Y. 12202

John Mesick
Mendel, Mesick and Cohen
388 Broadway
Albany, N.Y. 12207

Mesick, John et. al., *Report of the Committee on South Mall Environs.*

Community Development Program, City of Albany, N.Y.
Project No. B-75-MC-36-0010, 1975

Zoning Ordinance, City of Albany, N.Y.
May 21, 1968 as amended through January 6, 1975

Anacostia

Dept. of Housing and Community Development
Housing Division
Neighborhood Improvement Administration
614 H St., N.W.
Washington, D.C. 20001

Neighborhood Housing Services Program
1312 V St., S.E.
Washington, D.C. 20020

Urban Reinvestment Task Force
Federal Home Loan Bank Board
320 First St., N.W.
Washington, D.C. 20552

Washington Planning and Housing Association
1225 K St., N.W.
Washington, D.C. 20020

City Planning Dept.
Municipal Building
Duke of Gloucester St.
Annapolis, Md. 21401

Annapolis	Historic Annapolis, Inc. 18 Pinckney St. Annapolis, Md. 21401	Report of the Berkeley Housing Survey, December 1973. Prepared by Willis Research & Development Company, 571 5th Street, Oakland, Calif. 94607	
	Maryland Historical Trust 21 State Circle Annapolis, Md. 21401	Berkeley Department of Housing and Community Development, *A Proposed Housing Strategy and Housing Program for Community Development Funding.*	
Atlanta	City Planning Dept. Commissioner of Budget and Planning City Hall 68 Mitchell St., S.W. Atlanta, Ga. 30303	Boston Redevelopment Authority City Hall 1 City Hall Square Boston, Mass. 02201	Boston
	Inman Park Restoration, Inc. 192 Hurt St., N.E. Atlanta, Ga. 30307	Landmarks Commission City Hall 1 City Hall Square Boston, Mass. 02201	
	Thomas, Diane, "There Go the Neighborhoods," *Atlanta Magazine*, July 1973.	Massachusetts Housing Finance Agency Old City Hall 45 School St. Boston, Mass. 02108	
	The Inman Park Advocator, a monthly bulletin.	Roxbury Action Program 10 Linwood St. Roxbury, Mass. 02119	
Austin	Community Development Office City of Austin P.O. Box 1088 Austin, Tex. 78767	The Boston Harbor Associates, Inc. 88 Broad St. Boston, Mass. 02210	
Baltimore	Dept. of Housing and Community Development Planning Division 222 East Saratoga St. Baltimore, Md. 21202	Engle, Robert F. and Avault, John, *Residential Property Market Values in Boston*, Boston Redevelopment Authority, 1973.	
	Dept. of Planning City Planning Commission 222 East Saratoga St. Baltimore, Md. 21202	Historic Charleston Foundation 51 Meeting St. Charleston, S.C. 29401	Charleston
	Society for Preservation of Federal Hill, Montgomery St. and Fells Point 804 S. Broadway Baltimore, Md. 21231	Charleston Dept. of Planning and Redevelopment 205 King St. Charleston, S.C. 29402	
Berkeley	Berkeley Masterplan Revision Committee 2030 Milvia St. Berkeley, Calif. 94702	Preservation Society P.O. Box 521 Charleston, S.C. 29402	
	Dept. of Housing and Development City of Berkeley Berkeley City Hall Berkeley, Calif. 94704	Save Charleston Foundation 1 Meeting St. Charleston, S.C. 29401	

Delaney, Barbara Snow, "Preservation 1966," reprint from *Antiques*; Describes restoration activities in Charleston.

Historic Charleston Foundation, Revolving Fund regulations, adopted 1957.
Historic Preservation Plan, June 1974.

Neighborhood Analysis Report, Charleston Department of Planning and Redevelopment, 1975.

Zoning Ordinanace of the City of Charleston, amended through 1973.

Chicago

Dept. of Development and Planning
Urban Design Unit
City Hall
123 North LaSalle St.
Chicago, Ill. 60603

Historic Pullman Foundation, Inc.
614 E. 113th St.
Chicago, Ill. 60628

Landmarks Preservation Service
407 South Dearborn St., Suite 1705
Chicago, Ill. 60605

Lincoln Park Conservation Association
2373 North Lincoln Ave.
Chicago, Ill. 60614

Renewal Effort Service Corporation
(RESCORP)
7 South Dearborn St.
Chicago, Ill. 60603

Cincinnati

City Planning Commission
Cincinnati, Ohio 45202

Friends of Cincinnati Parks, Inc.
3012 Section Road
Cincinnati, Ohio 45237

Office of the City Manager
Cincinnati, Ohio 45202

The Cincinnati Institute
Cincinnati, Ohio 45202

Dallas

Dallas County Heritage Society
Old City Park
1717 Gano St.
Dallas, Tex. 75215

Dept. of Urban Planning
Office of Urban Design
City of Dallas
500 South Ervay, Suite 200-B
Dallas, Tex. 75201

Goals for Dallas
1 Main Place
Dallas, Tex. 75250

Historic Preservation League, Inc.
5707 Swiss Ave.
Dallas, Tex. 75214

Lakewood Bank & Trust Co.
6323 La Vista Drive
Dallas, Tex. 75214

Neighborhood Housing Services of Dallas, Inc.
4923 W. Lover's Lane
Dallas, Tex. 75209

Dept. of Urban Planning, *Historic Landmarks Preservation Ordinance*, 1973.

———, *Preservation ordinance and development plan for Downtown Historic District*, 1975.

———, *Swiss Avenue Historic District Ordinance.* 1973.

———, *Design Guidelines for Inner City Neighborhoods*, 1972.

———, *Swiss Avenue Survey Report, 1972.*

Neighborhood Housing Services of Dallas, Inc., Dallas: Neighborhood Housing Services of Dallas, Inc., 1973.

Wright, Don, "Economics of Urban Restoration," from *Texas Real Estate News*, September 12, 1974.

Detroit

Community and Economic Development Dept. (includes historic preservation functions)
350 East Congress
Detroit, Mich. 48226

Detroit Renaissance, Inc.
1127 First Federal Building
1001 Woodward Ave.
Detroit, Mich. 48226

Michigan State Housing Development Authority
1200 Sixth St.
Detroit, Mich. 48226

Professional Skills Alliance
2551 John R St.
Detroit, Mich. 48201

Woodward East Project, Inc.
2915 John R. St.
Detroit, Mich. 48201

Osman, Mary E., "Designing the renaissance of
a proud but decayed neighborhood in Detroit," *AIA Journal*, May 1975.

Galveston

Director of Planning
Planning and Traffic Dept.
City Hall
823 Rosenberg
Galveston, Tex. 77550

Galveston Historical Foundation, Inc.
U.S. National Bank, Trust Dept.
2202 Market St., 11th floor
P.O. Box 179
Galveston, Tex. 77550

Galveston Zoning Code Sec. 25-16, Special Historical District Regulations

Hartford

Community Life Association
100 Constitution Plaza, 6th floor
Hartford, Conn. 06103

Greater Hartford Arts Council
250 Constitution Plaza
Hartford, Conn. 06103

Hartford Architecture Conservancy
65 Wethersfield Ave.
Hartford, Conn. 06114.

Hartford Commission on the City Plan
Office of Planning Director
City Hall
Hartford, Conn. 06103

Hartford Redevelopment Agency
City Hall
550 Maine St.
Hartford, Conn. 06103

Knox Foundation; Downtown Council
15 Lewis St.
Hartford, Conn. 06103

Office of Housing and Neighborhood Preservation
Community Development Agency
84 Washington St.
Hoboken, N.J. 07030

Hoboken

Ehrman, Michael, "The Hoboken Municipal
Home Improvement Project: A Pioneer Effort in Neighborhood Preservation," 1974.

Silverman, Ivan, "The City as a Mortgage Broker," *Nation's Cities*, September 1973.

Hudson Urban Renewal Agency
32 Warren St.
Hudson, N.Y. 12534

Hudson

Raymond, Parish and Pine, Inc.
555 White Plains Rd.
Tarrytown, N.Y. 10591

Raymond, Parish & Pine, Inc., *Urban Design
Principles and Guidelines for Hudson Urban
Renewal Project No. 1*, NYR-244, 1970.

Raymond, Parish & Pine, Inc. and Raymond A.
Ruge, *Street Historic Area of Hudson, 1974.*
prepared for the Hudson Urban Renewal
Agency.

Butchertown, Inc.
911 East Washington St.
Louisville, Ky. 40402

Louisville

Historic Landmarks and Preservation Districts
Commission
City of Louisville
617 West Jefferson
Louisville, Ky. 40202

Louisville and Jefferson County Planning Com-
mission
Kentucky Home Life Building
Louisville, Ky.

Neighborhood Development Corporation
520 West Magnolia
Louisville, Ky. 40208

Office of the Mayor
City Hall
Louisville, Ky. 40402

Preservation Alliance of Louisville and Jefferson County, Inc.
712 West Main St.
Louisville, Ky. 40202

Butchertown study produced by Louisville and Jefferson County Planning Commission. Includes zoning map, articles of incorporation of Butchertown, Inc., 1968.

Annual reports of Preservation Alliance.

Madison

City Planning Dept.
City of Madison
City-County Building
210 Monona Ave.
Madison, Wis. 53709

Dept. of Housing and Community Development
Rehabilitation Loan Office
P.O. Box 1785
Madison, Wis. 53701

13th Aldermanic District
Neighborhood Association
1815 Madison St.
Madison, Wis. 53711

Middlebury

Chamber of Commerce
Court St.
Middlebury, Vt. 05753

Green Mountain Place
Middlebury, Vt. 05753

Middlebury Planning Commission
27 Washington St..
Middlebury, Vt. 05753

Vision Inc.
2 Hubbard Park
Cambridge, Mass. 02138

Middlebury, Vt., Townscape Improvement Project Study, available from Ilsley Public Library, Middlebury.

Historic Walker's Point, Inc.
414 West National Ave.
Milwaukee, Wis. 53204

Milwaukee

Milwaukee Economic Development Corp.
Neighborhood Improvement Development Corp.
Dept. of City Development
734 North 9th St.
Milwaukee, Wis. 53233

Milwaukee Landmarks Commission
Dept. of City Development (q.v.)

Junior League of Milwaukee
316 East Silver Spring
Milwaukee, Wis.

Junior League of Milwaukee, *Walker's Point Project*.

Final Report of Steering Committee to Board of Directors, Historic Walker's Point, Inc., 1973.

Minneapolis Housing and Redevelopment Authority
217 South Third St.
Minneapolis, Minn. 55401

Minneapolis

Minnesota State Arts Council
314 Clifton Ave.
Minneapolis, Minn. 55403

Urban Design Studio
210 City Hall
Minneapolis, Minn. 55401

Urban Homesteading Program
Minneapolis Housing and redevelopment Authority
217 South Third St.
Minneapolis, Minn. 55401

Minneapolis Housing Redevelopment Authority, annual reports.

New Haven

Historic District Commission
709 Townshend Ave.
New Haven, Conn. 06512

New Haven City Plan Dept.
157 Church St.
New Haven, Conn. 06510

New Haven Preservation Trust
29 Loomis Place
New Haven, Conn. 06511

New Haven Redevelopment Agency
157 Church St.
New Haven, Conn. 06510

New Haven Preservation Trust, *An Introduction to Historic Wooster Square*, 1969.

New Orleans

Curtis and Davis
111 Rue Iberville
New Orleans, La. 70130

Historic District Landmarks Commission
City Hall, Room 9W
1300 Perdido St.
New Orleans, La. 70112

Vieux Carré Commission
630 Chartres St.
New Orleans, La. 70130

Plan and Program for the Preservation of the Vieux Carré, Historic District Demonstration Study, Bureau of Governmental Research, New Orleans, La., 1968. Photographs, maps.

Curtis and Davis, *New Orleans Housing and Neighborhood Preservation Study*, 1974. Does not include Vieux Carré.

Laws governing Vieux Carré Commission, Code of the City of New Orleans.

New York

City Planning Commission
2 Lafayette St.
New York, N.Y. 10007

Landmarks Preservation Commission
305 Broadway
New York, N.Y. 10007

Pratt Conference Coalition
(a citywide organization of 100 community, neighborhood-improvement and housing groups)
240 Hall St.
Brooklyn, N.Y. 11205

New York City Planning Commission, *Neighborhood Preservation in New York City*, a source book for planning workshop; New York: City Planning Commission, 1973.

Esposito, John, with Fiorillo, John, *Who's Left on the Block: a Study of New York City's Working Class Neighborhoods*, New York: New York Center for Ethnic Affairs, 11 West 42nd St., New York, N.Y. 10036, 1975.

Macchiarola, Frank J., "Decentralization: The Right Answer to the Wrong Questions?" *New York Affairs*, vol. 1, no. 4, 1974.

Urban Design Council of New York City, *Housing Quality: a Program for Zoning Reform*, New York: Dept. of City Planning, 1974.

Mayor's Policy Committee, *Housing Development and Rehabilitation in New York City*, New York: Office of the Mayor, 1974.

North Adams

Hoosuck Community Resources Corporation
121 Union St.
North Adams, Mass. 01247

Langenback, Randolph, *Old Buildings as a Resource for Growth in Cities*, Massachusetts Dept. of Community Affairs, 1974. A handbook for preservation in New England industrial cities; special chapter on North Adams.

Oklahoma City

Office of the City Manager
200 North Walker
Oklahoma City, Okla. 73102

Oklahoma City Urban Renewal Authority
15 North Robinson
Oklahoma City, Okla. 73102

Paterson

Great Falls Development Corp.
176 Maple St.
Paterson, N.J. 07522

Great Falls Project
Dept. of Community Development
52 Church St.
Paterson, N.J. 07505

Norwood, Christopher, *About Paterson: the Making and Unmaking of an American City.* New York: Dutton, 1974. Describes historical development of S.U.M.

Great Falls/S.U.M., survey prepared by the Historic American Engineering Record (HAER), 1973.

Peekskill

Peekskill Community Development Agency
901 Main St.
Peekskill, N.Y. 10566

HUD Challenge, U.S. Department of HUD, January 1975.

"Shake the Money Tree," *Newsweek*, July 10, 1972.

Articles in *The New York Times*, November 2, 1971; December 28, 1973.

Philadelphia

Benjamin Franklin Federal Savings & Loan
1624 Chestnut St.
Philadelphia, Pa. 19107

City Planning Commission
City Hall Annex
Philadelphia, Pa. 19107

Redevelopment Authority
City of Philadelphia
1234 Market St. East
Philadelphia, Pa. 19107

Pittsburgh

Department of City Planning
7th Floor, Public Safety Building
Pittsburgh, Pa. 15219

Neighborhood Housing Services
1419 Arch St.
Pittsburgh, Pa. 15212

Pittsburgh History and Landmarks Foundation
701 Allegheny Square West
Pittsburgh, Pa. 15212

Urban Redevelopment Authority
Civic Building
200 Ross St.
Pittsburgh, Pa. 15219

Evaluation of Pittsburgh's Neighborhood Housing Services Program, Washington: U.S. Dept. of Housing and Urban Development, Office of Policy Development and Research, Washington, D.C. 20410, 1975.

Portland

Community Development Services, Inc.
175 Danforth St.
Portland, Me. 04101

Greater Portland Landmarks, Inc.
Station A. Box 4197
Portland, Me. 04101

Maine Historic Preservation Commission
31A Western Ave.
Augusta, Me. 04330

MICAH
Equal Housing Opportunity
132 Park St.
Portland, Me. 04101

Portland Planning Dept.
City Hall
Portland, Me. 04111

Portland Renewal Authority
Room 315, City Hall
Portland, Me. 04111

Providence

Elmwood Foundation for Architectural and Historical Preservation
125 Princeton St.
Providence, R.I. 02907

Executive Office
City Hall
City of Providence, R.I. 02903

Historic Preservation Commission
150 Benefit St.
Providence, R.I. 02906

State Office of Historic Preservation
Dept. of Community Affairs
150 Washington St.
Providence, R.I. 02903

PACE (People Acting through Community Efforts)
557 Public St.
Providence, R.I. 02907

Richmond

Historic Richmond Foundation
2407 East Grace St.
Richmond, Va. 23223

Richmond Redevelopment and Housing Authority
P.O. Box 26887
Richmond, Va. 23261

Sacramento

City Planning Commission
Room 308, City Hall
915 I St.
Sacramento, Calif. 95814

Office of Community Development
State of California Dept. of Housing and Community Development
1807 13th St.
Sacramento, Calif. 95814

Old Sacramento
1029 2nd St.
Old Sacramento, Calif. 95814

Historical Structures Advisory Committee,
Sacramento Old City: a Preservation Program,
1974

American Association of University Women,
Vanishing Victorians.

St. Charles

Land Clearance for Redevelopment Authority
City of St. Charles
118 Monroe St.
St. Charles, Mo. 63301

St. Charles County Historical Society, Inc.
P.O. Box 455
St. Charles, Mo. 63301

St. Joseph

Land Clearance for Redevelopment Authority
510 Francis St.
St. Joseph, Mo. 64506

St. Joseph Historical Society
3411 East Colony Square
St. Joseph, Mo. 64506

Minneapolis Housing and Redevelopment Authority
217 South Third St.
Minneapolis, Minn. 55401

Minnesota State Arts Council
314 Clifton Ave.
Minneapolis, Minn. 55403

Old Town Restorations, Inc.
158 Farrington St.
St. Paul, Minn. 55102

St. Paul

City of St. Paul, Ordinance for Historic District.

State Enabling Statute.

Property Conservation Division
Dept. of Public Works
City and County of San Francisco
480 McAllister St.
San Francisco, Calif. 94102

San Francisco

Foundation for San Francisco's Arthictectural Heritage
2007 Franklin St.
San Francisco, Calif. 94109

Office of Community Development
State of California Dept. of Housing and Community Development
1807 13th St.
Sacramento, Calif. 95814

Principal Planner for Urban Design
Dept. of City Planning
100 Larkin St.
San Francisco, Calif. 94102

SAMCO (Savings Associations Mortgage Co.)
2483 E. Bayshore Blvd., Suite 200
Palo Alto, Calif. 94303

San Francisco Twin Bicentennial Commission, Inc.
555 Market St.
San Francisco, Calif. 94105

The Victorian Alliance
4143 23rd St.
San Francisco, Calif. 94114.

Urban Design Plan for the Comprehensive Plan
for San Francisco, 1971.

Association of Bay Area Governments (ABAG),

264

Conserve, a report on community strategies for conserving the region's housing stock, San Francisco: ABAG, Hotel Claremont, Berkeley, Calif. 94705, 1974.

Santa Fe

City of Santa Fe Planning Dept.
P.O. Box 909
Santa Fe, N.M. 87501

Old Santa Fe Association, Inc.
545 Canyon Road
Santa Fe, N.M. 87501

"H" Historical District Regulation, 1957.

"Santa Fe Capitalizes on Its Atmosphere," *Business Week*, April 10, 1971.

Savannah

Historic Savannah Foundation, Inc.
P.O. Box 1733
119 Habersham St.
Savannah, Ga. 31402

Dept. of Urban Renewal
Housing Authority of Savannah
P.O. Box 1179
200 E. Broad St.
Savannah, Ga. 31402

Historic Preservation Plan Brochure, Savannah Dept. of Urban Renewal, 1973.

Historic Savannah Architectural Inventory, Savannah Dept. of Urban Renewal, 1965.

Lane, Mills, *Savannah Revisited: A Pictorial History*. Savannah: The Beehive Press, 1973.

Seattle

Historic Preservation and Development Authority for Seattle
Smith Tower
Seattle, Wash. 98104

Office of Historic Preservation
Dept. of Community Development
Arctic Building
Seattle, Wash. 98104

Victor Steinbrueck FAIA
2622 Franklin Avenue East
Seattle, Wash. 98102

Makers group, Smith Tower, Seattle, *Pioneer*

Square Historic District Plan, a public improvements study prepared for the City of Seattle, 1974.

City of Seattle, Dept. of Community Development, Urban Renewal Plan, Pike Place Project, 1974.

———, Design Report, 1974.

Steinbrueck, Victor. *Seattle Cityscape #2*. Seattle and London: Univ. of Washington Press, 1973.

———. *Market Sketchbook*. Seattle and London: Univ. of Washington Press, 1968.

Bureau of Planning and Community Development
City Hall
Monument Square
Troy, N.Y. 12180

Troy

TRIP-Troy Rehabilitation and Improvement Program
5 First St.
Troy, N.Y. 12180

Delaware Avenue Association
c/o Butcher & Singer
Bank of Delaware Building, Suite 1106
300 Delaware Ave.
Wilmington, Del. 19899

Wilmington, Delaware

Dept. of Planning and Development
City Hall
10th St. and King
Wilmington, Del. 19899

Greater Wilmington Development Council
911 Washington St.
Wilmington, Del. 19899

Historical Society of Delaware
505 Market St.
Wilmington, Del. 19899

Historic Preservation Commission
911 Washington St.
Wilmington, Del. 19899

Historic Wilmington Foundation, Inc.
400 South Front St.
Wilmington, N.C. 28401

Wilmington, North Carolina

Printed Resources

Books and reports

General

Advisory Council on Historic Preservation. *Federal Programs for Neighborhood Conservation.* Washington: Advisory Council on Historic Preservation, 1975.

The Conservation of Cities. London: UNESCO Press, 1975.

Greer, Scott. *Urban Renewal and American Cities.* New York: Bobbs-Merrill, 1965.

Housing Assistance Council, Inc. *Rural Housing Preservation: Programs and Prospects.* Washington, D.C.: Housing Assistance Council, 1974.

Houstoun, Lawrence O., Jr. *Places to Live.* Address by the Acting Director, Planning and Management Assistance, U.S. Dept. of Housing and Urban Development, to annual meeting of American Society of Planning Officials, Vancouver, B.C., April 14, 1975.

Jacobs, Jane. *The Death and Life of Great American Cities.* New York: Random House, 1961.

Kliment, Stephen A., ed. *Community Leader's Workbook*, Division 7 (Preservation). N.Y. State Council on Architecture and National Endowment for the Arts. Limited inspection copies at National Endowment for the Arts, Washington, D.C., 1973–75.

Listokin, David. *The Dynamics of Housing Rehabilitation: Macro and Micro Analyses.* New Brunswick, N.J.: Center for Urban Policy Research, 1973.

The Logan Circle Historic Preservation Area, A Report prepared for the District of Columbia Redevelopment Land Agency. Washington, D.C., 1973.

Miner, Ralph W. *Conservation of Historic and Cultural Resources.* ASPO Planning Advisory Service Report No. 244. Chicago: American Society of Planning Officials, 1969.

National Trust for Historic Preservation. *Annual Report* (latest). Washington, D.C.: National Trust for Historic Preservation.

President's Council on Environmental Quality. *Environmental Quality: The Fourth Annual Report of the Council on Environmental Quality.* Washington, D.C.: U.S. Government Printing Office, 1973.

Public Affairs Counseling, a division of Real Estate Research Corp. *The Dynamics of Neighborhood Change.* Washington: U.S. Dept. of Housing and Urban Development, Office of Policy Development and Research, 1975.

———. *HUD Experimental Program for Preserving Declining Neighborhoods: An Analysis of the Abandonment Process.* Prepared for the U.S. Department of Housing and Urban Development. San Francisco: Public Affairs Counseling, no date.

Pynoos, John; Schafer, Robert; Hartman, Chester, ed. *Housing Urban America.* Chicago: Aldine, 1973.

Real Estate Research Corporation. *Neighborhood Preservation: A Catalog of Local Programs* and *Neighborhood Preservation Catalog: Field Methods.* Prepared for U.S. Dept. of Housing and Urban Development, Office of Policy Development and Research. Washington: U.S. Dept. of Housing and Urban Development, 1975.

Reilly, William K., ed. *The Use of Land: A Citizens' Policy Guide to Urban Growth.* A Task Force Report sponsored by The Rockefeller Brothers Fund. New York: Thomas Y. Crowell Co., 1973.

Wilson, James Q., ed. *Urban Renewal: The Record and the Controversy.* Joint Center for Urban Studies, Massachusetts Institute of Technology and Harvard University. Cambridge, Mass.: The MIT Press, 1966.

Worskett, Roy. *The Character of Towns.* London: The Architectural Press, 1969.

Articles and periodicals

Adubato, Stephen N., and Krickus, Richard J. "Stable Neighborhoods: A Strategy for the Cities," *Nation*, May 18, 1974.

Advisory Council on Historic Preservation. *Newsletter* (monthly). Washington, D.C.

Aldrich, Howard. "Ecological Succession in Racially Changing Neighborhoods," *Urban Affairs Quarterly*, March 1975.

Cahn, Robert. "Where Do We Grow from Here?" *Architectural Forum*, December 1973.

Middleton, Michael. "Conservation activities, goals and accomplishments of the Civic Trust, London." Presented at annual conference of the National Trust for Historic Preservation in Cleveland, Ohio, October 13, 1973. Washington: National Trust for Historic Preservation.

Murtagh, William. Statement on the criteria for determining historical districts, the background of preservation in the United States and the economic, financial and social issues of historical preservation. Presented at the General Assembly of the International Center for Conservation, April 1973. Washington: National Trust for Historic Preservation.

Peters, Richard C. "Towards a Redefinition of Preservation." *Society of Architectural Historians Journal*, October 1972.

Phillips, Kenneth F., and Agelasto, Michael A., II. "Housing and Central Cities: The Conservation Approach." *Ecology Law Review* (University of California, Berkeley, School of Law), vol. 4. no. 4, 1975.

"The Revival Spirit of Dayton." *Business Week*, May 19, 1975.

Administrative/political

Books and reports Banfield, Edward C. *Political Influence.* New York: The Free Press of Glencoe, 1965.

Banfield, Edward C., and Wilson, James Q. *City Politics.* Cambridge, Mass.: Harvard University Press and The MIT Press, 1963.

Barnett, Jonathan. *Urban Design as Public Policy.* New York: Architectural Record Books, 1974.

Bellush, Jewel, and Hausknecht, Murray, eds. *Urban Renewal: People, Politics, and Planning.* Garden City, N.Y.: Anchor Books, 1967.

Block, Peter B. *Equality of Distribution of Police Services.* Washington, D.C.: The Urban Institute, 1974.

Boots, Andrew J. et al. *Inequality in Local Government Services: A Case Study of Neighborhood Roads.* Washington, D.C.: The Urban Institute, 1972.

Costonis, John J. *Space Adrift: Saving Urban Landmarks through the Chicago Plan.* Published for the National Trust for Historic Preservation. Urbana, Ill.: University of Illinois Press, 1974.

Downs, Anthony. *Federal Housing Subsidies: How Are They Working?* Lexington, Mass.: D.C. Heath, 1973.

Fisk, Donald M., and Lancer, Cynthia A. *Equality of Distribution of Recreation Services.* Washington, D.C.: The Urban Institute, 1974.

Grigsby, William G. *Housing Markets and Public Policy.* Philadelphia: University of Pennsylvania Press, 1963.

Hallman, Howard W. *Neighborhood Government in a Metropolitan Setting.* Beverly Hills, Calif.: Sage, 1974.

Housing Management Technical Memoranda— 180 management improvement techniques. Washington, D.C.: Office of Housing Management, Department of HUD, 1976.

Hughes, James W., and Bleakly, Kenneth D., Jr. *Urban Homesteading.* New Brunswick, N.J.: Center for Urban Policy Research, 1976.

Kaplan, Harold. *Urban Renewal Politics.* New York: Columbia University Press, 1963.

Keyes, Langley Carleton, Jr. *The Rehabilitation Planning Game: A Study in the Diversity of Neighborhood.* Cambridge, Mass.: The MIT Press, 1969.

Massell, Adele P. *Compensating for Landlord Nonresponse in the Housing Supply Experiment.* Santa Monica, Calif.: RAND Corp., 1973.

Meyerson, Martin, and Banfield, Edward C. *Politics, Planning and the Public Interest.* New York: The Free Press of Glencoe, 1955.

Nordlinger, Eric. *Decentralizing the City: A Study of Boston's Little City Halls.* Cambridge: MIT Press, 1973.

Rand Corp. *Housing Assistance Supply Experiment*, latest annual report. Washington, D.C.: U.S. Dept. of Housing and Urban Development (HUD Contract H-1789). Undated.

Real Estate Research Corporation (RERC). *Recommendations for Community Development Planning.* Proceedings of U.S. Dept. of Housing and Urban Development/RERC workshops. Chicago: RERC, 1975.

Real Estate Research Corporation with RTKL Associates, Inc. *Evaluating Local Urban Renewal Projects.* A Simplified Manual. Washington, D.C.: U.S. Dept. of Housing and Urban Development, 1975.

Real Estate Research Corporation with RTKL Associates, Inc. *The Future of Local Urban Redevelopment.* A Guide for Community Policy Makers. Washington, D.C.: U.S. Dept. of Housing and Urban Development, 1975.

Rossi, Peter H., and Dentler, Robert A. *The Politics of Urban Renewal.* New York: The Free Press of Glencoe, 1961.

Stipe, Robert E. *State of Problems.* A description of the factors which have hindered preservation efforts in North Carolina, by the state's historical preservation officer. Raleigh, N.C.: Dept. of Community Affairs, Div. of Archives and History, 1974.

Urban Land Institute. *Management and Control of Growth.* Prepared for U.S. Dept. of Housing and Urban Development. Washington, D.C.: Urban Land Institute Publication Division, 1975.

Urban and Rural Housing Opportunities 1975. Washington, D.C.: The Urban Strategy Center, Chamber of Commerce of the United States, 1975.

Washnis, George. *Municipal Decentralization and Neighborhood Resources.* Survey of 12 cities. New York: Praeger, 1972.

Ziegler, Arthur P., Jr. *Historic Preservation in Inner City Areas: A Manual of Practice.* Pittsburgh: The Allegheny Press, 1971.

Cooper, Aileen. "HUD 'Realigns' Area Offices as Accommodation to Housing and Community Development Act of 1974." *The Journal of Housing* (Official Publication of the National Association of Housing and Redevelopment Officials), vol. 32, no. 1, 1975.

Kessler, Robert P. and LeGates, Richard T. "Municipal Housing Code Enforcement and Low-Income Tenants." *AIP Journal*, March 1974.

Mallon, Frederick W. "Neighborhood Conservation in the District of Columbia." *The Journal of Housing*, January 1966.

Markus, Marvin, "Urban Design through Zoning." *Planners Notebook*, vol. 2, no. 5, American Institute of Planners, October 1972.

Marshall, Patricia. "Locally-funded Rehabilitation Programs in Nine Cities." *The Journal of Housing*, July 1975.

"Neighborhood Housing Services Program Said to Work." *Nation's Cities*, "Washington Report" section. February 1975.

Russo, Ronald A. "Preservation of a Washington Neighborhood." *The Journal of Housing*, October 1974.

Articles and periodicals

Legal

Bosselman, Fred; Callies, David; and Banta, John. *The Taking Issue: An Analysis of the Constitutional Limits of Land Use Control.* Washington, D.C.: President's Council on Environmental Quality, 1973.

Historic Preservation through Land Use Legislation. State of Vermont: Division of Historic Sites, 1973.

Books and reports

Morrison, Jacob H. *Historic Preservation Law.* Washington: National Trust for Historic Preservation, 1965.

———. *Supplement to Historic Preservation Law.* New Orleans: By the Author, 315 Carondelet Building, 1972.

Articles and periodicals

Elliott, Donald H., and Marcus, Norman. "From Euclid to Ramapo: New Directions in Land Development Controls." *Hofstra Law Review,* Spring 1973.

"Historic Preservation." *Law and Contemporary Problems* (Duke University Law School), Summer 1971.

Stipe, Robert E. "Easements and Zoning: The Advantages and Disadvantages." *Popular Government,* "Tools for Historic Preservation" section, December 1967.

Turnbull, H. Rutherford. "Aesthetic Zoning and Property Value." *Wake Forest Law Review,* March 1971.

White, Harry E., Jr. "The Police Power, Eminent Domain and the Preservation of Historic Property." *Columbia Law Review,* April 1963.

Woodbury, Steven R. "Transfer of Development Rights: A New Tool for Planners." *Journal of the American Institute of Planners,* January 1975.

Business/financial

Books and reports

Downie, Leonard, Jr. *Mortgage on America: The Real Cost of Real Estate Speculation.* New York: Praeger, 1974.

Downs, Anthony. *Stimulating Capital Investment in Central-City Downtown Areas and Inner-City Neighborhoods.* Paper prepared for conference at Racine, Wis. sponsored by National Urban Coalition and the Johnson Foundation. Washington, D.C.: National Urban Coalition, 1973.

Kuchling, Ray. *Rehabilitation: Tax Abatements and Downward Assessments.* Columbus, Ohio:

Mid-Ohio Regional Planning Commission, 1974.

National Council for Urban Econimic Development Information Service. *Tax Increment Financing.* Report no. 1, September 1975. NCUFD, 1620 Eye St., N.W., Washington, D.C. 20036.

New York University Real Estate Institute. *Saving New York's Neighborhoods,* vol. 1. New York: New York University Real Estate Institute, 1975.

Price Waterhouse. *A Study of the Effects of Real Estate Property Tax Incentive Programs upon Property Rehabilitation and New Construction.* Washington, D.C.: U.S. Dept. of Housing and Urban Development (HUD Contract H-1300), 1973.

Slitor, Richard E. *The Federal Income Tax in Relation to Housing.* Washington, D.C.: U.S. Government Printing Office, 1968.

Sternlieb, George. *The Tenement Landlord.* New Brunswick, N.J.: Rutgers University Press, 1969.

———, and Burchell, Robert W. *Residential Abandonment: The Tenement Landlord Revisited.* New Brunswick, N.J.: Center for Urban Policy Research, Rutgers University, 1973.

Ziegler, Arthur P., Jr.; Adler, Leopold, II; and Kidney, Walter C. *Revolving Funds for Historic Preservation: A Manual of Practice.* Pittsburgh: Ober Park Associates, Inc., 1975.

Articles and periodicals

Black, J. Thomas. "Private-Market Housing Renovation in Central Cities: a ULI Survey." *Urban Land* (published by Urban Land Institute, Washington, D.C.). November 1975.

Mitchell, Maxine. "Municipal Rehabilitation Loan Funds: What Type Works Where?" *Journal of Housing,* June 1975.

Williamson, Roxanne Kuter. "The Economic Benefits of Historic Zoning: A Sense of Place." *Texas Business Review,* May 1974.

Social

Books and reports

Davis, J. Clarence, III. *Neighborhood Groups and Urban Renewal.* New York: Columbia University Press, 1961.

Gans, Herbert J. *Peoples and Plans: Essays on Urban Problems and Solutions.* New York: Basic Books, 1968.

———. *The Urban Villagers.* New York: Free Press, 1962.

Glazer, Nathan, and Moynihan, Daniel P. *Beyond the Melting Pot.* Cambridge, Mass.: MIT Press, 1970.

Heinberg, John D.; Spohn, Betty W.; and Taher, Grace M. *Housing Allowances in Kansas City and Wilmington: Appraisal.* Washington: Urban Institute, 1975.

Keller, Suzanne. *The Urban Neighborhood.* New York: Random House, 1968.

Levy, Frank J. et al. *Urban Outcomes: Schools, Streets and Libraries.* Berkeley: University of California Press, 1974.

Newman, Oscar. *Defensible Space.* New York: Macmillan, 1972.

Private Revitalization of Downtown (PROD, Inc.). *Revitalization of Downtown: Self-help Guidelines for a Smaller City.* Report, package of 160 slides, narrative text. Santa Cruz, Calif.: PROD, Inc., 406 Lincoln St., Santa Cruz, Calif. 95060. Undated.

Sternlieb, George et al. *Residential Abandonment*, Monticello, Ill.: Council of Planning Librarians Exchange Bibliography 342, December 1972.

Various. *Abandoned Housing Research: A Compendium.* Summary of four studies: Linton, Mields, Coston: *A Study of the Problems of Abandoned Housing.* Institute for Environmental Studies: *Housing and Poverty.* National Urban League: *A National Survey of Housing Abandonment.* Sternlieb, George: *The Urban Housing Dilemma.* Washington, D.C.: U.S. Government Printing Office, Stock no. 023-000-00210. Undated.

Ward, Colin. *Tenants Take Over.* London: The Architectural Press, 1974.

Washington University, St. Louis. *The Neighborhood Succession Process: Executive Summary.* Washington, D.C.: U.S. Dept. of Housing and Urban Development, Office of Policy Development and Research. Undated.

Yin, Robert K. *Participant-Observation and the Development of Urban Neighborhood Policy.* New York: The New York City-Rand Institute, 1972.

Yin, Robert K., and Yates, Douglas. *Street-Level Governments: Assessing Decentralization and Urban Services.* Lexington, Mass.: Heath, 1975.

Articles and periodicals

Arnstein, Sherry R. *"A Ladder of Citizen Participation." AIP Journal*, July 1969.

Downs, Anthony. "What most Communities are now doing about Citizen Participation in Community Development—and Why Some Changes are Needed." Unpublished article. Available from Real Estate Research Corp., 72 West Adams St., Chicago, Ill. 60603.

Freiberg, Peter. "How to Stop a Neighborhood from Dying." *Harper's Weekly*, April 11, 1975.

Fried, Marc, and Gleicher, Peggy. "Some Sources of Residential Satisfaction in an Urban Slum." *Journal of the American Institute of Planners*, November 1961.

Gans, Herbert J. "The Balanced Community: Homogeneity or Heterogeneity in Residential Areas." *Journal of the American Institute of Planners*, August 1961.

———. "The Failure of Urban Renewal." *Commentary*, April 1965.

———. "Social and Physical Planning for the Elimination of Urban Poverty." *The Washington University Law Quarterly*, February 1963.

Kriesberg, Louis. "Neighborhood Setting and the Isolation of Public Housing Tenants." *Journal of the American Institute of Planners*, January 1968.

Physical Design

Books and reports

Canter, David, and Lee, Terence. *Psychology and the Built Environment.* London: The Architectural Press, 1974.

Dunsavage, Lyn, and Talkington, Virginia. *Swiss Avenue, Dallas: The Making of a Historic District.* Washington, D.C.: National Trust for Historic Preservation, 1975.

Educational Facilities Laboratories and National Endowment for the Arts. *Reusing Railroad Stations*, books 1 and 2. New York: Educational Facilities Laboratories, 1974 and 1975.

Federal Architecture Project. (1) Craig, Lois et al. *Federal Architecture: A Framework for Debate.* (2) Binder, Gordon. *Federal Architecture: Multiple Use Facilities.* (3) Ware, Merrill. *Federal Architecture: Adaptive Use Facilities.* Washington, D.C.: National Endowment for the Arts, 1975.

Lynch, Kevin. *The Image of the City.* Cambridge, Mass.: MIT Press, 1960.

———. *What Time is This Place.* Cambridge, Mass.: MIT Press, 1972.

Papageorgiou, Alexander. *Continuity and Change: Preservation in City Planning.* New York: Praeger, 1971.

Proshansky, Harold et al, eds. *Environmental Psychology.* New York: Holt, Rinehart and Winston, 1970.

Rudofsky, Bernard. *Streets for People:* A Primer for Americans. Garden City, N.Y.: Doubleday, 1969.

Whyte, W. H. *The Last Landscape.* Garden City, N.Y.: Doubleday, 1968.

Articles and periodicals

Jacobs, Stephen W. "A Current View of Area Preservation." *AIA Journal*, December 1964.

Kliment, Stephen A. "Fall and Rise at Society Hill." *Progressive Architecture*, June 1973.

"Large-Scale Preservation: Saving Places for People." *Progressive Architecture*, November 1972.

"New Life for Old Buildings." *Architectural Record*, December 1971.

"Reclaiming the Urban Environment: San Francisco Urban Design Plan." *Ecology Law Quarterly*, (University of California, Berkeley, School of Law), vol. 3, no. 3, 1973.

State-oriented resources

Advisory Commission on Intergovernmental Relations. *State Actions 1974: Building on Innovation.* Washington, D.C.: Advisory Commission on Intergovernmental Relations, Doc. M-90, 1975.

Advisory Council on Historic Preservation. *Guidelines for State Historic Preservation Legislation.* Washington, D.C., 1972.

Center for Urban Social Science Research, Rutgers University. *The Role of the States in Solving Urban Problems* (HUD Contract #H-1039). New Brunswick, N.J., 1969.

Council of State Housing Agencies. *State Housing Agencies: Roles and Accomplishments.* Washington, D.C., 1975.

National Governors Conference Center for Policy Research and Analysis. *States' esponsibilities to local governments: An Action Agenda.* 1150 17th St., N.W., Washington, D.C. 20036, October 1975.

National Trust for Historic Preservation. *A Guide to State Programs.* Washington, D.C., 1972 (also, 1973 update).

Report of the National Conference on the States' Role in Strengthening Local Government Capabilities. Harrisburg, Pa.: Dept. of Community Affairs, Commonwealth of Pennsylvania, 1975.

Smart, Charlotte B., ed. *State of New York Local Government Handbook.* Albany, N.Y.: Department of State, 1975.

U.S. Dept. of Housing and Urban Development. *Examples of Local and State Financing of Property Rehabilitation.* Community Planning and Development Program Guide No. 1. Washington, D.C., 1974.

———. *Housing in the Seventies*, Washington, D.C., 1973.

Wilson, Paul E., and Winkler, H. James. "The Response of State Legislation to Historic Preservation." *Law and Contemporary Problems*, (Duke University School of Law), Summer 1971.

Conference on Neighborhood Conservation

Program

8:00 — 9:00	Registration at McGraw-Hill Conference Center 1221 Avenue of the Americas, New York City	Coffee . . . Book Fair . . . Federal Shopping Center
9:00 — 9:15	Opening Session Welcome to Participants	Beverly Moss Spatt, Chairman, New York City Landmarks Preservation Commission New York City Mayor Abraham D. Beame, Conference Host
9:15 — 9:30	"Neighborhood Conservation: The Endowment's Involvement, Concern, Hopes"	Nancy Hanks, Chairman, National Endowment for the Arts
9:30 — 10:00	Opening Address The Value of Older Neighborhoods: Stability and Change; Purpose of the research; Conference program.	Robert H. McNulty, Conference Director and National Endowment for the Arts
10:15 — 12:00	Cincinnati: One City's Neighborhood Conservation Controversies Chairman: William K. Reilly, President, The Conservation Foundation	E. Pope Coleman, President, Cincinnati Institute Carl Westmoreland, V.P., Madisonville Housing Service George Behmyer, Pres., Home Federal S&L of Cincinnati Estelle Berman, Chairperson, City Planning Commission
12:00 — 1:30	Informal Lunch . . . Book Fair . . . Federal Shopping Center	
1:30 — 3:00	**Four Workshops: Some Basic Value Consideration in Conserving Neighborhoods**	

1

	Property Rights and Public Regulation, including Rezoning, Transfer of Development Rights Chairman: Fred P. Bosselman, atty., Ross, Hardies, O'Keefe, Babcock & Parsons, Chicago	Frank Gilbert, Dir., Landmarks & Pres. Law, Natl. Trust for Historic Preservation Henry R. Lord, Deputy Att'y. General, State of Maryland B. Budd Chavooshian, Land Use Specialist & Program Adviser for Resource Mgmt., Rutgers Univ. John J. Costonis, Visiting Prof. of Law & Urban Design, Univ. of Calif., Berkeley

2

	The Interests of Owners versus Renters: Displacement, A Social Cost; Housing Allowance Chairman: M.gr. Geno Baroni, Pres., National Center for Urban Ethnic Affairs, Washington	Edith Woodbery, Pres., Woodward East Project, Detroit Bruce Zielsdorf, Skid Road Community Council, Seattle George Sternlieb, Dir., Center for Urban Policy Research, Rutgers Univ. Herbert Gans, Columbia Univ. Center for Policy Research Michael Ehrmann, Dep. Dir:, Westchester Housing Council, Inc., White Plains, N.Y. Peggy Spohn, Dept. Dir., Housing Allowance Office, South Bend, Ind.

3

	Tax Policies—Incentive or Disincentive for Improvement: Local Assessments and Property Taxes; Federal Policies and Possible Reforms Chairman: Majorie W. Evans, atty; Consultant to Bank of America on Land Use & the Environment, San Francisco	Roger S. Ahlbrandt, Jr., Dir., Housing Dev't. & Research Action Housing, Inc., Pittsburgh Richard Morris, Staff, Speaker of the NYS Assembly William Apgar, Research Assoc. Nat'l Bureau of Economic Research, Cambridge Lee E. Koppelman, Exec. Dir., Nassau-Suffolk Regional Planning Board, New York C. Lowell Harris, Prof. of Economics, Columbia Univ., Economic Consultant to the Tax Foundation, Inc.

4

	Decentralized Government and the Neighborhood Political Environment: Citizen Participation and Service Delivery Chairman: Maxwell Lehman NYS Charter Revision Commission for NYC	Robert Yin, Research Psychologist, The Rand Corp. Milton Kotler, Dir., Institute for Policy Studies, Washington Larry Reich, Dir. Dept. of Planning, Baltimore Peter G. Meade, Dir., Mayor's Office of Public Services, Boston Arthur J. Naparstek, Dir., Policy & Planning, Nat'l. Center for Urban Ethnic Affairs, Washington Hortense Dixon, Exec. Asst. to the Mayor, Houston

Wednesday	September 24, 1975

3:15 — 4:15	**Special Issue Symposium:** Special Treatment for Special Neighborhoods: The Creative Use of Zoning Chairman: William L. Slayton, Exec. V.P., Amer. Inst. of Architects	Daniel R. Mandelker, Prof. of Law & Urban Studies, Washington Univ., St. Louis Weiming Lu, Dir., of Urban Design, City of Dallas Arthur M. Skolnik, State Conservator, State of Washington Robert E. Stipe, Lecturer in City & Regional Planning, Univ. of No. Carolina Robert E. Manley, atty., Cincinnati Norman Marcus, Counsel, New York City Planning Commission
4:30 — 5:30	**The New York City Story** Chairmen: Beverly Moss Spatt, Chairman, Landmarks Preservation Commission; and Deputy Mayor James Cavanagh	John E. Zuccotti, Chm., City Planning Commission Tupper Thomas, Housing & Dev't. Administration Frederic S. Papert, Pres., Carnegie Hill Neighborhood Assoc. Kent Barwick, Exec. Dir., Municipal Art Society Ron Shiffman, Dir., Pratt Institute Center for Community & Environmental Dev't. Ada Louise Huxtable, Member, Editorial Board, The New York Times
5:30 —	**Mobile Workshops:** Buses leave for New York Neighborhoods—historic districts, special zoning districts, non-designated neighborhoods— for walkabouts, dinner, and briefing by community leaders and city officials

Thursday	September 25, 1975

| 9:00 — 9:30 | Roundtable talk-back on neighborhoods visits | Led by Kenneth Ricci, AIA, Chm., New York Center for Ethnic Affairs,
and Judy Laffoon, Supervisor, Community Dev't. Div., Kansas City |

| 9:45 — 11:15 | **Four Workshops: Physical Settings for Neighborhood Conservation** | |

5

| | Municipal Commitment to Urban Design and
Neighborhood Conservation

Chairman: Wes Wise, Mayor of Dallas | Bob Brandhorst, representive, Board of Aldermen, St. Louis
Paul Schell, Dir., Dept. of Community Dev't., Seattle
Richard Hedman, Principal Planner for Urban Design,
City Planning Dept., San Francisco |

6

| | Design for Old and New Buildings:
Controls and Follow-through to Reinforce
Neighborhood Identity

Chairman: Bill N. Lacy, Dir., Architecture + Environmental
Arts, National Endowment for the Arts | Ronald Lee Fleming, Exec. Dir., Vision, Inc., Cambridge
Lavid A. Crane, Chm., The Crane Design Group, Houston
Harry W. Weese, Harry W. Weese & Assoc., Ltd., Chicago
Charles W. Moore, Charles W. Moore Assoc., Essex, Conn.
Hugh Hardy, Hardy, Holzman Pfeiffer Assoc. |

7

| | Neighborhood Appearance:
Streetscape, Pedestrianization, Recreation;
Community Facilities as Symbolic Buildings

Chairman: Grady Clay, Editor, Landscape Architecture | Susan Southworth, City Designer, Cambridge
M. Paul Friedberg, Landscape Architect, NYC
Simon Breines, Architect Partner, Pomerance and Breines, NYC
John Andrew Gallery, Assoc. Dean, School of Architecture & Planning, U. of Texas
Byron Rushing, Dir., Museum of Afro-American History, Roxbury, Mass.
William H. Whyte, Consultant, American Conservation Assoc., NYC |

8

| | Integrating Conservation Neighborhoods into
Comprehensive Planning

Chairman: Lawrence O. Houstoun, Jr., Acting Dir.,
Planning & Management Assistance, HUD | William B. Shore, Vice Pres. of Public Affairs, Regional Plan Association, NYC
Richard A. Miller, Pres. & Gen. Counsel, Landmarks Preservation Service, Chicago
George M. Raymond, Pres., Raymond, Parish & Pine, Tarrytown, N.Y.
Marilyn Klein, Council on Environmental Quality, Washington
Elliot Rhodeside, Chief Landscape Architect, Urban Design Dept., Boston
Redevelopment Authority
Marjorie L. McCann, Chief; Research Div., Philadelphia City Planning Commission |

Thursday	September 25, 1975

11:30 — 12:00   **The Needed Partner for Neighborhood Conservation:**   Richard Babcock, attorney, Ross, Hardies, O'Keefe, Babcock & Parsons, Chicago
The Role of Corporate Support

12:00 — 1:15   Informal Lunch . . . Book Fair . . . Federal Shopping Center

1:15 — 2:30   **Special Issue Symposium:**   Frances Levinson, Dir. of Urban Housing, NY Bank for Savings, NYC
Inner City Financing and the Lending Institutions   Gail Cincotta, Dir., Housing, Training & Information Center, Chicago
William Whiteside, Dir., Urban Reinvestment Task Force, Washington
Chairman: John R. Price, Jr., Vice Pres.,   George Behmyer, Pres., Home Federal S&L Cincinnati
Manufacturers Hanover Trust Corp., NYC   Gerald R. McMurray, Staff Dir., House Subcommittee on Housing
& Community Dev't., Washington

2:45 — 4:00   **Two General Workshops: Support for Neighborhoods: Management of Programs**

9

A Compendium of Economic Mechanisms   Inthony Downs, Chm. of the Board, Real Estate Research Corp., Chicago
Chairman: George Sternlieb, Dir.,   Arthur Ziegler, Pres., Pittsburgh History & Landmarks Foundation
Center for Urban Policy Research, Rutgers Univ.   Philip G. Hammer, Chm. of the Board, Hammer, Siler, George Assoc., Washington
Charles Orlebeke, Ass't. Secy. for Policy
Development & Research, HUD

10

Choosing Development Formats   William Lee Roberts, Exec. Dir., Greater Portland Landmarks Foundation,
Public, Private, Profit, Non-Profit   Portland, Me.
Chairman: Richard Weinstein,   Tersh Boasberg, atty., Boasberg, Hewes, Klores & Kass, Washington
Consultant, Rockefeller Brothers Fund   Patrick J. Mogan, Exec. Dir., Human Services Corp., Lowell, Mass.
Edgar A. Lampert, NYC Community Preservation Corp.

4:15 — 5:30   **Four Workshops: Support for Neighborhoods: Tools and Tactics**

11

Housing Rehabilitation: Sources and Uses of Funds;   Robert Schur, Exec. Dir.-Coordinator, Association of Neighborhood Housing
Administrative Innovations   Developers, Inc., NYC
Matt C. Andrea, Program Analyst, Neighborhood Improvement Admin.
Chairman: Robert Maffin, Exec. Dir., NAHRO   D.C. Dep't. of Housing & Community Dev't.
George J. Morrison, Exec. Dir., Roxbury Action Program, Mass.
Anita Miller, Program Officer in Urban & Metrop. Dev't., Ford Foundation
Charles A. Noon, Dir., Neighborhood Dev't. Div.,
Baltimore Dept. of Community Dev't.

12

Operating with Muscle: Self-Help, Urban Homesteading,   Ian Donald Terner, Dir., U-HAB, NYC
and Community Equity Programs   Robert Kolodny, Asst. Prof. of Urban Planning, Columbia Univ. School of
Architecture & Planning
Chairman: Samuel Jackson, att'y,   Carolyn Cresswell, Jubilee Housing
Stroock, Stroock & Levan, Washington

53

Strategies for Revitalizing Neighborhood   Lynn DeBlois, Assoc. Dir., Urban Strategy Center,
Commercial Areas   U.S. Chamber of Commerce. Washington
Arthur M. Skolnik, State Conservator, State of Washington
Chairman: Robert W. Kennedy, Dir.,   David Ornstein, Exec. Dir., Peekskill, N.Y. Community Dev't. Agency
Boston Redevelopment Authority   N. Manfred Shaffer, Pres., PROD, Santa Cruz, Cal.
Benjamin Goldstein, Pres., Nat'l. Council for Equal Business Opportunity,
Washington
Peter Brink, Dir., Galveston Historical Foundation
Dana Crawford, Larimer Sq. Assoc., Denver

Thursday	September 25, 1975	

14

	Saving and Adapting the Large, Hard-to-Save Building	Herbert McLaughlin, Kaplan/McLaughlin, Architects-Planners, San Francisco
		Margaret Tuft, Dir. of Preservation, LPC, NYC
	Chairman: Alan C. Green, Exec. Vice Pres., Educational	Roger Webb, Architectural Heritage, Inc., Boston
	Facilities Laboratories, NYC	Frederick L. Rath, Jr., Dep. Commissioner for Historic Preservation,
		NYS Office of Parks & Recreation, Albany
		Rev. Henry W. Sherrill, Dir., The Cheswick Center, Cambridge

5:45 — 6:15	**Toronto, The Critics' Choice:**	David Crombie, Mayor of Toronto
	A City where Neighborhood Conservation and the	
	Quality of Life have High Priority	

6:30 — 8:30	Reception hosted by Mayor Beame	Presentation of The Bronze Medallion to Lewis Mumford
	North Balcony, Grand Central Station	

Friday	September 26, 1975	

8:45 — 9:15	**Major Urban Policy Address**	The Hon. Henry S. Reuss, Chairman,
		House Banking, Currency & Housing Committee

9:30 — 11:00	**Four Workshops: Implementing Neighborhood Conservation Programs: Organization, Strategies, Roles**	

15

	Leadership for Action: Institutions, Foundations,	Marilyn Levy, Program Officer, Rockefeller Brothers Fund
	Community Groups	Antoinette F. Downing, Chm., Rhode Island Historic Preservation Commission
		Saundra Graham, Cambridge City Councilwoman
	Chairman: Harvey I. Sloane, Mayor of Louisville	Judge William R. Brennan, Pres., Harlem Savings Bank, NYC

16

	Imaginative Uses for Community Development	Wayman D. Palmer, Dir., Dept. of Community Dev't., Toledo, Ohio
	Block Grant funds	Mary Elizabeth Lattimore, Savannah, Neighborhood Action Program
		Judy Flynn, Dir., Training & Program Dev't.,
	Chairman: Beverly Moss Spatt, Chairman	Issociation of Neighborhood Housing Developers, NYC
	New York City Landmarks Preservation Commission	Lewis W. Hill, Dept. of Dev't. & Planning, Chicago
		Robert Hunter, Asst. Dir., Dept. of Community Dev't. & Planning, San Antonio
		George A. Karas, Dep. Dir., Environmental Planning Div., HUD

17

	Municipal Organization and Reorganization:	Judy Laffoon, Supervisor, Community Dev't. Div., Kansas City
	Managing for Neighborhood Conservation	Maxwell Lehman, NYS Charter Revision Commission
		Lawrence Irvin, Dir. of Planning & Dev't., Minneapolis
	Chairman: John Orestis, Mayor of Lewiston, Maine	Ralph Widner, Dir., Academy for Contemporary Problems, Columbus

18

	Creative Uses of Building Codes,	Richard P. Rosenthal, Dir., Office of Design, NYC HDA
	Code Enforcement and Code Variances	Bernard Cummings, Chief, Property Conservation Div., FACE, DPW, San Francisco
		Melvyn Green, Melvyn Green & Assoc., Structural Engineers, El Segundo, Cal.
	Chairman: Carolyn J. Odell, Staff Assistant, COHUD,	Charles A. Noon, Dir., Neighborhood Dev't.
	Community Service Society, NYC	Div. Baltimore Dept. of Community Dev't.

11:15 — 12:30	**Special Issue Sympositum:**	William J. White, Dir., Mass. HFA, Boston
	Focus on State Actions to Support	Fred C. Williamson, Dir., Dept. of Community Affairs, Providence
	Neighborhood Conservation	Lonald Burns, Secy., Business & Transportation Agency, State of Calif.
	Chairman: Robert B. Rettig, Asst. to the Keeper,	
	Nat'l. Register of Historic Places	

12:30 — 1:00	Summary	Robert H. McNulty, Conference Director

1:00	Informal Concluding Lunch	Cash Bar

Photocredits

Index

Edited by Robert H. McNulty and Stephen A. Kliment AIA
Designed by Ivan Chermayeff and Stephan Geissbuhler
Composed in 10 point Times Roman by Publishers Graphics, Inc.
Printed and bound by Interstate Book Manufacturers, Inc.